4/09

D0742933

Consciousness Revisited

Representation and Mind
Hilary Putnam and Ned Block, editors

For a list of the series, see page 231.

for Lauretta, Margie, Dorothy and Jim

For information on quantity discounts, email special_sales@mitpress.mit.edu.

Set in Times New Roman and Syntax on 3B2 by Asco Typesetters, Hong Kong. Printed and bound in the United States of America.

Library of Congress Cataloging-in-Publication Data

Tye, Michael.
Consciousness revisited : materialism without phenomenal concepts / Michael Tye.
    p.   cm. — (Representation and mind series)
"A Bradford book."
Includes bibliographical references and index.
ISBN 978-0-262-01273-7 (hard cover : alk. paper)
1. Consciousness. 2. Phenomenology. 3. Materialism. I. Title.
B808.9.T943   2009
126—dc22   2008030920

10   9   8   7   6   5   4   3   2   1

Consciousness Revisited

Materialism without Phenomenal Concepts

Michael Tye

A Bradford Book
The MIT Press
Cambridge, Massachusetts
London, England

Contents

Acknowledgements

I have a general debt to Mark Sainsbury for discussion and helpful criticism. I have been influenced by conversations with my student Derek Ball, whose doctoral dissertation is on phenomenal concepts, and I have had much worthwhile feedback from the members of my graduate class at UT/Austin to whom I presented the main ideas in this book in fall 2007. I also recall the following individuals as having made useful remarks at colloquia and elsewhere: John Bengson, Ned Block, Ray Buchanan, Alex Byrne, David Chalmers, Jonathan Cohen, Tim Crane, Maite Escuardia, Enrico Grube, Dan Korman, Fiona Macpherson, Aidan McGlynn, David Papineau, Adam Pautz, Susanna Siegel, Tim Schroeder, Dan Simons, Malte Willer, Briggs Wright. I am especially grateful to Margie Venieri for giving me her house on Mykonos to use for the summer of 2007. Her generosity made it possible for me to complete a full draft of the book earlier than I would have been able to manage otherwise and to do so in a very beautiful setting.

Nearly all of the material in this book is new. Section 5.2 draws on my "Nonconceptual Content, Richness and Fineness of Grain," in *Perceptual Experience*, ed. T. Gendler and J. Hawthorne (Oxford University Press, 2006). Section 8.6 contains several pages from my "Phenomenal Externalism, Lolita and the planet Xenon," forthcoming in a volume of essays in honor of Jaegwon Kim (MIT Press). Chapter 4 is taken with very few changes from my paper "The Admissible Contents of Visual Experience," forthcoming in *Philosophical Quarterly*.

Introduction

"Living in a material world, and I am a material girl." So sang Madonna. She was right. We do live in a material world, and she is a material girl. We are all material beings. But we are also beings who have experiences and feelings. We perceive things with our senses, and in so doing we undergo perceptual experiences; we have bodily sensations; we feel a variety of emotions and moods. These things are subjective, or, at any rate, they have a subjective side. How can they *just* be a matter of matter? Modern philosophical materialists try to account for the intuition that there is more to our consciousness than is countenanced in the materialist worldview by allowing that it is conceivable and thus consistently thinkable that the subjective, felt character of our experiences is not a material phenomenon. They have denied, however, that *in actual fact* there is more to our conscious minds than our material assembly.

This general reaction has led more specifically to what might be called "the phenomenal-concept strategy" for defending materialism. This strategy has it that we are possessors of a range of concepts for classifying the subjective aspects of our experiences—concepts very different in how they function from concepts applied elsewhere. These concepts permit us to think of our experiences in a first-person, subjective way even though the aspects of our experiences about which we so think are, in reality, purely material or physical entities.

I have come to the view that the phenomenal-concept strategy is mistaken. There simply are no phenomenal concepts, as materialists standardly suppose them to be. Indeed, there is *nothing* special about the concepts whereby we form a conception of what it is like for us subjectively. This leaves the materialist with the large task of finding some other strategy for defending the position. In particular, the materialist must now confront four major puzzles of consciousness that can no longer be handled by an appeal to phenomenal concepts:

• How is it possible for Mary to make a discovery when she leaves her black and white room?
• In what does the explanatory gap consist and how it can be bridged?
• How can the hard problem of consciousness be solved?
• How are zombies possible?

Coming to grips with these puzzles or challenges to the materialist's position requires discussion of a wide range of issues, including the nature of perceptual content, whether all worldly knowledge is factual knowledge, the conditions necessary for consciousness of a given object, the nature of phenomenal character and our awareness of it, and whether we have privileged access to our experiences (and, if we do, in what such access consists).

This book is intended to present solutions to the above-mentioned puzzles of consciousness—solutions that relieve the pressure on the materialist created by the failure of the phenomenal-concept strategy. The package of views I develop here is new, although I have certainly been influenced by others. My biggest debt is to Bertrand Russell. When I first read his little book *The Problems of Philosophy*, I could not make heads or tails of his "knowledge by acquaintance." I thought I understood "knowledge by description" perfectly well, but Russell's comments on knowledge of things as opposed to knowledge of truths seemed to me unintelligible. That is no longer my view. Indeed, I hold that Russell's distinction holds the key to understanding central aspects of the correct solutions to the above puzzles.

What Russell needed when he advanced his distinction between knowledge by acquaintance and knowledge by description was a better grasp of the nature of perceptual content. Lacking such a grasp, he was not in a position to provide a fully satisfactory answer to the question of the conditions necessary for an experience to be an experience of some particular thing (or quality, for that matter). This is why, in my view, Russell's comments on knowledge by acquaintance have not had more impact. Be that as it may, the missing links are provided here. These links not only help place materialism back on a secure footing; they also have consequences for claims made about change blindness by well-known philosophers and psychologists.

I now hold that the conservative line on change blindness—that we always see the things that are the differences in pairs of pictures even though we do not notice them—is mistaken. In the recent philosophical literature, there has been a trend back toward the conservative line. I

maintain that this trend should be resisted, and further that such resis-
tance does not commit us to endorsing all the very strong theses of the
original change-blindness theorists. The position I develop leads me to
suggest that seeing things is a bit like drawing pictures of them with the
eyes.

Even though there is a constructivist element in my present account
of seeing objects, I still hold that visual experiences have nonconceptual
content. I no longer hold, however, that veridical and hallucinatory perceptual experiences share a common representational content. And so,
relatedly, I no longer accept strong intentionalism—the view that the
phenomenal character of an experience is the same as its representational
content. In its place, I offer a new proposal that locates phenomenal character in the world-as-represented.

There is one other thesis I have held in past work that I no longer
unqualifiedly accept. This is that knowledge of phenomenal character is
provided by introspective awareness of experiences, conceived of as a
form of displaced or secondary perception. My change of heart here
does not indicate that I now have doubts about the thesis of transparency
(the thesis that, when we introspect, the qualities of which we are directly
aware are qualities of external things, if they are qualities of anything at
all). I remain fully committed to that thesis and unmoved by criticisms
of it.

The present work covers a wide range of territory. When put together
with my previous work on phenomenal consciousness (suitably modified
to allow for the new proposals), it provides for a comprehensive theory
that, in my view, does a better job of handling the data than any other.

In chapter 1, I introduce the notion of phenomenal consciousness, discuss various hypotheses about the relationship of phenomenal consciousness to other sorts of consciousness, and make a proposal about the
conditions necessary for consciousness to become consciousness of a specific object. I also discuss various real-world cases, including some that involve impairments of one sort or another.

In chapter 2, I lay out the thesis of physicalism (a more general form of
the view I am calling "materialism" in this introduction). I also explain
the major challenges that consciousness presents for physicalism and the
major reasons for being a physicalist.

In chapter 3, I offer criticisms of extant theories of phenomenal concepts and general arguments for abandoning the phenomenal-concept
strategy.

In chapter 4, I discuss in detail whether perceptual content is singular or general. Here I opt for an overall disjunctivist view on content: veridical experiences have singular contents whereas hallucinatory experiences have gappy ones.

In chapter 5, I discuss certain parallels between seeing and knowing and introduce Russell's distinction between knowledge by acquaintance and knowledge by description. I then make a new proposal about the nature of phenomenal character and our knowledge of it.

In chapter 6, drawing on views developed in chapters 3–5, I offer solutions to the four major puzzles of consciousness distinguished in chapter 2.

In chapter 7, I apply the views elaborated in earlier chapters to the issue of change blindness.

In chapter 8, I consider the question of what happens to privileged access with respect to the phenomenal character of our experiences and feelings under my new view. I argue that in one sense we have no privileged access while in another sense we do. Indeed, I maintain that there is a sense in which our knowledge of phenomenal character is immune from error altogether. In this chapter, I also take up the issue of externalism and phenomenal character.

Philosophy is a hard subject—too hard, I sometimes think, for human beings. This seems especially true when it comes to the topic of consciousness. But philosophy is also a fascinating subject, and the puzzles of consciousness are as fascinating as any. In thinking about consciousness, I have often had the sense that I am like the man in a room described by Wittgenstein. The man is expending great effort to find a way out, but it does not occur to him to pull on the door instead of pushing. The door, which is unlocked, opens inward, and he can simply walk outside.

The views in this book came to me unusually easily, notwithstanding the difficulty of the subject matter. Perhaps that is because they are just wrong. I prefer to suppose that on this occasion I managed to open the door. I leave it to the reader to judge.

Consciousness Revisited

1 Phenomenal Consciousness

At the very heart of the mind-body problem is the question of the nature of consciousness. It is consciousness, and in particular phenomenal consciousness, that makes the mind-body relation so deeply perplexing. Many philosophers agree that phenomenal consciousness (P-consciousness, for short) cannot be reductively defined. For example, Ned Block writes:

Let me acknowledge at the outset that I cannot define P-consciousness in any remotely non-circular way. I don't consider this an embarrassment. The history of reductive definitions in philosophy should lead one not to expect a reductive definition of anything. But the best one can do for P-consciousness is in some respects worse than for many other things because really all one can do is *point* to the phenomenon.... Nonetheless, it is important to point properly. (2002, p. 206)

How, then, should we point properly to P-consciousness? Block answers as follows:

Well, one way is via rough synonyms. As I said, P-consciousness is experience. P-conscious properties are experiential properties. P-conscious states are experiential states; that is, a state is P-conscious just in case it has experiential properties. The totality of the experiential properties of a state are "what it is like" to have it. Moving from synonyms to examples, we have P-conscious states when we see, hear, smell, taste and have pains. P-conscious properties include the experiential properties of sensations, feelings and perceptions, but I would also include thoughts, wants and emotions. (ibid., p. 206)

Remarks similar to these form the starting point for most discussions of phenomenal consciousness or phenomenal character. Here are two more examples:

Conscious experience is a widespread phenomenon.... Fundamentally an organism has conscious mental states if and only if there is something it is like to be that organism—something it is like *for* the organism.... We may call this the subjective character of experience. (Nagel 1974, p. 436)

On a natural view of ourselves, we introspectively discriminate our own experiences and thereby form conceptions of their qualities, both salient and
subtle.... What we apparently discern are ways experiences differ and resemble
each other with respect to *what it is like to undergo them.* Following common usage, I will call these experiential resemblances *phenomenal qualities.* (Loar 1997,
p. 597)

The conception that many philosophers have of P-consciousness, then,
goes as follows: Experiences and feelings are inherently conscious states.
Each experience, in being an experience, is phenomenally conscious.
States that are not conscious cannot be experiences or feelings at all.
There is no clear agreement as to just which states are experiences, however. Everyone agrees that there are such experiences as pain, feeling angry, having a visual experience of red, and feeling a tickle. But is, for
example, the state of suddenly remembering something an *experience* of
suddenly remembering something? However this is settled, each experience, in being phenomenally conscious, is such that there is something it
is like to undergo it.[1]

1.1   Preliminary Remarks

What it is like to undergo an experience varies with the experience.
Think, for example, of the subjective differences among feeling a sore
wrist, experiencing an itch in an arm, smelling rotten eggs, tasting Marmite, having a visual experience of bright purple, running one's fingers
over rough sandpaper, feeling hungry, experiencing anger, and feeling
elated. Insofar as what it is like to undergo each of these experiences is
different, the experiences differ in *phenomenal character.*

Not only do experiences have phenomenal character; in many cases, it
is uncontroversial that they also carry information—that they tell us
things about ourselves or the world around us. Visual experiences purport
to inform us about the colors and shapes of things in our environments;
pain experiences signal bodily damage. The informational aspect of experiences is something that many philosophers suppose is entirely separable
from their phenomenal character, as indeed is anything external to the
experiences themselves. On this view, all that matters to the phenomenal
"feel" of an experience is how it is intrinsically. If you duplicate the
causal relations the experience stands in, the cognitive responses the experience generates, the informational links between the experience and other
things outside it you need not thereby have duplicated the experience. It
is, in principle, possible that all these external things are present and yet

there is no internal state with phenomenal character. This is the so-called absent qualia hypothesis (Block 1980).[2]

Another way to help explain the notion of phenomenal character is to reflect on the famous inverted spectrum hypothesis—the hypothesis that possibly what it is like for you when you see red things is the same as what it is like for me when I see green things and vice versa, with corresponding inversions for the other color experiences, even though you and I function in the same ways in color tests and in our everyday behavior toward colored things (Shoemaker 1975). Whether or not this hypothesis is true, it can be used to focus our attention on the phenomenal character of an experience, just as the description "the man drinking champagne" can be used to single out a person who in actual fact is female and drinking water (Donnellan 1966).

Once P-consciousness is introduced in the above way, it is natural to suppose that P-conscious states can be present without their subjects' being conscious of them. As I type now, for example, I have the bodily experience of my ankles' being crossed and my left shoulder's having a slight ache. I also feel my feet touching the floor and my wrists touching the keyboard. I have the auditory experience of my computer humming quietly, some students talking down the hall, and distant traffic. I am subject to the olfactory experience of the remnants of an orange sitting on my desk. These and other such sensations do not require for their existence that I focus on them. Experiences can occur even though their subjects are not conscious that they are occurring. Or so it is often supposed.

A popular example illustrating this point is the case of the distracted driver (Armstrong 1968). Lost in thought about his marital problems as he drives down the freeway, he does not pay attention to the visual experiences he is undergoing. He does not notice those experiences. He does not think to himself that he is having so-and-so experiences. But he is having them, all right. After all, he is still *seeing* other cars and the road ahead. The beliefs he forms on the basis of his visual perceptions about the direction of the road and the locations of the other cars guide his driving. If he weren't seeing the road and the cars, he would end up in the ditch or worse.

Phenomenal consciousness, then, according to many philosophers, is conceptually separable from higher-order consciousness. We are sometimes conscious *of* our phenomenally conscious states, or at least we are sometimes conscious *that* they are occurring. But there is no conceptual barrier to phenomenally conscious states' occurring without higher-order consciousness. This is the case, moreover, whether higher-order consciousness is construed on the model of perception of things or as the formation of a higher-order thought that the subject endorses (a thought to the effect that the subject is having such-and-such an experience).[3]

Some philosophers maintain that it is a mistake to hold that higher-order consciousness and phenomenal consciousness can be separated in the above way. In their view, phenomenal states always involve awareness of themselves.

1.2 Phenomenal Consciousness and Self-Representation

The central claim of the self-representational view (Levine forthcoming; Horgan and Kriegel 2007) is that phenomenally conscious states represent themselves. My current visual experience of the page I am typing not only represents the page but also represents itself. The latter representation is supposedly built into the experience. Every experience involves such self-representation. Since experiences make us aware of what they represent, my current visual experience makes me aware both of the page and of the experience. The latter awareness is peripheral, however. I am aware primarily of the page and not of my experience of the page. My awareness of the experience is only at a dim, background level.

Consider, for example, the case of my peripheral awareness of a dark object on the far right side of my visual field. In front of me is a beautiful piece of jewelry. My attention is taken up largely by it, but I have a dim awareness of something on the right, even though I cannot say what it is. Here there is focal awareness of the jewelry in front of me and there is peripheral awareness of the object on the right.

According to the self-representation view, normally in undergoing an experience I am focally aware of things outside and their features and only peripherally aware of the experience, but my experiences can upon occasion make me focally aware of themselves. When this happens, all that is required is that my attention shift from one thing to another in much the same way in which I shift my attention from the piano to the cellos at a concert so that my awareness of the cellos becomes focal instead of my awareness of the piano.

Once an experience becomes the object of my focal attention, I automatically form a belief about it, just as in the case of ordinary perceptual attention. Shifting attention suffices for the formation of such a belief. Thus, shifting attention can serve as the foundation for knowledge of our own phenomenal states via introspection. On this view, it is not the case that phenomenal states are sometimes accompanied by higher-order states in virtue of which their subjects are introspectively aware of those phenomenal states. Awareness of a phenomenally conscious state is not a matter of there being a quasi-perception of the state (as on the view of consciousness associated with John Locke[4]) or of there being a higher-order thought or belief about the state (as on the higher order thought theory). Such views open up a gap between our awareness of our phenomenal states and the phenomenal states themselves; and once this gap is introduced, it brings with it the possibility of radical error about the phenomenal character of those states. Such a gap supposedly is closed on the self-representation view, since the phenomenally conscious states inherently involve awareness of themselves.

That, in a nutshell, is the self-representation view. It seems to me unappealing for a variety of reasons (although, as we shall see in chapter 5, there is a grain of truth in it).

First, the motivation for the view is weak. One foundational claim motivating the self-representational approach is that having an experience necessarily involves being conscious of the experience. This necessary connection is lost on the higher-order account of consciousness of an experience. The truth supposedly is that experiences inherently involve consciousness of themselves. But in fact, although having an experience of something necessarily involves experiencing an experience of something (just as having a laugh at someone necessarily involves laughing a laugh at that person), experiencing an experience is not a matter of being conscious of the experience. Supposing otherwise is no more plausible than supposing that if I have a laugh at a joke and in so doing I laugh a laugh at the joke, I am laughing at my laugh. The laugh is directed at the joke; likewise, the experience is directed at the appropriate thing. The experience is not directed at itself.

Second, the self-representation view simply does not fit the phenomenological facts. I cannot be focally aware of my own current token visual experiences in the way I can be aware of a book, say, in my visual field. We all know what it is like to shift our attention from one object in the field of view to another. But we cannot shift our attention to our own current token visual experiences. Indeed, we cannot attend to them at all. Of course, we can be aware *that* we are having such experiences. No one denies that. But such factive awareness is not supported by awareness of, or attention to, the token experiences themselves. This is the familiar and widely accepted doctrine of transparency, of course, about which I shall have more to say later.[5] Suffice it to say for now that this doctrine seems to me to undercut the self-representation strategy from the start.

Third, cases like that of the distracted driver create problems for the view. The distracted driver surely sees the road ahead, and that seeing surely involves visual experiences caused by the road. But the distracted driver is lost in thought. He is not aware of his experiences, nor is he aware that they are occurring. On the self-representation view, the case as described is impossible. The driver must be aware of his experiences, albeit in a peripheral way. But then what is the difference between this case and the case of the attentive driver, on the self-representation account? The attentive driver is aware of his experiences in a peripheral way, just as the distracted driver is. The difference, then, must consist in the fact that the attentive driver has focal awareness of the road ahead, whereas the distracted driver has only peripheral awareness of it. But this seems unsatisfactory. The distracted driver does a much better job of keeping the car on the road than would someone whose awareness of the road is like my awareness of the objects at the periphery of my vision.

Fourth, what is the content of an experience, according to the self-representation view? The answer seems to be that there is no single content. Instead there are two: the externally directed content of the experience and the self-referential content. This is enough to give one pause already. But what exactly is the latter content? It cannot be that a token experience of something red (call it t) represents that one is having (or that there is occurring) an experience of something red. This content is not self-referential: the token experience itself, the representational vehicle, is not a constituent of the content. Nor can the content be simply that one is undergoing t. Advocates of the self-representation view agree that the subjectivity of experiences—what they are like for their subjects—is captured by the self-referential content and this proposal leaves out the phenomenal redness that is part and parcel of that subjectivity in the case of t.

Horgan and Kriegel (2007, p. 134) say that "the inner awareness of one's phenomenal experience is a constitutive aspect of the experience's phenomenal character." They add (p. 134):

... what it is like *for the subject* to have the experience is determined by the way the subject is aware of her experience. If the subject is aware of the experience as reddish, then what the experience is like *for the subject* is reddish. (In the ordinary case, the subject is focally aware of an external object as red, via an experience deploying a reddish mode of representation of that red object; the subject thereby is peripherally aware of the experience itself as reddish, since the reddish experience represents both the red object and itself.)

Horgan and Kriegel's proposal about the self-referential content in the case of t would then seem to be this: t represents that it is reddish. Thus, awareness of t via introspection is focal awareness of t and of reddishness,

where reddishness is a property of color experiences (a property such experiences use to represent real-world red). This is very close to the classic "qualia freak" view, according to which, when the subject introspects, she is aware of the token experience and its phenomenal properties. The new twist is that this awareness uses t itself and one of its contents.

Such a view flies in the face of transparency. By my lights, it is completely implausible introspectively. Furthermore, talk of *an experience's* being reddish seems to me unintelligible.

There are other difficulties facing this option. How exactly does t represent itself? How exactly does t represent reddishness, construed as a property of experiences? Horgan and Kriegel liken the relevant modes of presentation to indexicals. Thus, they see the self-referential content as being akin to the following: *that this experience has this property*, where 'this experience' denotes t and 'this property' denotes reddishness.[6] The problem now—assuming that we are prepared for the moment to go along with talk of reddish experiences—is that if t really does represent that it has *this* property, then t is accurate if and only if it is reddish. What, then, rules out the possibility that t is inaccurate, being really greenish and not reddish at all? Horgan and Kriegel (2007, p. 134) comment: "... it seems all but incoherent to suppose that one could have a phenomenal experience which was greenish, but of which one was aware as reddish." The trouble is that this possibility is not ruled out on their view except by stipulation. If this is not obvious, here is a comparison: A color experience e might be held to represent that surface s has this shade.[7] But then it must be possible for s to appear to have this shade and yet in reality lack it.[8] Thus, this shade cannot be just *whatever* shade s has. It must be some one specific shade. To suppose otherwise is to make the representational content of e empty. Likewise, without some further account that brings out the disanalogy with the case just mentioned, it must be possible for t to lack the represented property. That property cannot just be *whatever* property t has that it uses to represent red, on pain of leaving out of the content the specific property the representation of which is (according to Horgan and Kriegel) crucial to t's phenomenal character. But if the represented property is one that t can lack, then the proposal fails by Horgan and Kriegel's own lights, for an unacceptable gap has opened up again between what it is like for the subject and the actual character of t.

I agree with the self-representation theorists that higher-order accounts of introspective awareness do not do justice to our knowledge of phenomenal character via introspection. The problem is that the proposal they offer is no improvement. There is a much more plausible alternative, as we will see later—an alternative that respects transparency and that has no need of the recherché device of self-reference or self-representation.

1.3   The Connection between Phenomenal Consciousness and Creature Consciousness

Phenomenal consciousness, as introduced above, is a feature of mental states, for it is mental states that are phenomenally conscious. But we also use the term 'conscious' with respect to ourselves and other sentient creatures. For example, I am conscious of the loud noise to my left, the hissing of the cappuccino machine behind me, and the purple wisteria hanging from the trellis. My dog is aware of the toads in the glass tank, the barking sounds on the other side of the fence, and the bone in his bowl. As I noted above, I am also sometimes conscious of my own phenomenally conscious states. This is creature consciousness.

Intuitively, phenomenal consciousness requires creature consciousness. But what exactly is the connection? Evidently a creature cannot undergo phenomenally conscious states without being conscious. But might a creature have a phenomenally conscious state that is about some entity without being conscious of that entity? For example, might I have an experience of a particular flower without being conscious of that flower? Surely not. Experiences cannot exist un-experienced any more than laughs can exist un-laughed or screams can exist un-screamed. Thus, if I have an experience of a flower, I must experience an experience of a flower. But patently I cannot experience an experience of a particular flower unless I experience a particular flower. In that event, I must be conscious of the flower. So, generalizing, if I undergo a phenomenally conscious state about entity E, I must be conscious of E.

Here is a possible counterexample to this claim based on an imaginary case due to Ned Block (2001) with some minor modifications: I was tortured in a red room in my youth. I have deeply repressed visual images of this room. (They cause me to react violently at the sight of red dining rooms, red walls, etc.). These images are phenomenally conscious. Even so, I am not conscious of the red room.

This case is not persuasive. If the images of the red room are phenomenally conscious then I must have experiences of the red room. That is, I must undergo conscious states about the red room. But if the images are deeply repressed, then I am no longer conscious of this room and what happened to me in it. Thus, by the argument above, these images are not phenomenally conscious after all. Indeed, perhaps it would be better not to call them 'images', since that term arguably brings it with the connotation of phenomenality.

Nothing I have said here counts against the existence of a deeply repressed *representation* of a red room. My claim is simply that such a representation is not phenomenally conscious.

There is another way to make the point I am making. Consider the experience of a loud noise. There is something it is like to have an experience of a loud noise. What it is like is the same as what it is like to experience a loud noise. This patently is not a coincidence. Why do these things necessarily go together? Because having an experience of a loud noise just is experiencing a loud noise. But necessarily, if one is experiencing a loud noise, one is conscious of a loud noise. Thus, having an experience of a loud noise entails being conscious of a loud noise. Generalizing, it follows that one cannot have a phenomenally conscious state of an *F* unless one is conscious of an *F*.

Let me offer one further argument for this claim. The phenomenal character of an experience is what it is like to undergo the experience. If you don't know what it is like to experience Marmite, you do not know the phenomenal character of the experience of Marmite. And if you do know the phenomenal character of that experience, you know what it is like to taste Marmite. This much is immediately clear and agreed upon.

Now, we can talk of experience types as having phenomenal character and also of experience tokens. Consider the type pain. There is something it is like to feel pain, to undergo that type of mental state. Consider next a particular pain. There is also something it is like to undergo that token. What it is like may be somewhat different from what it is like to undergo other pain tokens, for pains vary somewhat in phenomenal character: there are stinging pains, burning pains, throbbing pains, aches, and so on.

What it is like to undergo a token state *e* is what it is like *for the subject* of *e* to undergo *e*. Experiences—the bearers of phenomenal character— are private to their owners. You cannot undergo my token experiences, and I cannot undergo yours. Thus, if there is nothing it is like for me to undergo a given visual representation *v* of mine at time *t*, then there is nothing it is like for anyone to undergo *v* and thus nothing it is like to undergo *v*, period. That visual representation, *v*, is not an experience at *t*. It has no phenomenal character at *t*.

Now consider again the case of the deeply repressed image. If I am presently the subject of such a deeply repressed image, patently there is nothing it like *for me* to undergo it now. But if there is nothing it is like for me to undergo it and that image could not be undergone by anyone else, then there is nothing it is like to undergo it, period. Accordingly, it has no *phenomenal* character.

Perhaps it will be replied that there is something it is like for me to undergo the repressed visual image now. I just don't *know* what it is like from introspection. However, *for me* it is as if no image is present. *I* am not conscious of the red room in which I was tortured. Of course, I find myself bolting from red rooms and feeling nauseated when I am in them, but *subjectively* the token 'images' I undergo are missing. Surely, intuitively, they are not a part of my phenomenal life.

Here is another possible counterexample to the position I am taking on phenomenal consciousness and creature consciousness: My refrigerator makes a humming noise. I am used to it, and most of the time I do not notice it. Suddenly the noise stops. I notice this, and I then realize that I have been hearing the humming for some time in the background, even though I did not notice the noise earlier on. Since I was hearing the humming noise, I was undergoing auditory experiences caused by it, but I was not conscious of the noise. There was phenomenal consciousness of the noise, but not creature consciousness of it (Block 1997).

Not so. If I really did hear the noise earlier, I *was* conscious of the noise. After all, if I heard it, it must have sounded some way to me. How could it have sounded any way to me if I was not conscious of it? For it to have sounded some way, I must have experienced it. Thus, I must have been conscious of it. Of course, whether I really did hear the noise earlier on can be disputed. I certainly heard the noise stop. That change was a particular event, and I was conscious of it. Further, I was aware at that moment *that* the noise had stopped. But it does not follow from this that I was conscious of the noise at earlier times. It is a well-known fact that changes can be experienced within the specious present.[9] Thus, I need not have been conscious of the noise in the past in order to experience the noise stopping. Still, perhaps I have a phenomenal memory of the noise. In that event, the memory is genuine, I really did hear the noise in the past, and correspondingly I really was conscious of it, even though, if I did not notice it, I was not conscious of the fact that there was a noise.

1.4   Consciousness of Things

Under what conditions does an experience of mine make me conscious of a particular entity? Suppose that on the tree trunk before me there is a perfectly camouflaged brown moth. I do not notice that there is a moth on the trunk. I do not notice that there is an insect of any sort on the trunk (where the moth is located). Do I see the moth? Here is a similar case: On the white sheet of paper before me, there is a blob of white-out. I do not know where it is. I do not know that there is any white-out on the page. Do I see it?

One argument that I do see these things is as follows: Suppose that the white-out covers the letter 'p'. The white-out blocks my view of the letter. It does so by occluding it. In that case, surely I must see the white-out. Similarly, suppose that the moth covers a bright purple postage stamp stuck to the tree trunk. The moth blocks my view of the postage stamp. But if the moth blocks my view, I must see it.[10]

This is too fast, however. The earplugs I am wearing block my hearing the sound my alarm clock is emitting, but I do not hear the earplugs. The numbing taste paste I spread on my tongue blocks me from tasting the chocolate I am eating, but I do not (or need not) taste the taste paste. The black tape touching my eyeballs and covering them blocks my seeing the clock before me, but I do not see the black tape.

Still, it might be replied, in these cases the blocking items do not cause my experience. The facing surface of the moth does; more precisely, the facing surface of the moth causes me to undergo an experience as of a brown surface in a certain place P in the field of view. But why should this fact make it the case that I actually see the moth? One answer is that the causal link here is such that the experienced color (in the relevant spatial region) systematically varies with variations in the moth's surface color. Had the moth's color been red, for example, I would have experienced red in place P; had the moth's color been green, I would have experienced green in P; and so on. One sees the moth, it may be suggested, since one sees something just in case there is a causal connection between the facing surface of the thing and one's experience as of a surface in a certain region of the field of view, where that causal connection supports such a color-involving counterfactual dependence.[11] Likewise for the blob of white-out.

Again, this is not persuasive. For one thing, it is not obvious how to specify the relevant region of the field of view. P, for example, need not be the place the moth actually occupies, since one can see an object even if it is not where it appears to be. Another serious difficulty is that, insofar as it is agreed that the experience as of a brown surface in place P is an experience that represents that *there is* a brown surface in place P, the proposal not only removes the seen object from the content of the

experience (which seems wrong-headed, as I note below) but also introduces into the content an arbitrary undetached surface region. This seems
very hard to swallow. Surely one's overall experience does not have in its
content a huge number of minimally overlapping surface regions of the
tree trunk and the moth.

A further problem is that there are obvious counterexamples to the
proposed account of what it is to see an object. In the case of very distant
objects (for example, a star), changes in the object's color do not affect
the experienced color. Dimly seeing objects through thick, distorting,
darkened glass is similar. And what about people who lack normal color
vision and see the world in black and white? These people see things, but
the colors they experience do not change with changes in the colors of the
objects they see.

There is no straightforward way to revise the above proposal so that
the moth still counts as seen. The explanation for this, I suggest, is that
one sees an object just in case it looks some way to one, and that an object looks some way to one just in case one has an experience that represents *it* as being that way. An object's looking *F* is not a matter of that
object's causing an experience which is a sensing of an *F* sense datum (as
on the sense-datum theory) or a sensing *F*-ly (as on the adverbial theory);
nor is it a matter of the object's causing an experience which represents
simply that *something* is *F*. The experience one has of the seen object is
one into whose content the seen object itself enters.[12] But intuitively, the
moth is *not* in the content of my experience. My experience is not *about*
the moth at all. And neither is my experience of the sheet of paper *about*
the white-out.

Why not? Because if the moth were in the content of my experience,
then, by the argument of the preceding section, I would be conscious *of*
the moth. But surely I am not conscious of the moth. That seems to me
just intuitively obvious, a datum from which to argue, not something for
which argument is needed.[13] Still, what is it about the moth that makes
me fail to be conscious of it? The answer, I suggest, is that the moth is
not differentiated from its surroundings in any way whatsoever in my
conscious experience, and thus my experience does not enable me directly, without using any collateral information, to form any *de re* propositional attitudes about it.[14] Solely on the basis of my experience, I am
not *enabled* even so much as to wonder "What is that?" with respect to
the moth. Of course, my experience might put me in such a position *indirectly*, if I am told that there is something on the tree trunk and I am told
further just where to look. In these circumstances, even if I cannot differ-

entiate the moth from the bark of the tree, I can now wonder what *that* is. But such indirectly based wondering is not to the point. What matters is whether my experience directly (that is, non-inferentially) enables me to query what *that* is, where *that* is the moth. Since my experience does not enable me to do this, the moth is hidden from me. I am blind to its presence. I am not conscious of it. Similarly for the white-out. But if I am not conscious of the moth and the white-out, then I do not see these things.

There is another reason to insist that the moth is not seen. If someone asks me whether I am American, and I reply (sincerely) 'No', I am expressing my belief that I am not American. I am not expressing my failure to believe that I am American. Similarly, if someone says to me "Do you see the moth?" and I say 'No' (as I certainly will say if the moth is perfectly camouflaged), I am expressing my belief that I do not see the moth. I am not simply indicating that I do not believe that I do see the moth. Admittedly, there is sometimes evidence that runs against some such beliefs, and that evidence should not be ignored. I might, for example, believe that I am not seeing a spy when there is plenty of evidence that the man I am seeing is a spy. But suppose I am asked whether I am seeing anything on the tree trunk with *this* shape, where the shape of the moth is shown to me separately (drawn on a piece of paper, say). Again, even if I view the tree trunk for an extended period of time, I will reply 'No', this time expressing my belief that I am not seeing something on the tree trunk with the given shape. Now my belief is not so easily overturned.

Of course, beliefs to the effect that there is a thing with a certain shape in a certain direction can be overturned if there is evidence that the subject is hallucinating or subject to a visual illusion with respect to shape, but in the absence of evidence of this sort such beliefs deserve to be taken very seriously. In general, philosophical theories should (as much as is possible) respect ordinary beliefs. We should try to fit our theories to the ordinary beliefs as much as we can. If we don't, we run the risk of offering theories that we cannot really believe. Thus, *prima facie* the right thing to say about the moth case is that the moth is not seen, and *not* that it is seen but not noticed. The moth is neither seen nor noticed. And what goes for the moth goes for the white-out too.

The moth is a particular thing. What about properties or types? Take the color red, for example. I do not see the color red, for red itself looks no way to me. What I see is the red surface. Still, I am aware or conscious of the color red. And clearly I cannot be conscious of red unless I am in a conscious state—unless I am undergoing an experience. What is needed for me to be conscious of red is that my experience enable me at least to wonder "What is that color?" with respect to red. If I cannot even do that, *whether or not I actually do so wonder*, on the basis of my experience, then surely the color red is hidden from me, just as is the moth. I am not conscious of it. Red, therefore, does not enter into the content of my experience at all.

Here is a further way of illustrating these points: Have someone stand in front of you and hold several colored pencils next to one another out to his side while you look straight ahead at his nose. You will not be able to make out the pencils as such, and you will not be able to make out their colors either. At this stage you are in a position to ask yourself, with respect to the pencils, "What are they?" Thus, you are conscious of the plurality of pencils. But you will not be able to wonder this with respect to any given pencil. Thus, you are not conscious of individual pencils. Nor are you conscious of any pencil color. While you may wonder "What is the color of that?" (where 'that' refers to the collection of pencils[15]), there is no pencil color such that you can wonder, on the basis of your experience, "What is that color?" As the pencils are moved in from the holder's side and they approach the center of your field of view, there comes a time at which you are able to ask yourself (with respect to individual pencils' colors) "What is that color?" or to think to yourself "That color is red," for example.[16] As this occurs, the individual pencils' colors make their way into your consciousness. You become conscious of them, one by one. They enter into the content of your visual experience.

This is not to suggest that subjects need, *in fact*, to ask themselves anything about colors of which they are conscious. I certainly need not be conscious that the color on which I am focusing is the color red in order to be conscious of it.[17] Suppose, for example, I am color-blind and my color vision is suddenly restored. I am locked in a room with paint patches on the wall, some red, some blue, some green, and some yellow, and I am staring at the red patch. I am conscious of its color, but I am not conscious *that* its color is red.

The general suggestion, then, is as follows: If a phenomenally conscious state of mine is such that at a minimum it at least enables me to ask "What is that?" with respect to some entity, and it does so directly on the basis of its phenomenal character alone, then I am conscious of that entity. But if a phenomenally conscious state of mine is not so situated, then I am not conscious of the relevant entity.

It follows from these remarks that simply having a mental picture that is produced by the use of the eyes and that is caused by light reflected from an object does not suffice for being conscious of that object. The mental picture must play an appropriate role with respect to the object—a role that involves possible *de re* conceptual responses to it. Furthermore, the picture (if there is one) involved in being conscious of an object cannot be like a clear color photograph of the object and the scene involving it. This is shown by the pencil case.

A better model is a drawn picture with many details left out. There is evidence that generating a mental image is like drawing a picture. Perhaps being conscious of an object and relatedly seeing an object is a bit like that too.[18] I shall return to this topic in detail in chapter 7.

Ned Block has recently suggested (2007b) that there is empirical evidence for the view that the 'grain' of seeing is finer than the 'grain' of attention, and this may seem to create difficulties for my claim that one sees an object only if one's conscious state at least enables one to bring the seen object under a demonstrative concept; for demonstration requires attention. The empirical evidence Block has in mind derives from some experimental studies by Patrick Cavanagh (1999). Fixate on the central dot in figure 1.1. Whether or not you attend to each line on the right, you do see each of those lines, and you are *able* to attend to each one. However, even though you see the lines on the left, you will not be able to attend to each one (at least if you are a typical subject) if you continue to fixate on the central dot. One way to persuade yourself of this is to try to count the lines on the left or to go through them mentally one by one. So, allegedly, the density of the display on the left exceeds "the resolution limit of attention," as Cavanagh puts it. Even so, you definitely see the lines on the left.

Contra Block, the empirical evidence here does not show that there are things you see to which you are unable to attend. This needs a little explanation. Some verbs have a collective (non-distributive) character.

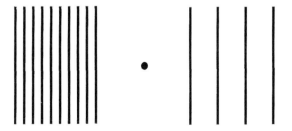

Figure 1.1
The density of the bars on the left of the central dot is greater than the density of bars on the right. As you fixate on the dot, you cannot attend to each bar on the left but you can attend to each bar on the right.

For example, I can weigh the marbles without weighing any one marble in particular. If the marbles are of different sizes, after having weighed all the marbles (by putting them together on the scales), I cannot say what *this* marble weighs. I haven't weighed *it*. Similarly, I can think about my colleagues without thinking about any one colleague in particular. I can form the plural analogue of a singular thought about my colleagues without having a singular thought about any one—for example, I can think of my colleagues that they get on well together. Likewise, I can be conscious of the vertical lines on the left of the dot without its being true that I am conscious of, for example, the fourth line in from the left in particular, and thus without its being true that each line on the left is such that I am conscious of it. So the fact that there are individual lines on the left which are such that my experience does not enable me to bring them under a demonstrative concept does not show that I am not conscious of the lines on the left. I am conscious of the lines; I do see them. *They* are what my experience is about. And my experience clearly does enable me directly to ask such questions as "Are they parallel?" or to believe of them that they are vertical. Even so, there are individual lines on the left that I do not see. For each such line, my experience does not enable me to bring it individually under a demonstrative concept. These lines are ones to which I cannot attend individually. There is, then, no difficulty for the view I am proposing.[19]

This view, incidentally, seems to me to fit the phenomenology very well. Fixate again on the central dot in figure 1.1. I predict that it will seem to you that you are seeing the lines on the left, but if you continue to fixate on the dot it will not seem to you that with respect to each line on the left (say, the fourth line away from the dot on the left) that you are seeing *it*.

In this case, it seems plausible to suppose that there genuinely is a composite entity on the left that is seen, namely a grating composed of the vertical lines. And this is actually the way Cavanagh himself puts it:

While fixating on the central dot, we can clearly see the grating on the left and report that there are several fine bars vertically oriented. However, it is much more difficult to individuate and count the bars on the left (again while fixating on the central dot).... In contrast on the right, the bars can be accessed individually, counted, and inspected. (1999, p. 43)

Some of the above points may be applied to the famous problem of the speckled hen, suggested to A. J. Ayer by Gilbert Ryle. One sees a speckled hen (figure 1.2) in good light in a single glance, but one cannot enumerate the experienced speckles with accuracy. How many speckles does one see?

Figure 1.2
A speckled hen.

Ayer (1940) held that, since one is unable to count the experienced speckles accurately, it is a mistake to assert that there is a definite number of
speckles one sees. Ayer was not denying, of course, that there is a definite
number of speckles on the hen; his view was proposed with respect to
what he took to be the immediate object of experience, namely the sense
datum presented by the hen. The sense datum has many speckles on it,
according to Ayer, but there is no definite answer to the question "How
many speckles does it have?" *Prima facie*, this view is contradictory.

Block (2007b) takes this case, and in particular the phenomenological
disagreement about it, to derive from a conflation of seeing and attending. A better diagnosis, in my view, is that the disagreement (or at least
the puzzlement) the case has generated derives from a failure to understand non-distributive verbs and plurals properly.

One cannot mark all the trees in an orchard with Xs unless each tree in
the orchard is marked with an X, but one can be conscious of the speckles
on the hen without each speckle's being such that one is conscious of *it*.
The reason that one cannot enumerate the number of speckles is that the
enumeration would require one to attend to each of the speckles. This one
cannot do in a single glance, even in good light. Even so, one does see
the speckles. One is conscious of *them*. Further, there surely are individual speckles of which one is conscious in seeing the speckled hen. But
these speckles are such that one's experience enables one to form beliefs
(or other conceptual attitudes) about them individually, if one so chooses.
Thus, one can attend to *these* speckles in particular.

Does one see *all* the speckles? That depends on how 'all' is understood.
One does not see *each* speckle, since there are speckles one does not see—
speckles of which one is not conscious. Thus, if 'all' is read 'distributively',

it is false that one sees all the speckles. But there remains a collective sense of 'all' under which it is true that one sees all the speckles: one sees them collectively. This is the sense of 'all' under which it is true that (in the earlier example) one weighs all the marbles.

I should emphasize that I am not offering a conceptual analysis in this section of what it is for any creature whatsoever to be conscious of any given entity. What I am offering is a test for such consciousness in creatures sophisticated enough to have *de re* propositional attitudes.

I suspect that some will respond to the framework I have been developing by saying that I am legislating with respect to matters that are properly a matter of empirical investigation. This I deny. It is all too easy to confuse the question "Am I subject to a representation that represents so-and-so when I undergo such-and-such an experience?" with the question "Do I experience so-and-so?" or the question "Am I conscious of so-and-so?" The first question is certainly empirical. But it is a mistake to slide from empirically based conclusions about the richness of non-conscious or pre-conscious visual representation, for example, to conclusions about that of which we are conscious. Consider David Marr's representations of zero crossings (sudden, localized changes in light intensity at the retina).[20] The visual system computes such representations from information in the retinal image, and it does so in order to generate representations of edges and ridges in the visual field. But patently there is nothing it is like for human beings to undergo representations of zero crossings. This is something we know *a priori* in our own case from the actual character of our visual experience, which is directed on distal stimuli. Nor, relatedly, are we conscious of zero crossings, for on the basis of our visual experiences we are not in a position to ask "What is that?" with respect to any zero crossing. Thus, an affirmative answer to the question "Am I subject to a representation that represents zero crossings when I undergo an ordinary visual experience?" does not bring with it an affirmative answer to the question "Am I conscious of zero crossings?" This result should surprise no one. But slides from a question of the first sort to a question of the second sort are not uncommon in philosophical and psychological discussions of consciousness.

1.5 Real-World Puzzle Cases

One issue that has confused much recent discussion of consciousness has been how to describe various real life examples. Consider first the phenomenon of meta-contrast.

Figure 1.3
A disk and a masking ring of the same color.

When a stimulus (e.g., a red disk) is briefly flashed on a screen and then it is followed by a second masking stimulus (e.g., a red ring, the inner side of which is just larger than the disk), subjects report having seen only the second stimulus. That is certainly how it seems to them. And that is how it is standardly described in the psychological literature. The usual claim is that the second stimulus prevents conscious experience of the first. Even so, subjects in the experiment, if forced to guess whether there was one or two stimuli, do much better than chance with their guesses. (See figure 1.3.)

Dan Dennett, in his description of the above-mentioned case, says that there are two possible alternatives here. According to the "Stalinesque theorist," "the first stimulus never plays on the stage of consciousness, but has whatever effects it has entirely unconsciously" (Dennett 1991, p. 142). This can be countered by its "Orwellian alternative": "Subjects are indeed conscious of the first stimulus (which explains their capacity to guess correctly) but their memory of this conscious experience is *almost* entirely obliterated by the second stimulus (which is why they deny having seen it, in spite of their tell tale better-than-chance guesses)." (ibid.)

One reason to prefer the Stalinesque account is that it fits with what the subjects themselves believe and report. Not only do the subjects deny afterwards having seen the first stimulus; if told in advance to say during the presentation of the stimuli when they are conscious of a disk or to press a button at the moment at which they are conscious of a disk, and not to respond otherwise, they fail to respond. Try it yourself. You will find that you have a very strong sense that you are not conscious of the disk at all. But if you are not conscious of the disk, you do not undergo a visual experience that is about it. Thus, you do not see it.

This is also the result delivered by the account I developed in the preceding section. For the subjects to be conscious of the disk, they must undergo experiences that at least enable them to wonder "What is that?" with respect to it. So wondering about the disk requires bringing it under the demonstrative concept *that*. But surely there is no time at which the subjects' experiences enable them directly to think any thought about the disk or subsume it under any concept. The process that would have led to a conceptual response (or could have done so) is interfered with by the almost immediate presentation of the second stimulus (the ring). The result is that there is no time at which the subjects are conscious of the disk. And if they are not conscious of the disk, then they are not in a phenomenally conscious state *about* it. They do not undergo an experience with respect to the disk. That is why things seem to them as they do. There is nothing it is like for them to undergo the mental representation elicited by the first stimulus. Still, they do undergo such a representation. That is why they guess correctly that there were two stimuli. Both stimuli are represented, but only one stimulus is experienced. To suppose that both stimuli must be experienced, since both are represented, is to engage in the slide commented on earlier.

But might it not be the case that the subjects' experiences do at least *enable* them to wonder "What is that?" with respect the disk? They do not *actually* so wonder because of the presentation of the second stimulus. Still, they are enabled to so wonder.

This seems very implausible. The presentation of the second stimulus effectively removes the subjects' ability to wonder anything about the first stimulus or to form any beliefs about it on the basis of their experience. To be sure, had the second stimulus *not* been presented, they would have been able to do these things. But in actual fact, they cannot. Thus, in actual fact, their experiences do not enable them to form *de re* propositional attitudes about the first stimulus.

Compare: I cannot win the race on Thursday. I lack the ability to run fast enough. Thus, training hard earlier in the week does not enable me to win the race. To be sure, I would have had the ability if my right foot had not been swollen badly from an injury in a recent car accident. But in actual fact, given the swelling, I cannot win. Training hard, thus, is pointless if my goal is to win, for in the actual circumstances training hard will not *enable* me to win.

Something similar is true in the case of the perfectly camouflaged moth. I am not conscious of the moth. My experience does not enable me to pick out the moth from its surroundings. In actual fact, solely on the basis of my experience, I am not able to wonder anything about the moth. Of course, had the cones in my eyes been sensitive to the ultraviolet light reflected off the moth's wings, I would have been able to pick out the moth. Then I would have been conscious of it. But in actual fact, I am not.

In adopting the above position, I am not denying that some experiences of things in the world can be very brief. An experimental set-up can easily be devised in which, although a stimulus is flashed on a screen too quickly for subjects to be able to identify it (and perhaps even too quickly to identify its shape or color), they still have an experience of *something* (in addition to the screen). In this case, the subjects can at least ask themselves what *that* is, on the basis of their experiences, and so I accept that they are conscious of the stimulus. However, in the meta-contrast case the situation is different. The subjects in the experiment cannot tell, on the basis of their experience, when the disk was flashed on the screen at all. Going on the basis of their experiences, they have no information about the disk. They simply are not conscious of it. The disk does not look any way to them. Even though there is a visual representation of the disk, as evidenced by their guessing behavior, the only representation that makes it into consciousness is that of the ring. At a conscious level, then, the ring effectively functions as a mask with respect to the disk, even though it is in a different position in the field of view.[21]

Again, let me emphasize that the requirement for consciousness of a stimulus is not that one actually wonder anything about the stimulus. Perhaps one is a very dull person who rarely wonders anything. The requirement is that one's experience have such a character that, directly on the basis of that experience, one *can* wonder things about the stimulus (or can form other *de re* propositional attitudes about it).

Consider next the case of unilateral visual neglect. Subjects with this impairment have damage to one of the hemispheres (typically the right one), resulting in an attentional deficit with respect to the opposite side of space.[22] These subjects often behave as if the relevant side of space is nonexistent. For example, they might complain of being hungry while not eating the food on the left side of the plate. Alternatively, if asked to draw a clock, they might draw the side with the numbers from 12 to 6 correctly while leaving the other side blank. (See figure 1.4.) The behavior of these subjects is evidence that their impairment prevents them from wondering anything with respect to any item or items on the neglected side.[23] The visual experiences they undergo do not enable them to form *de re* propositional attitudes with respect to the neglected stimuli. Accordingly, on my proposal, they are not conscious of the items on the neglected side. Thus, for the same reasons as before, they do not see those items.

Figure 1.4
Right: Drawings by a subject with unilateral visual neglect. Left: Models. Source: B. Kolb and I. Whishaw, *Fundamentals of Human Neuropsychology* (Freeman, 1990).

I am not claiming that my use of 'see' is the only proper use. Zombie replicas of human beings are conceptually possible, according to many philosophers, and it does not seem clearly wrong to say that they see things even though they undergo no experiences. This, however, is a non-phenomenological use of the term 'see'. There are other related uses. Take, for example, the case of a simple surveillance robot programmed to detect activity in a yard. A thief might be intent on getting across the yard without being seen by the surveillance robot. In being so intent, the thief is not committed to supposing that the robot has experiences. He simply assumes that if he is registered or detected by the robot eyes then he is seen and the game is up. In this sense of 'see', blindsight subjects may be said to see the items in their blind fields, since they evidently do detect or register some stimuli there, as witnessed by their correct guesses about those stimuli.[24] Likewise, in this sense, some unilateral visual neglect subjects may be said to see the neglected items—at least, if they guess correctly.

My concern has been with what might be called "conscious seeing." It is evident that neither the blindsight subject nor the surveillance robot nor the zombie *consciously* sees anything.

Consider finally this case: I am viewing a room full of people. My friend Barnabus Brown is in clear view before me. I do not notice that Barnabus is present. Do I see him? Again the crucial question, on the proposed account, is whether my experience enables me *directly* to form *de re* judgments or beliefs about him. In actual fact I form no such attitudes; for I do not notice him. Could I have done so? Well, maybe. But suppose that undergoing *de re* attitudes with respect to Barnabus necessitates that I shift the focus of my eyes appropriately. Then I would have had a somewhat different experience. Phenomenologically, things would have been different. In those circumstances, Barnabus, let us suppose, would have been in the center of my field of view, whereas in actual fact he is a bit to the left. Furthermore, certain details that were not manifest in my experience before would be manifest now, and others that were manifest would have been lost.

If you have any doubts about this, position a familiar object (say, a camera) in the center of your field of view, then shift the fixation point of your eyes just a little to the right (to a magazine, say). You will find that your experience changes, and not only with respect to the positions of things relative to your point of focus. Certain letters on the camera— for example, "Canon Zoom Lens"—will no longer be discernible. You will be able to tell that there are small letters on the camera, but your experience will not be such that you can tell what they are. Other smaller letters on the magazine cover that you couldn't read before without shifting your focus will now be easily readable. In short, the scene will not *look* to you exactly as it did before. Of course, the scene itself remains the same. But the way it looks to you is slightly different. Thus, changing the fixation point of your eyes really does change your experience phenomenally.

In the case of Barnabus, thus, had I altered where I was looking, I would have had a *different* experience. Phenomenologically, things would have been different—which is not to say, of course, that my counterfactual experience might not have been very similar to my actual experience.[25] And, given my counterfactual experience, I might well have been in a position directly to form a *de re* attitude about Barnabus. But the experience I *actually* undergo is not that experience. My actual experience (let us agree) does not enable me directly to respond with a *de re* attitude to Barnabus Brown. So, I am not conscious of him. I am blind to his presence. He is hidden from me, in one sense, even though he is in plain view. Thus, I do not see him.

Suppose it is replied that Barnabus is not like the moth. The phenomenology really does differentiate him from his surroundings, whereas the phenomenology in the moth case does not mark out the moth. Given this, is it not reasonable to hold that Barnabus is seen after all?

My reply is that it depends. To be sure, there *would* be something in the phenomenology that marked out Barnabus if I *were* to shift my focus somewhat with respect to the scene before my eyes so that I was staring right at him. But that is *potential* phenomenology. Under those circumstances, I certainly would see Barnabus. But it does not follow that *in actual fact* I do. The crucial question is whether, without any shift in the focal point of my eyes, my experience enables me directly to form a *de re* conceptual attitude about Barnabus—whether, without any shift in my focus, I can differentiate him cognitively from his surroundings on the basis of my visual experience alone, without engaging in any process of inference.

Consider again the lines to the right of the dot in figure 1.1. As you fixate on the central dot, you need not actually form a *de re* conceptual attitude with respect to each of the four lines, taken separately. But your visual experience is such that, while you stare at the central dot, you *can* form such attitudes with respect to each of the lines, one by one. For each line, you can bring it under the demonstrative *that* directly on the basis of your experience. In this case, you really do see each of the four lines as you fixate on the dot. In the case of Barnabus, the situation is different, or so it is being supposed. Barnabus is more like one of the lines in the middle of the group to the left of the dot. And if he is, you do not see him.

2 Why Consciousness Cannot Be Physical and Why It Must Be

There is a familiar line of reasoning that goes as follows: Modern science tells us that we are biological organisms. We belong to one species among many: the species *Homo sapiens*. Biological organisms are a part of the natural world, and things in nature are made of matter. We ourselves, then, are material systems made of the same stuff as flowers, trees, caterpillars, and kangaroos. The difference between us and other things in nature is not that we have some additional spiritual, nonphysical component; the difference is, rather, one of the arrangement of the basic material parts and the complexity of the resultant material systems.

Of course, not everything in the natural world is a material object in the sense that a mountain or a piece of wood is a material object. Think of lightning flashes or electromagnetic fields, for example. Still, these entities have a wholly physical nature. That nature can be studied within the physical sciences alone, and ultimately that nature is microphysical.

2.1 What Is the Thesis of Physicalism?

Physicalism, in its most general form, is the thesis that no nonphysical ingredients are needed to account for anything in the actual world: the physical ingredients alone suffice (Braddon-Mitchell and Jackson 1996). Indeed, the *microphysical* ingredients alone suffice. Once the microphysical facts about the world are fixed, *everything* else in the world is automatically determined. For example, once *all* the microphysical facts are fixed, automatically there is a lightning flash in place *p*, an electromagnetic field in place *q*, a caterpillar in place *r*, a tree in place *s*, a river in place *t*, a human being in place *u*, and so on. No further nonphysical ingredients are needed to generate these things.

One way to picture what is being claimed here is to imagine God laying out all the microphysical phenomena throughout the universe. Having

done so, and having settled all the microphysical properties of those phenomena along with the basic microphysical laws, God did not then have
to ask Himself "Shall I make lightning flashes or caterpillars or mountains or human beings?" No further work was needed on His part.[1]

The basic microphysical phenomena, the physicalist may say, are those
fundamental entities and properties picked out within a completed physics. Just what counts as physics is a question that merits further discussion, but it is not one the physicalist is compelled to answer in presenting
a general statement of her view. All she needs to insist is that there are no
fundamental mental entities or properties that fall within the domain of
physics (Chalmers and Jackson 2001).

The physicalist's central idea is standardly put in terms of the notion of
a possible world. Think of the actual world as a way things actually are—
a complete way. There are many other complete ways things might have
been. These are the non-actual possible worlds. The physicalist's view (in
first approximation) is that any possible world that is a microphysical duplicate of our world is a duplicate *simpliciter*.[2] This will not quite do as it
stands, however. Consider another possible world W that is just like our
world microphysically but that contains in addition some nonphysical
angels. If physicalism is true, then W is not a duplicate of our world, for
physicalism cannot allow there to be actual nonphysical angels. Yet
according to the above statement of physicalism, if physicalism is true, it
is such a duplicate.

The usual way to handle this problem is to require that the relevant
possible worlds be minimal microphysical duplicates, where a minimal
microphysical duplicate of the actual world is a possible world that contains no more than it must to duplicate our world microphysically. Now
the world with nonphysical angels is beside the point. The physicalist's
thesis, then, comes down to this: Any possible world that is a minimal
microphysical duplicate of the actual world is a duplicate period.

There is still a difficulty for the above formulation, however. Suppose
that God exists. Since God is a necessary being, if He exists at all, He
exists in all metaphysically possible worlds. As stated above, the thesis
of physicalism claims that every possible world that is a minimal microphysical duplicate of the actual world is a duplicate *simpliciter*. Since any
world that contains no more than it must to duplicate our world microphysically contains God if God actually exists, there is no inconsistency
in supposing both that physicalism (as stated) is true and that God exists.
But there should be an inconsistency, for God is a nonphysical being and
intuitively if there are any actual, concrete, nonphysical entities then
physicalism is false.

Clearly something is missing. One simple diagnosis of the problem is that the bare-bones physicalist proposal needs to be fleshed out with the requirement that every concrete particular either be identical with a microphysical particular or be constituted by such particulars. On this view, physicalism is partly a worldly determination thesis and partly a thesis about the makeup of actual, concrete particulars.

The above account of physicalism still seems to leave unexplained certain facts that need explaining.[3] After all, why should it be the case that duplication at the microphysical level guarantees duplication across the board? It seems inimical to the spirit of physicalism simply to retort "It's a brute fact, and that's an end to it." Of course, if all particulars have a microphysical nature and all properties (and other types, for example state types) are microphysical then the explanation is straightforward. But many physicalists would deny this. And on the face of it, the suggestion is absurd. Consider, for example, the properties of being a mountain, being a river, being a continent, being a neuron, and being an earthquake. There are multiple microphysical ways of *realizing* these properties, and hence there is no single microphysical property with which each is identical.

What the above account of physicalism seems to need, then, is some explanation of a physicalistically acceptable sort as to why once the microphysical states of affairs are fixed, all the states of affairs are fixed.[4]

What is not so clear is just what form the relevant explanation should take. One reasonable proposal is that the physicalist should hold that the higher-level properties are second-order properties of the type, being a (or the) property that has feature F. Likewise for higher-level states: they are second-order states of the type, being a state that has feature F. Similarly for processes. Each higher-level entity, then, may be held to have lower-level realizations which themselves are microphysical or which have further still lower-level realizations that meet the same constraint, and so on down until each property "bottoms out" in microphysical realizations. Here it is assumed that a property P realizes a property Q if and only if Q has a second-order essence of the type, being a (or the) property that has feature F and P has F.

Consider, for example, the property of being the color of a British postbox. That is a second-order property. It is realized by the property of being red, since red is the color of British postboxes. In this case, there is just a single realization of the second-order property. The realizing property, red, is not itself a microphysical property, however, since surfaces that are microphysically very different may nonetheless share the property of being red. Thus, according to the physicalist, it too must be a second-order property having further lower-level realizations and so on down to the microphysical.

Or consider the process of reproduction. Arguably that is the process of undergoing a process the function of which is to enable living beings to transmit their genes and in so doing generate further living beings. The relevant process in paramecia is that of dividing into two; in seahorses the process involves the female's laying eggs and placing them in a pouch in the male; in humans the process is that of bearing live young. Reproduction, thus, is multiply realizable by further processes that themselves have further lower-level realizations. Ultimately, according to the physicalist, the realizations bottom out in the microphysical realm.

It is important to appreciate that the entities that partly make up the essences of other higher-order entities—the feature, Q, in the case of the property of being a property that has Q—must themselves conform to the above picture too. *All* higher-level properties, states, etc. must have lower-level realizations all the way down to the microphysical level.

This is not the only way to view the realization relation. An alternative picture at least of mental-physical realization is provided by the relationship of determinables to their determinates (Yablo 1992). The thought here is that, just as being scarlet and being crimson (determinate shades) are different ways for an object to be red, so being in physical state P_1 and being in physical state P_2 are different ways for a subject to be in mental state M. One virtue of this approach is that it makes it no more reasonable to demand an explanation of why, once the physical facts are in place, mental states are distributed as they are than it is to insist that a further explanation be given as to why once an object is scarlet it is red. Another virtue that has been claimed for this approach (ibid.) is that it leaves room for the mental to be causally efficacious with respect to the physical.[5]

Some philosophers impose a much stronger constraint on the physicalist than is required by the above views. They say that if physicalism is true, it must be the case that the microphysical truths *a priori* entail all the truths.[6] A little more carefully, they claim that the conjunction C of the microphysical truths together with a "that's all" statement (T) *a priori* entail all the truths. This as yet is no part of the picture sketched above. The addition of T amounts to an *a priori* way of capturing the minimality constraint, on the physicalist's view, on possible worlds that are microphysical duplicates of the actual world. Consistent with the earlier account of physicalism, it could be that the higher-level properties, states, processes, etc. do not have essences that can be articulated *a priori* from the armchair.

This version of the physicalist's view faces an immediate and obvious difficulty. Indexical truths such as 'I am tall' are not *a priori* entailed by the microphysical truths. This difficulty can be overcome by adding a further qualification to the statement of *a priori* physicalism. The conjunction of C and T needs to be supplemented by some indexical information, specifically the conjunction of two further truths 'I am A' and 'Now is B', where A is an identifying description of myself (or the relevant subject) and B is an identifying description of the current time (Chalmers and Jackson 2001).[7] These descriptions are to be understood to be such that the conjunction of C and T *a priori* entails that there is a single individual or time satisfying the relevant description. The idea here is that once the conjunction of C and T is supplemented by this information, the subject will then be able to locate himself on the objective map provided by the conjunction of C and T, and thus the conjunction of C and T and the above indexical information will *a priori* entail all truths.

To get a sense for what this version of physicalism is committed to, consider the truth that water covers most of the Earth. How is this truth to be *a priori* deduced from the microphysical facts? Well, suppose that

(1) H_2O covers most of the Earth

is *a priori* deducible from the microphysical truths. Suppose also that

(2) H_2O is the watery stuff of our acquaintance

is *a priori* deducible from the microphysical facts along with the above indexical truths. Given

(3) Water is the watery stuff of our acquaintance,

which is supposed to be an *a priori* truth supportable by reflection on the concept *water*,[8] we may deduce

(4) Water covers most of the Earth.

What goes for the truth (4) goes for all non-microphysical truths, according to the *a priori* physicalist.

2.2   Why Consciousness Cannot Be Physical

There are a number of well-known puzzles or problems that consciousness, and in particular phenomenal consciousness, presents for physicalism. I shall distinguish four here. These four puzzles are widely seen as creating the biggest obstacles to the truth of physicalism.

The first puzzle is what we might call "the zombie problem." A philosophical zombie is not someone who looks like the individual depicted in

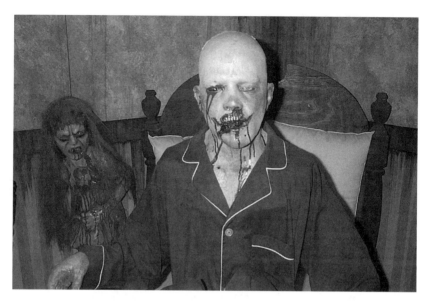

Figure 2.1
A Hollywood zombie.

figure 2.1. That is a Hollywood zombie. A philosophical zombie is someone who looks like an everyday human being, for example, the individual
depicted in figure 2.2.

The difference between a zombie and a real person is simply that the
zombie lacks any phenomenal consciousness. My zombie twin is a perfect
microphysical duplicate of me—and thus, given an identity of physical
setting, he processes information just as I do in all respects, both wide
and narrow—but he experiences nothing. There is *nothing* it is like for
him.

Philosophers who bring up the case of zombies are not claiming that
zombies are *naturally* possible—i.e., that they could exist in the actual
world without violating any actual laws. The claim is, rather, that the
idea of a zombie is internally consistent. Zombies, thus, are logically possible: there is a logically possible world in which zombies exist even if they
don't exist in the actual world. Call this the "zombie hypothesis."

Consider, then, a zombie replica of the actual world—a world just like
ours microphysically but without any phenomenal consciousness. If the
zombie hypothesis is internally consistent, then it seems that there is a
possible world that is such a replica. Such a world would be a minimal
microphysical duplicate of the actual world; however, it would not be a

Figure 2.2
Evelyn Waugh (author of *Brideshead Revisited* and one of my favorite authors) in
a characteristic pose.

duplicate period, for phenomenal consciousness would be lacking in that
world. It follows that physicalism is false.[9] The zombie hypothesis, then,
seems to suggest that the existence of consciousness in the actual world is
a *further* nonphysical fact about it. To put the point in the picturesque
form used earlier to make the hypothesis of physicalism vivid: Even if
God had no further work to do in determining whether there would be a
tree in place p or a river in place q or a neuron-firing in place r, say, having settled all the microphysical facts, God *did* have more work to do to
guarantee that we were not zombies. He had to add something extra,
namely phenomenal consciousness. That is left out by the physicalist
account.

A second problem is presented by the example of Mary in her black-
and-white room (Jackson 1982). Mary has been trapped in the room since
birth. She has at her disposal computers and monitors and books, but the
monitors and the books are all black-and-white. Through time Mary
becomes an expert on color vision. Eventually she comes to know everything there is to know about what goes on physically and functionally in
human beings when they see various colors. But still there is something
she does not know: the phenomenal character of the experience of red,
the phenomenal character of the experience of blue, the phenomenal
character of the experience of green, and so on. When she leaves her

room and sees objects with these colors, Mary discovers something new: she finds out what it is like to experience red, blue, green, etc. This is a genuinely new piece of knowledge. But how can this be, if in her room Mary knew all the physical facts? It appears that physicalism leaves something out again, namely what it is like to experience the various colors.

This point is especially straightforward on the *a priori* version of physicalism. Mary in her room cannot *a priori* deduce what it is like to see red from her store of microphysical information, her indexical knowledge of her own location, and a "That's all" claim. But if this is not so deducible, then the phenomenal character of the experience of red is not physical. Physicalism is false. Let us call this "the Mary puzzle."[10]

The third puzzle has come to be known as the *explanatory gap* (DuBois-Reymond 1885–1887; Wittgenstein 1953; Levine 1983; McGinn 1991). Tell me everything you like about what goes on physically and functionally in someone who is experiencing red and, it seems, you still will not have told me what it is *like* to experience red, for even after I have all the relevant physical and functional information, I can still intelligibly ask "Why do those physical and functional goings-on generate *that* phenomenal character (the phenomenal character of the experience of red)? Why *couldn't* another phenomenal character be present?"

Since the physicalist seems compelled to hold that the determination of non-microphysical phenomena by microphysical phenomena is something that can be explained, the existence of the explanatory gap puts pressure on physicalism. For what *is* the explanation? It seems that we haven't a clue. One reasonable response, then, is to say that physicalism is false, that the physicalist story is incomplete and that is why there is an explanatory gap.

The so-called Hard Problem is a cousin of the explanatory-gap puzzle just bruited. It asks not why physical processes give rise to *this* experience as opposed to *that* one but rather why they give rise to conscious experience at all (Chalmers 1996). Why couldn't the same physical processes that are present in me be present and yet I not have *any* experiences? After all, in that situation, if I were a zombie, I would function in just the same way as I actually function. Given the same physical stimuli, I would respond just as I actually respond, assuming all the underlying physical processes were the same. So why am I not a zombie?

Again, the natural thought occasioned by these reflections is that the physical story is incomplete, insofar as it lacks the resources to account properly for the phenomenon of conscious experience.

There are well-known physicalist responses to these puzzles, but I have come to think that all of them are lacking.

2.3   Why Consciousness Must Be Physical

It seems very hard to deny that consciousness has effects on our behavior. The anguish Jane feels over a broken love affair causes her to keep reliving certain moments in her memory, to call up her friends and ask them for support, and to say various things to them and to herself as she reflects on the sorry state she has got herself into. The wonderful taste John experiences as he bites into some crabmeat lasagna causes him to smile and to thank his host for cooking such a good meal. The pain Sebastian feels in his buttocks as his headmaster lashes him with a cane causes him to scream loudly. The embarrassment Samantha experiences as she slips and falls on her way to a table in an expensive restaurant causes her to flush.

That phenomenally conscious states have effects of this sort seems undeniable (which is not to say, of course, that some philosophers have not denied it). But we now know enough to know that physical behavior in all probability has a complete explanation in neurophysiological terms. Muscles twitch as a result of the electrical messages that come down the axons of the motor neurons. Those messages are generated by the responses of the cell bodies of those neurons to the electrical messages passing along their dendrites, which in turn are triggered by the messages from the cranial neurons to which they are connected. Those neurons fire in response to incoming messages from other neurons, all the way back (in typical cases) to messages from the sensory neurons. The sensory neurons, in turn, respond to the messages they receive from transducers in the eyes, the ears, the nose, the mouth, and the skin, and these transducers themselves respond to physical energy of various sorts—light, sound, smell, chemical flavor, pressure, heat, damage, and so on. In short, the evidence strongly suggests that there is a complete chain of physical causes. This is true at both the token level and the type level. Token physical events in the brain cause muscle twitchings, and they do so in virtue of their neurological properties. How, then, can token experiences have any effect on our behavior if they are nonphysical? Alternatively, if token experiences are physical and they have additional nonphysical properties, how can their nonphysical properties have any causal impact on our behavior?

As an illustration of the problem at the type level, suppose that Tom's current feeling of pain is one and the same as (or is constituted by) token neuron-firing N in Tom's brain. N causes the event of Tom's groaning G. The empirical evidence supports the view that N causes G in virtue of its physical properties. If N has an additional, nonphysical property P, then N does not cause G in virtue of having P, for even if P had been missing, N would have caused G so long as it had the same physical properties, just as the sounds emitted from my stereo system would still have caused the shattering of the wine glass even if those sounds had possessed different semantic properties so long their physical properties (pitch, loudness, etc.) remained the same.[11]

One reply the anti-physicalist might make to the above points is that they rest on a false assumption. Experiences really cause actions, not behavior. But this seems woefully inadequate. For one thing, in some of the examples given above it seems clear that the effects of experiences are straightforwardly behavioral. For another, even if a distinction is drawn between actions and behavior, an action A and its realizing behavior B may both cause the same effect in the physical world. Thus, my reaching for the glass of water and bringing it to my mouth causes the glass to move from point P to point P' in space. Likewise, my arm's going out and my hand's encircling the glass and moving back to my mouth has the very same effect. That effect is physical and has a complete set of physical causes. How, then, can it be caused by an action resulting from a desire to drink some water (plus an appropriate belief about the location of the water), where the desire is caused by my feeling of thirst, if feelings are not physical?

A second possible reply is that quantum mechanics casts doubt on the idea that there is a complete physical explanation of behavior on the grounds that if quantum mechanics is true, some physical events in the brain are not determined by prior physical causes. This is confused, however, for two reasons. First, the claim that there are no nonphysical causes does not require a deterministic reading. For all we know, the basic physical causal generalizations themselves have a probabilistic character. Second, so long as prior physical causes alone fix the probabilities of later physical events, there will be no room for nonphysical causes.

To see this, suppose that nonphysical experiences really do influence neurotransmitter movements. Then certain movements of neurotransmitters would occur more frequently when preceded by such experiences than when not. In this situation, independent nonphysical causes would have an effect on the probabilities of various physical results. This would be at odds with the idea that prior physical causes alone fix the probabilities of later physical events. Of course, such a possibility cannot be ruled out *a priori*. But this would be inconsistent with the quantum-mechanical version of the causal closure of the physical world (Papineau 2000).

A third line that might be taken by those who wish to hold on to the view that experiences are nonphysical notwithstanding the causal closure of the physical world is that there is over-determination of some human behavior. There is a neurological cause of my screaming after the dagger rips my flesh, but there is also an independent mental cause: my feeling pain. Each cause is sufficient for the behavior to occur. Thus, the behavior would have occurred if only one of the two causes had been present.

One significant difficulty for this view is that the usual cases of over-determination involve some differences in effects. For example, the shot through my heart caused my death, and so did the simultaneous lightning strike. But the shot also caused a hole in my heart whereas the lightning strike did not, and the lightning strike also caused burn marks on my shoulder whereas the shot did not. Such differences are not available in the mental case if the physical world is causally closed. For suppose that my feeling pain causes an additional physical effect, E, over and above my screaming. Given closure, E must have an independent physical cause. Thus, E must be over-determined, just as my screaming is. The problem of over-determination now recurs.

Another worry for the over-determination strategy is that it seems poorly motivated. To see this, suppose that the inhabitants of a small village take the view that little Albert's sickness was caused by a spell cast on him by a witch whom he met on his way home. Investigation by scientists reveals that Albert's sickness was caused by a virus created by the unsanitary living conditions in Albert's house. In this case, the folk could hold on to their view that the witches' spell caused Albert's sickness by appealing to over-determination. But then any causal explanation of anything could be saved in this way. And that patently is unacceptable. So what makes it acceptable to appeal to over-determination in the mental case but not in the case of little Albert?

A fourth possible reply is to claim that what the scientific evidence really shows is only that physical events in the brain are causally sufficient for behavior, not that they cause behavior (at least in many cases). To appreciate what is being suggested here, consider a case of trumping pre-emption proposed by Jonathan Schaffer (2000). Suppose that it is a law of magic that the first spell cast on a given day is the one that takes effect at midnight of the same day. Suppose further that at noon Merlin casts the first spell of the day—a spell to turn the prince into a frog. Later that day, at 6:00 p.m. Morgana casts the only other spell that day, which serendipitously is also a spell to turn the prince into a frog. Suppose finally that at midnight the prince becomes a frog. We should all agree, given the laws of magic, that Merlin's spell is a cause of the prince's becoming a frog and that Morgana's is not. Merlin's spell trumps Morgana's. Still, Morgana's spell is causally sufficient for the prince's becoming a frog. After all, if Merlin had not cast his spell, the prince would have become a frog in virtue of the effect of Morgana's spell. Thus, whether or not Merlin had cast his spell, Morgana's spell sufficed to turn the prince into a frog.

The suggestion, then, is that phenomenally conscious events trump neural events as causes of the relevant pieces of behavior. In Tom's case, neural event N is causally sufficient for his groaning G, but it is his pain that causes G, where his pain is neither identical with N nor constituted by it.

This maneuver does not do adequate justice to what scientists believe and say. In denying that neurological events really cause behavior, the anti-physicalist is adopting a revisionary position. Leaving this to one side, there is a further worry. The proposal requires us to believe that if Tom's pain had occurred without N, G would still have resulted (just as the prince's turning into a frog would have resulted if Merlin had cast his spell and Morgana had not). Arguably this counterfactual is true, since in the nearest world to the actual world in which Tom's pain occurs without N, a neural event very similar to N occurs even though N itself does not and so (arguably) the downstream neural consequences are the same and the same behavior results. But it is equally true that if N had occurred without Tom's pain, behavior G would have resulted. Thus, the situation with respect to Tom's pain and N seems symmetrical here. Why, then, count Tom's pain the cause of G and not N?

In the Merlin case, we choose Merlin's spell over Morgana's as the cause of the prince's turning into a frog, since it is a law of magic that the first spell of the day takes effect at midnight of the same day. But there is no comparable law that dictates the choice of Tom's pain over N. Rather, there is a law connecting pain and groaning and there is also a law connecting the relevant type of neural state and groaning. Thus, without some further story here, the trumping pre-emption proposal is *ad hoc*. It simply stipulates that Tom's pain is a genuine cause of his groaning and N is not.[12]

As far as the general issue of the nature of causation goes, one natural suggestion is that the causal relation be understood in terms of a suitable counterfactual dependence. But it is commonly held that the cases of trumping pre-emption undermine any simple counterfactual proposal (Lewis 1973).[13] I shall not try to settle the question of the correct approach to causation here. Instead, I shall close the chapter by briefly considering an account—due to Yablo (1992)—of how mental causation can occur in a material world. This account has points of contact with the anti-physicalist appeal to trumping discussed above.

Let us grant for present purpose that the realization relation is the determination relation, as Yablo holds. Yablo further claims that causes are normally *proportional* to their effects—that is, they don't incorporate irrelevant detail when it comes to bringing about their effects. This is captured in the following principle:

(PP) A state D incorporates detail which is irrelevant with respect to an effect E, and so does not cause E, if there is some state C such that C is a determinable of D and the following counterfactual is true: $(C \mathbin{\&} \sim D) > E$.

Yablo illustrates (PP) by reference to a trained pigeon, Sophie, who pecks whenever she sees red. One day, a scarlet triangle is placed before Sophie. She pecks at it. According to (PP), the triangle's being scarlet is not a cause of Sophie's pecking. This is because being red is a determinable of being scarlet, and if the triangle had been red without being scarlet (if, for instance, it had been crimson) Sophie still would have pecked. The triangle's being scarlet is causally sufficient for Sophie's pecking, but on Yablo's view it is not properly viewed as causing the pecking.

Now, if the realization relation between mental and physical states just is the determination relation, and mental states are realized by physical states, then, for each mental state M, there must be some physical state S that determines it. Thus, consider the mental state of Paul's being in intense pain. That state is realized by microphysical state S_1. Yablo's proportionality principle can now provide an answer to the question as to how the state of Paul's being in intense pain can cause his screaming. The answer, in brief, is simply that it can do so provided that the following counterfactual is true:

(C) If Paul had been in pain without S_1 occurring, then Paul would still have screamed.

And intuitively (C) is true, or so Yablo claims.[14]

The idea, then, is as follows: If (C) is true, S_1 incorporates details that are irrelevant to Paul's screaming. Thus, S_1 is not a cause of Paul's screaming. This now makes it possible for Paul's being in pain to be the cause—just as it is the triangle's being red and not its being scarlet that causes Sophie's pecking. In short, there is room for a mental cause to operate.

One objection to this account is that the truth of (C) doesn't demonstrate that the state of Paul's being in pain causes his screaming; consistent with the truth of (C), it could simply be that if Paul's pain state had been physically realized in a different way then that physical state would have caused the screaming, in which case Paul's pain state would be causally excluded.[15]

Still, if (PP) is true and mental states are realized by physical states in the way that Yablo supposes, there is reason to hold that the physical state realizing Paul's pain state does *not* cause his screaming. This is not an altogether happy result, it seems to me, since the denial of the claim that the physical state causes the behavior does not fit well with the scientists' view of the matter (as I noted earlier in this section). Still, there is *room*, on Yablo's account, for Paul's pain state to cause his behavior, and to do so without posing any threat to physicalism.

3 Physicalism and the Appeal to Phenomenal Concepts

For the reasons offered in chapter 2, there is widespread agreement that consciousness must be a physical phenomenon, even if it is one that we do not yet understand and perhaps may never do so fully. There is also widespread agreement that the way to defend physicalism about consciousness against a variety of well-known objections is by appeal to phenomenal concepts (Balog 1999 and forthcoming; Loar 1990; Lycan 1996; Papineau 1993; Sturgeon 1994; Tye 1995, 2000; Perry 2001). There is, however, no agreement on the nature of phenomenal concepts. The purpose of this chapter is to lay out how the phenomenal-concept strategy, as we might call it, is supposed to go and to argue that it encounters some serious difficulties. My diagnosis for these difficulties is that in a sense to be explained there are no phenomenal concepts. Physicalists have thought that they were wedded to such concepts since without them, physicalism is false. In subsequent chapters, I shall try to show that this view is seriously mistaken.

3.1 Some Terminological Points

As I shall be using them, the terms 'concept' and 'thought content' individuate in a fine-grained way. Consider the case of the thought that coriander is a spice. Intuitively, what I think—the content of my thought—when I have this thought is not what I think when I think that cilantro is a spice. The two thoughts play different roles in rationalizing explanations. This is why it is possible for me to *discover* that coriander is cilantro.

The concepts *coriander* and *cilantro* have the same referent, but the way in which the referent is presented in the two cases is different. One who thinks of coriander (cilantro) as coriander thinks of it under a different guise or in a different way from one who thinks of it as cilantro. Thus, the content of the one thought is different from the content of the other. In general, I take thought contents to be indicated by the 'that' clauses used to attribute thoughts. Moreover, in the first-person case, I take the content attributed via the 'that' clause to be the content of the thought, assuming that the thought ascription is true.[1] In the third-person case, the situation is more complicated. Here the thought ascription is sometimes counted as true even if the content of the thought is not the same as the content attributed, so long as there is sufficient similarity between the two. Accordingly, I take the 'that' clause in such a case to indicate that the thought has a content that, in the given context, is sufficiently similar to the content of the sentence embedded in the 'that' clause.

As I use the term 'concept', concepts are not linguistic terms in a public language. They are mental representations of a sort that can occur in thought.[2] Thoughts are composed of concepts and concepts individuate in a fine-grained way. As illustrated in the case above of the concepts *cilantro* and *coriander*, concepts that refer to the same entities can differ in their content. Indeed, concepts can differ in their content even if they refer to the same entity in all possible worlds. For example, the concept *Hesperus* has a different content from the concept *Phosphorus*, even though they both refer to the planet Venus in all possible worlds. This is why the thought that Hesperus is a planet is a different thought from the thought that Phosphorus is a planet. Similar comments apply to the concept *four* and the concept *two times two*. A small child who can count to four has the former concept, but she may not yet have learned how to multiply and thus may lack the latter concept. Such a child can think the thought that four is greater than three without being able to think the thought that two times two is greater than three. Likewise, in my view, the concept *fortnight* is a different concept from the concept *fourteen days*. One might be misinformed and believe that a fortnight is ten days without thereby believing that fourteen days is ten days. Concepts of which one has a partial understanding are still concepts one may exercise in belief and thought.

Concepts, then, are finely individuated mental representations of worldly entities—things, events, states, properties, etc. They are exercised whenever we undergo thoughts or other comparable mental states. One cannot notice something, recognize it, or make a judgment about it without conceptualizing it in some way, without bringing it under a concept. A child who is unable to count may see five pieces of candy but cannot notice that five pieces are present. A dog may hear a Beethoven symphony, but it cannot recognize the sounds as being a Beethoven symphony.

So far I have not said anything directly about concept *possession*. This too merits some brief preliminary discussion. What is it for a given concept to be a concept of *mine*? What is it for me to *possess* a concept? A straightforward answer is just this: I possess a given concept *C* if and only if I am able to exercise *C* in *my* thoughts. This answer is not very informative, however, for under what conditions can I exercise a concept in my thoughts? Given the phenomenon of partial understanding, the ability to exercise a concept in thought does not require full mastery of the concept. But this ability surely does require at least partial under-standing of the concept. And once one has at least a partial understand-ing, one can employ the concept in thought. Thus, another answer to the above question is that I possess the concept *C* if and only if I have at least a partial understanding of *C*. On this intuitively attractive view, one can-not possess the concept *fortnight*, for example, unless one grasps that a fortnight is a period of time. Similarly, one cannot possess the ordinary concept *red* unless one grasps that red is a color. Whether there are con-cepts the possession of which requires full understanding is a topic I will address later in this chapter.

A further requirement on concept possession is given by Gareth Evans's Generality Constraint (1982). A simple way to state the con-straint, idealizing away from limitations imposed by short-term memory and attention, is as follows: For any concepts a thinker possesses, the thinker can think any thought that can be formed from those concepts. This constraint places a necessary condition on concept possession and it is compatible with the above proposals so long as I am capable of exercis-ing a concept *C* in my thoughts only if I am capable of thinking any thoughts that can be formed from combining *C* with other concepts I pos-sess. Those who hold that thought is systematic and productive will hap-pily grant this, but not everyone will accede to such a requirement.

According to proponents of the phenomenal-concept strategy, phe-nomenal concepts are the concepts we exercise when (but not only when) we notice or become aware of the phenomenal character of our experi-ences and feelings via introspection. Our experiences have phenomenal character whether or not we attend to them, but when we notice how an experience feels, what it is like, in doing so we are bringing it beneath a phenomenal concept. Without phenomenal concepts, we would be 'blind' to our phenomenal feels (Dretske 1995; Tye 1995), just as the child who cannot count is 'blind' to the fact that there are five pieces of candy in front of her.

3.2   Why Physicalists Appeal to Phenomenal Concepts

Physicalists about consciousness typically agree with the following claims:

(a) Zombies are conceivable. We can conceive of physical duplicates, one of whom has experiences while the other has no experiences at all. Such duplicates may be metaphysically impossible, but they are conceivable (just as it is conceivable that I am not Michael Tye even though, given the actual facts, it is metaphysically impossible).

(b) Frank Jackson's Mary (1982)—the color scientist imprisoned since birth in a black-and-white room and possessed of all the physical information about color and color vision—doesn't know what it is like to experience red, green, etc. while she remains in the room. When she is freed and she starts to undergo color experiences, she makes some important discoveries.

(c) Presented with the full physical story about pain (or any other experience), we can still intelligibly ask "Why do those physical states feel like that? Why do they feel any way at all? How can it be that neurological changes generate 'technicolor phenomenology'?"

The usual line taken by physicalists to explain (a) is to say that phenomenal concepts are not physical concepts.[3] Since phenomenal concepts are different from physical concepts, we can conceive of zombies. There is no contradiction or incoherence in the thought that a given organism meets whatever are the relevant physical conditions for consciousness and yet feels nothing—any more than there is a contradiction or incoherence in the thought that I am not Michael Tye, or that water is not H_2O, or that now is not 2:15 p.m.

The usual way for physicalists to explain (b) is to say that Mary in her room does not possess the phenomenal color experience concepts the rest of us possess. She acquires these concepts as she notices the colors of flowers, trees, houses, etc. and as she attends to her color experiences in doing so. Once the new concepts are acquired, Mary can come to think new thoughts, and thereby she is able to make new discoveries. (I shall return to this point later.)

This line of reply to the Mary example requires again that phenomenal concepts not be physical concepts; if they were, Mary would possess them in her room, given her complete knowledge of all the physical facts. Nor can phenomenal concepts be demonstrative concepts utilizing physical sortals. To appreciate this, suppose that Mortimer is undergoing an experience of red and that Mary is viewing the physical state in Mortimer with which this phenomenal experience is identical through a cerebroscope suitably attached to her black-and-white room. She conceives of the state she sees as that F state, where 'F' is a physical predicate expressing the appropriate physical property. Patently, when she leaves her room and attentively experiences red she still makes a significant discovery.

A further conclusion that physicalists standardly draw from the Mary example is that phenomenal concepts are perspectival. Possessing the phenomenal color experience concepts that Mary lacks requires having a certain perspective on color experiences—the perspective conferred by undergoing the experiences. Mary in her room does not have the appropriate perspective.

The usual line taken by physicalists to explain (c) is to say that the intelligibility of the explanatory-gap questions requires again that phenomenal concepts not be physical concepts (at least if the physical story is complete) and further that there be no physical concepts that are *a priori* co-referential with any phenomenal concepts. To see this, suppose that 'pain*' below is used purely phenomenally for a state whose essence is the specific, unpleasant phenomenal character of pain, and suppose that 'F' is a physical predicate. Now consider the following argument form:

(i) Pain* is the F.

(ii) Physical state so-and-so is present.

(iii) Physical state so-and-so is the F.

Therefore,

(iv) Pain* is present.

Claims (ii) and (iii) are straightforwardly empirical, physical claims. Thus, if (i) is an *a priori* truth knowable by anyone who possesses the phenomenal concept *pain**, then, since (iv) is *a priori* deducible from (i)–(iii), there will be an explanation for why physical state so-and-so feels the way pain* does that is available without further empirical investigation to anyone who has that concept and who also has the requisite physical information. And this will be the case even if (i) is not a necessary *a priori* truth.

For the physicalist, then, it is usually supposed that any satisfactory account of phenomenal concepts must allow that, although phenomenal concepts refer to physical properties, they are not physical concepts, they are not demonstrative concepts utilizing physical sortals, they have no *a priori* associated co-referential physical concepts, and they are perspectival (in the sense given earlier).

So far I have said primarily what phenomenal concepts are not. What positive alternatives remain open?

3.3   Various Accounts of Phenomenal Concepts

One possibility is that phenomenal concepts are concepts that have explicitly non-physical definitions. A second possibility is that phenomenal concepts are primitive rigid concepts whose reference is fixed by an explicitly nonphysical description. A third alternative is that phenomenal concepts are indexical concepts utilizing explicitly nonphysical sortals. Each of these three alternatives entails that physicalism about consciousness is false.

Another alternative is that phenomenal concepts are concepts that have phenomenal definitions. This sets off a vicious regress and so gives us no satisfactory account of how phenomenal concepts operate. The same is true if we say that phenomenal concepts are primitive rigid concepts whose reference is fixed by a phenomenal description, for how do the concepts expressed in the phenomenal description refer? Given that phenomenal concepts have their reference fixed by a phenomenal description, the answer must be "by further associated phenomenal descriptions," and so on without end.

A further alternative is to hold that phenomenal concepts are demonstrative concepts utilizing phenomenal sortals. *Prima facie*, this proposal sets off a similar regress. But the threat of such a regress is staved off by a Ned Block's proposal (American Philosophical Association symposium talk, Pacific Division, 2001) that phenomenal concepts paradigmatically have the form *that phenomenal property*, where the indexical or demonstrative *that* refers to the phenomenal property exemplified in an associated mental sample (presumably an image or a quasi-image[4]). For example, suppose that I think in a phenomenal way of something's looking red. On this proposal, the image of red accompanying my thought exemplifies the phenomenal property RED* and my thought refers to the same phenomenal property by conceiving of it as that property—the one exemplified in my image.[5] If this account is applied to the concept *phenomenal property* as itself having the form *that phenomenal property*, the regress is stopped.

It is clear that Block's proposal meets the earlier desiderata on phenomenal concepts. One cannot possess a given phenomenal concept, on Block's account, without having the appropriate experience. So, phenomenal concepts are perspectival and relatedly they are not physical. However, leaving aside the point that it is far from obvious that there is always an associated mental sample when a phenomenal concept is exercised,[6] there are two insuperable difficulties. One is that a mental sample that exemplifies one phenomenal property will exemplify many. My image, when I think of something's looking red, will not only exemplify RED* but also (let us suppose) SCARLET*, DARK RED*, HAVING A COLOR*, and so on. Which of the exemplified properties is the one to which the demonstrative concept *that phenomenal property* refers? It seems that appealing to a mental sample does not help to fix the reference of the phenomenal concept at all. A second difficulty, related to the first, concerns the phenomenal concept *phenomenal property*. What is the relevant sample for this concept? It appears that *any* phenomenal image or quasi-image will do, in which case the problem of too many eligible candidates for reference rears its head again.

Perhaps it will be replied that the problem of too many eligible candidates goes away on the supposition that the property to which the demonstrative *that* refers is the phenomenal property (exemplified in the sample) to which the imager is attending. This does not help, however. Attention to a property is not like training the eyes on a point in space. Given the multiplicity of exemplified properties, attention to one of those properties in particular requires singling out the relevant property. And that involves bringing it under a concept—or, rather, it involves bringing it under a concept *if* attending to phenomenal character via introspection involves bringing that character under a concept, as those philosophers who accept the phenomenal-concept strategy suppose. The appropriate concept here will surely be a phenomenal one. Thus, the proposal is now circular.

In a recent essay (2006b), Block modifies his earlier view slightly and tries to meet the above objection. He now claims that phenomenal concepts have the form *the experience:* -----, where the blank is filled by the phenomenal property that is the referent of the concept. He claims further that it is only in fundamental uses that there is an actual occurrence of phenomenal properties, and that in such uses an actually occurring experience is used to think about that very experience. As for the above objection, here is what Block says:

What makes it the case that a token phenomenal property in a phenomenal concept serves as a token of one phenomenal type or property rather than another? For example, suppose that a token of a mental image of red serves in a phenomenal concept to pick out an experience as of red. Why red rather than scarlet or colored? One answer is an appeal to dispositions. Suppose you are looking at chips in an ideal paint store that has a chip for every distinct color.... You are looking at $Green_{126,731}$, thinking that the experience as of that color is nice, using a phenomenal concept of that experience. But what experience is it that your phenomenal concept is of? The experience as of $Green_{126,731}$? The experience as of green? The answer on the dispositionalist view is that it depends on the subject's disposition to, for example, treat another experience as falling under the same concept. You are thinking that the experience is nice—but what will you count as another one of those? If only another experience as of $Green_{126,731}$ will count as an experience of the same type, the phenomenal concept is maximally specific; if any bluish green experience will count as an experience of the same type, the concept is more abstract. If any experience of green will count as an experience of the same type, the concept is still more abstract. (2006b, p. 48, n. 31)

This attempt to deal with the objection does not work. Counting or treating another experience E as one of those—that is, as being of the same type as the experience F tokened in the use of a given phenomenal concept—involves judging or being prepared (or disposed) to judge that E is of the same type as F. The relevant typing here is phenomenal. Block's suggestion is that the phenomenal concept I am exercising in my thought as I look at a color chip picks out the experience as of $Green_{126,731}$ if I am only prepared to accept that another experience as of $Green_{126,731}$ is of the same phenomenal type. But this acceptance requires subsumption of the two experiences under the concept *having the same phenomenal character* and that concept involves the concept *having a phenomenal character* (or *being a phenomenal type*). So how does the referent of that most general phenomenal concept get fixed in a given use? In part, presumably, via my disposition to treat *all* other experiences as falling under it. But this now is patently circular.[7]

David Papineau (1993) has a view similar to Block's. His claim is that our brains are wired to form copies or replicas of the experiences we undergo, and these replicas play a role in fixing the reference of phenomenal concepts. Specifically, Papineau's proposal is that phenomenal concepts have the structure *that experience*, where the demonstrative refers to the experience type exemplified in an associated image or copy of the experience. On Papineau's account, exercising a concept of a phenomenal state involves re-creating it or simulating it and thinking of it as that state, the one tokened in the simulation. Such thoughts occur in introspective awareness of phenomenal states and also in memory of such states and imaginative acts.

This proposal, like Block's, secures the truth of the claim that phenomenal concepts are perspectival. One objection to it is that when I deploy a phenomenal concept in an introspective act (e.g., when I introspectively recognize the feel of a tickle), the only experiential state present is surely the one I am recognizing (e.g., the tickle feeling). There isn't a *further* image or copy of a tickle within my introspective act of recognition or associated with it. If there were, it would be accessible to me through my further awareness that I am engaging in an act of introspectively recognizing a tickle. But no such tickle copy or replica reveals itself to me.

Papineau's response to this objection (in conversation) is that in the case of introspective recognition the relevant sample is just the token experience I am undergoing. Block says the same thing in his 2006a account. This gets over the difficulty of there being too many experiences, but it has as a consequence that error with respect to the application of the concept in such a case is impossible. I return to this topic in chapter 8.

A second difficulty for Papineau's proposal is that the introspective act of recognizing pain now itself involves the token pain recognized. So, the thought involved in the introspective act has a part that itself hurts! But that seems wrong-headed. Intuitively, nothing *in* the thought is hurting me.

A third problem is that the earlier objection to Block applies to Papineau too. What Papineau—following Hugh Mellor (1992)—calls "exemplificatory reference by secondary experience" (Papineau 1993, p. 112) is not reference at all. Consider the idea when I think of pain in a phenomenal way, I exercise the concept *that experience (type)*, where the demonstrative picks out the type of experience tokened in an associated pain image or replica. There is, alas, no such thing as *the* type of experience so tokened. There are many types. My pain replica exemplifies the phenomenal quality PAIN* but also exemplifies such phenomenal qualities as THROBBING PAIN*, DULL PAIN*, and PRICKING PAIN* as well as such phenomenal properties as HAVING A PHENOMENAL QUALITY and HAVING AN UNPLEASANT PHENOMENAL QUALITY.[8]

Block's and Papineau's primary mistake, then, is to suppose that images play a *reference-fixing* role for phenomenal concepts. As far as reference goes, associated images play no role at all.

Another closely related view is that of Katalin Balog (forthcoming). Her basic idea is like those of Block and Papineau. In her view, phenomenal concepts are special in that they are partly constituted by the experiences they represent. More specifically, her claim is that a phenomenal concept *C*, as used by subject *S*, refers to a phenomenal property or type *P if*, were *S* confronted with any token of *P*, she would judge that that token is a token of the same kind of experience as this token of *P*, where this token is an experience that *S* is undergoing and that thereby partly constitutes *S*'s token of *C*. The condition Balog offers here seems to be a sufficient one (at least she uses 'if'), but presumably what she wants in the end are conditions that are necessary and sufficient.

There are various difficulties with this proposal. I'll mention two. First, since any token of *P* will also be a token of many phenomenal properties, as was noted above (an intense burning pain, for example, is a token of PAIN, of INTENSE PAIN, of BURNING PAIN, of EXPERIENCE, etc.), it should be obvious that Balog will not get sufficiency unless she adds a further condition, namely that if *S* were confronted with any token of phenomenal property *Q*, where *Q* is different from *P* and that token is not also a token of *P*, *S* would not judge that that token is a token of the same kind of experience as this token of *P*, where this token is an experience *S* is undergoing.[9] Second, and much more important, the relevant kind of sameness is phenomenal, where phenomenal sameness is sameness in phenomenal character. But, as I noted in connection with Block's view, to judge whether such sameness obtains one needs the concept *phenomenal character*. And this is itself a phenomenal concept (the most general such concept). Thus, Balog's account, as stated, looks as if it cannot succeed.

One reply that might be made here is that talk of judgment should be removed from the account and talk of nonconceptual dispositions introduced to replace it.[10] But this seems very obscure. Furthermore, appeal to such dispositions is in danger of undercutting the whole appeal to phenomenal concepts in the first place.

Brian Loar (1990/1997) has another view of phenomenal concepts. His claim is that they are recognitional concepts of a special kind. Recognitional concepts are concepts we use when we recognize items as being *one of those* and we do so without our using any theoretical knowledge. Take, for example, the ability to recognize rattlesnakes by sight. This ability requires the possession of a recognitional concept of a rattlesnake. This concept uses a non-theoretical mode of presentation, for example, *normally causing a so-and-so experience*. One who has this concept is disposed to apply it to rattlesnakes (under normal viewing conditions). Now consider the ability we have to recognize which phenomenal properties our inner states have via introspection. According to Loar, this ability is a matter of our being disposed to apply the appropriate recognitional concepts to phenomenal properties. The recognitional concepts so applied are special in that the properties they pick out also serve as modes of presentation for the concepts. These properties may sometimes be exemplified in associated mental samples that accompany application of the concepts, but this need not be the case. Sometimes there is no sample. Of course, one could have theoretical concepts of the phenomenal properties picked out by phenomenal concepts. One might, for example, have a neuroscientific concept of phenomenal pain. In this case, there would be two concepts of the same property, each using a different mode of presentation.

On Loar's view, as on the earlier quotational and mental sample views, phenomenal concepts are perspectival, for phenomenal concepts are recognitional concepts and obviously one cannot recognize a phenomenal character one has not experienced.

Loar's proposal offers a dispositional account of recognitional concept possession. As such, it encounters a version of the Kripke-Wittgenstein problem for dispositional analyses of meaning (Kripke 1982).[11] A second problem is that it is not at all clear that this view fully comes to grip with the explanatory gap, as it is supposed to do. Given Loar's account, we can now understand why identity claims such as

Painfulness = Brain state B

are informative. The concepts deployed use different modes of presentation even though they pick out the same entity. We can also understand why the physical truths do not *a priori* entail the phenomenal truths. Thus, we can understand why there is a conceptual gap here. But Loar's account does not begin to explain why we are *so* puzzled when we ask ourselves "How *could* this state be the same as that one?"

To see this, consider the following claim:

Hesperus = Phosphorus.

Again this is an informative identity. Again, the concepts it deploys use different modes of presentation. But the question "How could Hesperus be Phosphorus?" is not in the least perplexing. So why is there such perplexity in the explanatory-gap case? To say that phenomenal concepts are at play here and that they use special modes of presentation is to mark an important difference from the Hesperus-Phosphorus case. But it is not clear why or how this difference really makes a difference. After all, on

Loar's account there is no difficulty or puzzlement in seeing *how* physicalism about the phenomenal could be true: given physicalism, phenomenal concepts use physical properties as their modes of presentation to pick out physical properties. From whence does our puzzlement arise, then? Why is it that we ask ourselves "*How* could this be that?" and find ourselves to be so perplexed?

My point is that Loar's account does not begin to come to grips with the sort of perplexity that is expressed in the following passages:

How can pain (which hurts so) possibly be the same thing as insensate molecules rushing around the nerve fibres? (Papineau 2002, p. 161).

How could Technicolor phenomenology arise from soggy grey matter? (McGinn 1991)

[There is the] feeling of an unbridgeable gulf between consciousness and brain process [that occurs when I] turn my attention in a particular way on to my own consciousness, and, astonished, say to myself: THIS is supposed to be produced by a process in the brain!—as it were clutching my forehead. (Wittgenstein 1953, I, p. 412)

The difficulty I am raising here also applies to the quotational and mental sample views of Papineau, Block, and Balog. To see this, suppose that I am told that the experience of painfulness is one and the same as a certain brain state (brain state *B*). I find this puzzling. I ask myself "How could that be?" The Papineau-Block-Balog line makes available the following reply (explicitly endorsed by Papineau): As I am thinking about the identity, I am representing a certain state in two radically different ways. I am representing the state descriptively in my thought and I am also representing it by experiencing it. The result is that I am puzzled. I wonder how the state I am experiencing could just be the state I am describing.

However, if painfulness is brain state *B*, then the state I am experiencing is brain state *B*, and in representing that state by experiencing it, all I am doing is tokening brain state *B*. Thus, I am using brain state *B* to represent brain state *B*—the very state that I am also representing in a descriptive way. Why is that so puzzling or difficult to grasp? The simple fact is that it isn't. If I tell you, for example, that the typed expression 'these typed marks' is to be understood to refer to itself, does that make it difficult to see how the referent of that expression could be a physical entity located at a certain position in space? Clearly it does not.

The point, then, is that, in the painfulness case, it is only when I conceive of the state I am representing by being in that state as something I represent via a token of *painfulness* that I start to get really puzzled, for now I must conceive of the represented state *as* painfulness, and I find it mysterious how the state I am so conceiving could just be the state I am conceiving in objective, physical terms.

The above objection also may be extended to the view that phenomenal concepts are pure demonstrative concepts referring to phenomenal properties or demonstrative concepts that use physical sortals to do the same. If this is not immediately obvious, consider the statement "Now is 2 p.m." 'Now' is an indexical term, but no one thinks that there is a deep explanatory problem or gap here. Of course, one might ask "How could now be 2 p.m.?" in an incredulous tone of voice if, say, one's watch has stopped and one is under the misimpression that it is much earlier in the day. But patently there is no deep perplexity associated with supposing that now is one particular time. There is no feeling of an 'unbridgeable gulf' between now and 2 p.m. (or any other time). And likewise for the case of demonstrative concepts, either pure or accompanied by physical sortals.

This objection also applies to Perry's appeal (2001) to topic-neutral demonstrative/recognitional concepts. Another concern for demonstrative accounts generally (at least, for those that do not covertly introduce general phenomenal concepts too) is that whatever the demonstrative concept—call it 'this$_i$'—the claim that this$_i$ is phenomenal property/state *P* is informative.[12] But if the demonstrative concept is really a phenomenal concept, this should not be the case for some such claims (Chalmers 2003).

Where does this leave the physicalist who endorses the phenomenal-concept strategy? Well, one possibility not yet considered is that phenomenal concepts are non-demonstrative, general concepts that refer directly without the assistance of any associated reference-fixers, even though this is not what makes them phenomenal. This is the view I took in earlier work.

3.4   My Earlier View on Phenomenal Concepts

The natural way of developing this line further is as follows: Our phylogenetic nature determines which experiences we undergo. We are hardwired to experience various bodily sensations and to undergo various perceptual experiences. We cannot experience what a bat experiences when it uses echo-location, since we lack the appropriate sensory system. We are also equipped by evolution and nature to respond cognitively to our experiences in a certain range of ways once we undergo them. In responding cognitively, we bring the experiences under phenomenal concepts. Which concept is applied may depend on a number of factors, including how our attention is directed, previous experiences, learning, and attention span. But there are limits set on the phenomenal concepts available to us by our nature.

My earlier proposal (in first approximation) was that phenomenal concepts refer *directly*, where a concept C refers directly to a quality Q if and only if, under Normal cognitive conditions, C is tokened in an act of thought just in case Q is tokened and because Q is tokened. I say 'in first approximation' here since a further condition is needed to handle the possibility that, in the phenomenal case, C not only causally covaries with Q but also causally covaries with a further non-phenomenal, indeed non-introspectively accessible, quality of the experience under normal conditions.

This difficulty is, of course, part of a more general one for causal covariation accounts of representation, whether that representation is conceptual or not. The hair shedding of cats (under normal conditions) is causally correlated with the lengthening of days; and lengthening days correlate (roughly) with increasing temperature. Thus, hair shedding in cats causally covaries with both day length and temperature. Even so, given what we know of the relevant biological mechanisms, it seems wrong to say that the shedding of hair represents temperature in addition to (or instead of) day length.

In the cat case, the causal covariation between the shedding of hair and increasing temperature arises because the hair shedding causally covaries with day length and day length covaries with temperature. Were the covariation link between temperature and day length broken (by, for example, keeping cats indoors at a constant temperature or moving them to higher altitudes at the same latitude), the hair shedding would continue to covary with day length (albeit artificial day length for the indoor case generated by varying the hours of artificial light), but not with temperature. For this reason, hair shedding is best taken to represent day length—provided that we are prepared to talk of representation in this context at all.

Perhaps it will be objected that it is surely possible for a concept to refer directly to a phenomenal quality without being a phenomenal concept. Suppose, for example, that the distinctive phenomenal character of pain is a brain state and that Fred is a 21st-century neuroscientist who is incapable himself of feeling pain in virtue of a neurological defect he has had since birth. Fred has a device partly wired into his brain that causes him to think that another person is feeling pain when and only when the external part of the device is directed at the other person's brain and the relevant brain state is present there. Fred's thought exercises a concept of pain. But that concept isn't a *phenomenal* concept.

This example shows that it is necessary to distinguish the question "What is it that makes a phenomenal concept of quality Q be about or of Q?" from the question "What makes a phenomenal concept phenomenal?" Not all concepts that refer directly are phenomenal. Concerning the latter question, my thesis in Tye 2003b was that a concept that directly refers to a phenomenal quality is phenomenal if and only if it functions in the right sort of way. I denied, however, that this functioning could be specified *a priori* in a way that eschews any phenomenal language. My view was that the concept of a phenomenal concept is conceptually irreducible: no *a priori* definition or analysis is possible in non-phenomenal terms.

Why? Well, if such an analysis were possible, then a suitably cognitively informed automaton, without any experiences, would be able to acquire the concept of a phenomenal concept simply by reflecting on the analysis. But when I endorsed this view, I took it to be obvious that this isn't possible. Such an automaton could glean no phenomenal notion of an experience, and without such a notion the concept of a phenomenal concept would be beyond its grasp.

This does not have the consequence that we cannot say *a priori* anything illuminating about the relevant functioning of phenomenal concepts. Quite the contrary. A concept is phenomenal, I held in my earlier work, if and only if (1) it is laid down in memory as a result of undergoing the appropriate experiences (barring miracles, etc.), (2) it tends to trigger appropriate conscious images (or quasi-images) in response to certain cognitive tasks, and (3) it enables its possessors to discriminate the phenomenal quality to which it refers directly and immediately via introspection.[13] This proposal, originally made in Tye 1999, was motivated by what I took to be *a priori* links between possessing a phenomenal concept and knowing what it is like (one cannot possess a phenomenal conception of a given experience type unless one knows what that experience type is like) and further *a priori* links between the latter and certain phenomenal abilities underpinning the stated conditions (abilities to imaginatively re-create the experience, to remember it, to recognize it directly when it comes again). Moreover, the proposal, though non-reductive, is not vacuous or trivial. It imposes real requirements on a concept's being phenomenal—requirements that are not met by most of the concepts we possess.

The proposal also entails that phenomenal concepts are perspectival. On the above account, possessing the phenomenal concept *pain** requires having a certain perspective on pain: the one conferred by experiencing pain oneself (barring miracles, etc.). Why should this be? Because the phenomenal concept *pain** would not be a phenomenal concept at all if it didn't function in the right sort of way, and that functioning brings with it a distinctive first-person perspective on pain. This is why the 21st-century pain detector wired into the head of our neuroscientist Fred does not provide Fred with a *phenomenal* concept of pain, and why Mary in her black-and-white room does not have the phenomenal concept *red**. These individuals, given their special conditions, don't have any internal mental representations that function in the appropriate ways.

One objection that might be raised to the above view is that it faces a regress problem just as some of the earlier proposals do, for in saying what makes a concept phenomenal I have used phenomenal concepts. These concepts must refer to physical states and properties if physicalism about phenomenal consciousness is to be true.

I do not find this objection persuasive. There is no vicious regress set off by this requirement, since the reference of phenomenal concepts is direct. It is *not* the case, on the above view, that in order for a given phenomenal concept to *refer* successfully, other phenomenal concepts must do the same, where these concepts refer successfully only if other phenomenal concepts do, and so on without end.

Nor is there any regress in the above account of what makes a concept phenomenal. The account is not proposed as a reductive one. Thus, the fact that it uses phenomenal concepts does not create a regress. What the use of these concepts reflects is simply the conceptual irreducibility of the concept of a phenomenal concept.

However, it must be admitted that, since phenomenal concepts refer directly, they do not have fine-grained individuation conditions in the way that other concepts do. Thus, if having fine-grained individuation conditions is partly definitive of what it is for a mental representation to be a concept, phenomenal concepts (and any other supposed concepts that refer directly) are not *really* concepts at all.

Another concern is that the proposal above does not satisfactorily handle the case of Mary as far as the physicalist is concerned. In particular, it now seems to me that the proposal does not allow Mary to make any new

discoveries about the phenomenal character of color experience after she leaves her black-and-white room. This needs a little explanation.

To think a phenomenal thought, Mary must exercise a phenomenal concept. On the above account, she does not have phenomenal color experience concepts in her room. Thus, when she leaves her room, Mary begins to have *new* phenomenal thoughts. However, content-wise, these thoughts will not be new, given Mary's complete physical knowledge in her room, for, on the above proposal, phenomenal concepts refer directly, and thus the contribution they make to thought content is given by their referents alone—referents that are physical, if physicalism about consciousness is true.

One reply that might be made to this objection is that thought types need not be individuated by their contents alone. Intuitively, phenomenal thought types play a different role in rationalizing explanations than non-phenomenal thought types. If their contents are identical, a second factor must account for this difference. And intuitively that factor is simply that phenomenal thoughts exercise different concepts—*phenomenal* concepts (whose difference from non-phenomenal concepts, on my account, is given by their functional role). Accordingly, it might be said, the identity of a phenomenal thought type may be traced both to its content and to the fact that it employs concepts that function in a certain characteristic way.

This two-factor view of phenomenal thought types may be held to permit the physicalist to maintain that there is a perfectly good sense in which Mary discovers that so-and-so is the case after she is released, for she comes to think new thoughts and thereby to instantiate cognitive thought types (knowing-that types) she did not instantiate before, even though, given her exhaustive knowledge of the physical facts, the contents of her thought types before and after remain unchanged.

Still, a worry lingers. *What* Mary thinks is not new when she leaves her room. What is new is the *way* she is thinking what she is thinking. That isn't enough. What Mary knows before time t (the time of her release) is exactly the same as what she knows after time t. But if what she knows before and after her release is the same, she does not make a discovery in any really robust sense. This is counter-intuitive. Surely if anyone ever made a significant discovery, Mary does here. The proposal, in the end, is not convincing.

Thus, the phenomenal-concept strategy is in deep trouble. No one has yet managed to produce a plausible account of phenomenal concepts that gives them the features they must have in order to do the work needed to defend physicalism.

3.5   Are There Any Phenomenal Concepts?

As I noted in section 3.2, phenomenal concepts are supposedly the concepts we exercise when (but not only when) we notice or become aware of the phenomenal character of our experiences and feelings through introspection. Our experiences have phenomenal character whether or not we attend to them. But when we notice how an experience feels, what it is like, in doing so we are bringing it beneath a phenomenal concept.

One assumption that is being made here is that introspection requires the application of a concept, and that without the application of a concept we could not be aware of phenomenal 'feels' at all. I shall not take up this assumption in this chapter. It is one of the topics of chapter 5. Suffice it to say for now that I no longer wholeheartedly embrace the assumption. However, I still accept that on the basis of introspection I may form a thought or judgment about my phenomenal state. And such a thought or judgment uses a concept for that phenomenal state. Such a concept is a phenomenal concept if we stipulate that phenomenal concepts just are those concepts we use in thoughts or judgments formed on the basis of introspection about the phenomenal character of our phenomenal states. In this sense, then, it is obvious that there are phenomenal concepts.

What I argued in the preceding section is that no one has yet proposed an account of phenomenal concepts that will do the special job physicalists have usually wanted them to do. My diagnosis for this is that physicalists having been barking up the wrong tree. There is really *nothing* special about phenomenal concepts. The concepts we use in forming conceptions of our phenomenal states via introspection are just like many other concepts. Sometimes we use demonstratives and sometimes we use general concepts. These concepts, I grant, are *a priori* irreducible to physical concepts. That is, they are not definable in terms of physical concepts, nor are they such that their application can be deduced from the physical truths plus additional *a priori* truths. But this is true of many, many concepts that have nothing to do with phenomenal consciousness, as I shall now show.[14]

Consider the concept *water*. The application of this concept is straightforwardly connected to the application of chemical concepts, since water is identical with H_2O. However, the connection is *a posteriori*. After all, it was a significant scientific discovery that water is H_2O. Some philosophers have held that even though it is *a posteriori* that water is H_2O, still it is possible to deduce that the concept *water* applies from the physical truths, the indexical truths, and *a priori* truths in which the concept *water* figures.

As we saw in chapter 2, Frank Jackson (1998) claims that the truth

(1) Water covers most of the Earth

can be deduced from

(2) H_2O covers most of the Earth,

(3) H_2O is the watery stuff of our acquaintance,

and

(4) Water is the watery stuff of our acquaintance,

where (4) is *a priori* and (2) and (3) are physical truths. Jackson takes this argument to show that the water truths can be deduced *a priori* from the physical truths (and the permitted indexical truths[15]). Let us leave to one side the point that (2) and (3) are not obviously physical truths at all; not only do they contain terms outside of microphysics, chemistry, neurophysiology, and molecular biology, but it seems no more than wishful thinking to suppose that their truth is *a priori* deducible from the microphysical and indexical facts. (If you think otherwise, I have a previously unknown Monet painting in my attic that I am willing to let you buy from me for a very good price.) The point I want to emphasize is that it is simply a mistake to suppose that (4) is *a priori*.

I shall not press the objection that we could conceivably discover that water is not H_2O but instead is like jade, consisting of two very different natural kinds. In this case, it might be held that water is not *the* watery stuff of our acquaintance. My first concern about this objection is that the inference from (2)–(4) to (1) does not require uniqueness. In place of (4),

(4′) Water is *a* watery stuff of our acquaintance

would do equally well. Second, it could be held that if water turned out to be like jade, it would then count as a motley kind (just as jade may be held to be a motley consisting of jadeite and nephrite). In these circumstances, there is a single watery stuff, namely the relevant motley kind.

The objection on which I want to focus begins with the observation that things sometimes can look very different from the way they are. Furthermore, under certain circumstances, they can do this for extended periods of time. Think, for example, of the recent Hollywood film *Shallow Hal*. The antihero, Hal, loses his fixation on beautiful women after seeing a self-help guru. The result of this encounter is that Hal is left able to appreciate only the *inner* beauty of women. The woman he becomes enamored of—Rosemary—is fat and physically unattractive, but to Hal she now appears slim and gorgeous. Here Hal undergoes a persistent illusion: Rosemary appears one way to him when in reality she is a very different way. For a more extreme example, consider Odysseus's return to Ithaca after his travels around the Mediterranean. The goddess Athena appears to him as a beggar. He learns from her about the suitors who are besieging his faithful wife, Penelope. Odysseus here cannot see Athena as she really is. The goddess appears one way, but again in reality she is another.

Consider now the example of water. According to Jackson, what is definitive of something's being watery stuff is that it be a clear, colorless, tasteless liquid that comes out of taps, falls from the skies as rain, and fills rivers and lakes—or at least that it have *enough* of these features. The listed features are ones that enter into the concept's stereotype. However, these features or nearly all of these features are ones that water could lack.

What Jackson fails to realize is that water could turn out to have very few, indeed arguably none, of the relevant features. Just as we have found that whales are not fish, that tomatoes are not vegetables, and that glass is not a solid, so the stereotype for water could be revised in the face of future empirical findings. Indeed, it could be revised dramatically. For one thing, the features in the stereotype could be based on abnormal or atypical samples. This point is made by Putnam: "... the normal members of the natural kind in question may not really be the ones we think are normal" (1970, p. 142). For another, conceivably the conditions of observation have altered the apparent characteristics of the kind so that the kind is really very different from the way it appears.

Here is a conceivable scenario about the actual world that illustrates the last point: Suppose that wherever we take there to be a body or sample of water, there is really a pale pink, granular stuff. This granular stuff is made up of conglomerations of tiny, pink particles, each about the size of a grain of sand. These particles form clouds in the atmosphere. The pink, granular stuff does not appear to us to be pink or granular, however. Samples of it appear to us to be colorless and liquid. When we use the term 'water', we are really referring to this pink, granular stuff. We just don't realize this. We take the referent of 'water' to be colorless and

liquid, but we are wrong. That is merely how it *appears*. This is because the Martians, who are much cleverer than we, are deceiving us. They monitor our interactions with water, and (for reasons we cannot begin to fathom) they change the pattern of light that water samples reflect.

The Martian deception goes further: When we dip our fingers in water, we have the sensation of touching a liquid, but this is because the Martians change the way our brains process the information provided by touch about conglomerations of the relevant granules. As far as taste goes, water actually has a slightly acid taste, but the Martians apply a special taste paste to our tongues at night while we are sleeping so that water is tasteless to us. This paste contains chemicals that mask the taste of water without interfering with our taste for most other things.

Under the envisaged scenario, water does not really fall from the sky, even though it appears to do so. The pale, pink particles float in the atmosphere and form clouds from within which the particles are sucked back down to Earth by massive particle attractors hidden from our view just below the Earth's surface. Some clusters of such "falling" particles appear to us as colorless drops. All of this is far-fetched, of course, but that does not matter. My claim is that this is a coherent scenario. What it shows, it seems to me, is that it could conceivably turn out that water is not the or a watery stuff in our environment, and thus that it is not *a priori* that water is the or a watery stuff.[16]

One reply that might be made is that under this scenario water simply does not exist. But we don't conclude that Rosemary does not exist in the movie *Shallow Hal*, or that Athena does not exist when she appears to Odysseus as a beggar. Why hold that in the water case? Our word 'water', under the given scenario, really is reliably tracking a certain kind of stuff even though that stuff appears to us other than it is, just as uses of 'Rosemary' and 'Athena' are reliably tracking certain individuals in the movie and the story even though those individuals are not at all as they appear.

Another reply that might be made to the above case is that the scenario described merely shows that the proposed analysis of *watery stuff* is inadequate. A better analysis is this: Stuff that appears clear, appears to be a liquid, appears to fall from the sky, appears to come out of taps, and so on. Clearly this will not do either. Appears to whom? Me? But what if, unknown to me, I have been singled out for deception by extraterrestrials so that things often appear to me different from the way they appear to others. In that case, something I am viewing might conceivably appear to me to have the relevant qualities and yet not be water, just as something might appear in motion to a man who has taken LSD when in reality it is stationary.

Suppose that now it is said that the analysis should be as follows: Stuff that, to normal perceivers, appears clear, appears to be a liquid, appears to fall from the sky, etc. It seems to me incredible to suppose that a young child who thinks to herself that water is wet must, in so doing, be able to a make an *a priori* connection between water and normal perceivers. Such a child will typically not even have the concept *normal perceiver*. But leaving this to one side, who counts as a normal perceiver?

Suppose a normal perceiver is one who is biologically Normal. This will not work. Perhaps there really is a clear liquid that falls from the sky, etc., and this liquid is H_2O, but God has made it invisible to normal perceivers by tampering with their optic nerves so as to filter out any information about water provided to them by sight whenever samples of water are present before their eyes. Perhaps in addition, again for reasons we cannot begin to comprehend, God has made it appear to us that there is a clear, colorless liquid that falls from the sky, etc., in circumstances in which in reality there is none. In these circumstances, we are hallucinating. Nonetheless, rivers, lakes, and taps do exist, and H_2O flows from them; it is just that there are no rivers, lakes, or taps located in those places we experience these things as being. If we were to find out that this is how the actual world really is, would we deny that it contains any water? Surely the answer is No. We would accept that there is water even though we failed to discern it with our senses. In these circumstances, water is not the or a watery stuff, on the proposed analysis of *watery stuff*.

The same scenario undermines the suggestion that the relevant normal perceivers are those who are statistically normal. The overall point, then, is that we might well revise the properties we associate with typical samples of water in the face of empirical findings. Admittedly, some of the above putative empirical findings are quite fantastic. But they are conceivable. The properties we currently associate with samples we take to be typical conceivably are not properties that water really has. We simply cannot assume *a priori* which properties stereotypical examples of water have. The stereotype is revisable in light of empirical discoveries.

One possible reaction to what I have said above is that, in making judgments about the various scenarios put forward, I am using *a priori* reflection as to what counts as water. I decide *a priori* that, under a given possible scenario, so-and-so stuff would (or would not be) water. Thus, for example, reflecting on the first scenario, I know the following *a priori*:

(5) If in the actual world, even though there is no colorless liquid that falls from the sky, fills lakes, etc., Martians are making a pale, pink, granular stuff appear to us to be a colorless liquid that falls from the sky, fills lakes, etc., then that stuff would be water.

Am I not, then, assuming the viability of the very philosophical procedure my remarks seem intended to question? This misunderstands my intentions. I do not deny that there are such things as *a priori* truths, especially conditional ones. My claim is that no such truth, added to (2) and (3), will enable me to deduce *a priori* the earlier claim (1). It should be obvious that claims of the sort illustrated by (5) are not going to do the job. To get any mileage out of such conditionals, we would have to know their antecedents *a priori*. And we don't.

Of course, it might conceivably be insisted that the antecedents of the conditionals can themselves be deduced *a priori* from the microphysical facts. But why suppose that? After all, different conditionals put forward in connection with different possible scenarios will have different and conflicting antecedents. Can it really be held that we can decide by *a priori* reflection on the microphysical facts which of these scenarios actually obtains? That seems wishful thinking at best. The points I made above in connection with the water facts (such as the fact that water covers most of the Earth) will now repeat in connection with the facts pertaining to the entities supposed to exist in the antecedents. The game will then go on indefinitely, as further conditionals come into play and as their antecedents are held to be deducible *a priori* from the microphysical facts.

This is relevant to the position adopted by Chalmers and Jackson in their 2001 paper, in which they move away from the model of *a priori* entailment illustrated by the inference from (2)–(4) to (1) to a model that appeals to *a priori* sufficient conditions for the application of the concept *water*. Chalmers and Jackson illustrate their view by reference to an example involving the concept *knowledge*. Suppose that the following claims are true: Smith initially has no beliefs about where Brown is. Smith then forms a belief that Jones owns a Ford or Brown is in Barcelona. He does this on the basis of a valid inference from his belief that Jones owns a Ford. The latter belief, it turns out, is false, but serendipitously Brown is in Barcelona. Call the conjunction of these claims '*G*'. It seems plausible to hold that Smith does not know that Jones owns a Ford or that Brown is in Barcelona. Call this claim—the one it seems plausible to hold—'*K*'. It is plausible that G ⊃ K is *a priori*.

As Chalmers and Jackson note, it is also plausible to hold that the concept *knowledge* cannot be explicitly analyzed using the terms in '*G*'. They comment:

... *a priori* entailment does not require explicit analyses of the terms in the consequent using the terms in the antecedent. It is also somewhat plausible that there is no explicit analysis of the concept of knowledge at all. If so, *a priori* entailment does not require explicit analyses of the terms in the consequent. (2001, pp. 320–321)

A few pages later, Chalmers and Jackson write:

If a subject possesses a concept and has unimpaired rational processes, then sufficient empirical information about the actual world puts a subject in a position to identify the concept's extension. For example, if a subject possesses the concept 'water', then sufficient information about the distribution, behavior, and appearance of clusters of H_2O molecules enables the subject to know that water is H_2O, to know where water is and is not, and so on. This conditional knowledge requires only possession of the concept and rational reflection, and so requires no further *a posteriori* knowledge. (ibid., p. 323)

The suggestion, then, seems to be this: we can know *a priori* that if there is a watery stuff of our acquaintance in place *p* then there is water in place *p*. This will enable us to deduce *a priori* that there is water in place *p* from the microphysical facts and the indexical facts, *if* we can deduce *a priori* that there is a watery stuff of our acquaintance in place *p* from those facts. But why should we accept that we can move *a priori* from the microphysical and (allowed) indexical facts to watery stuff facts? After all, something is watery stuff just in case it is a clear, colorless, tasteless liquid that comes out of taps, falls from the skies as rain, and fills rivers and lakes—or at least, it has *enough* of these features. But the terms used here are as much a part of the manifest image as the term 'water'. They are not a part of the scientific image (to put the point in Sellarsian language.) Why think that the link these terms bear to the microphysical vocabulary is any more secure, *at an a priori level*, than the link the term 'water' bears? Why suppose that there are *a priori* sufficient conditions for the application of such concepts as *river*, *sky*, *tap*, and *colorless* that do not themselves involve concepts from the manifest image?

The fact is that the manifest image is made up of a complex web of concepts. Very few of them have explicit *a priori* analyses. Some do have *a priori* sufficient conditions for their application, but these *a priori* sufficient conditions employ other concepts *from the image*. And the image is not neatly and hierarchically organized, with the lowest-level concepts themselves having *a priori* sufficient conditions for their application using concepts from the scientific image (and the microphysical scientific image in particular).

The game Chalmers and Jackson are playing is called "passing the buck." But the buck has to stop somewhere. For there to be any plausibility at all to the Canberra program, we would need some examples of where and how the buck stops. We would need to see specific cases in which we can move *a priori* from purely microphysical claims (supplemented by indexical information) to claims in the manifest image. Chalmers and Jackson fail to provide us with any such cases.

The natural and obvious conclusion to draw, it seems to me, is that not even the concept *water* is *a priori* reducible to physical concepts. The application of the concept to something *cannot* be deduced *a priori* from the physical and indexical truths. This is an extremely important point, for if the application of the concept *water* is not so deducible, then the same is true for the vast majority of concepts.[17] Furthermore, even if it is granted that phenomenal concepts (understood as concepts exercised in thoughts or beliefs formed on the basis of introspection about our phenomenal states and their phenomenal character) are conceptually irreducible, the above discussion of the concept *water* shows that it does *not* follow that phenomenal concepts are special or different from all other concepts.

Putting the preceding point together with the critique of existing accounts of phenomenal concepts in the preceding section, we should begin to take very seriously the idea that phenomenal concepts do not stand apart from all other concepts. Relatedly, we should begin to question the supposition that phenomenal concepts cannot be possessed (barring miracles) without having had the requisite experiences.[18] Maybe *fully* understanding a general phenomenal concept requires having had the relevant experience; but if such concepts are like most other concepts, possessing them does not require *full* understanding. They can be possessed even if they are only partially understood.

3.6 Phenomenal Concepts and Burgean Intuitions

Consider a point made by Tyler Burge (1979): Color concepts can be over- or under-extended. For example, someone might have the usual beliefs as to what common objects are red, and in many cases this person might agree with others about which presented color patches are red while also thinking that in one particular case the shade of *that object over there* is clearly red even though everyone else agrees that it is on the border between orange and red. Such a person would likely accept correction from others who confidently agree about the right way to classify the given shade. In this way, color concepts are deferential. Typically, their users do not understand them fully and are willing to accept corrections about how to apply them in some cases. Likewise, I now want to suggest for phenomenal concepts.

Consider the phenomenal character of the experience as of red. That is a general character common to all and only token experiences as of red. Anyone who is willing to accept correction as to whether a given shade should really be counted as a shade of red should be willing to accept correction as to whether a given token experience she is undergoing while viewing that shade should properly be counted as having the phenomenal character of experiences as of red, assuming that she takes herself to be a normal perceiver in normal viewing conditions. To deny this is to be prepared to allow that someone who accepts that she is a normal perceiver in normal viewing conditions might also accept that she is not having an experience as of a shade of red, since the expert tells her that the object she is seeing is really orange in color, while simultaneously insisting that her experience has the phenomenal character common to experiences as of red. How could this be? If one concedes, in the face of the expert's correction, that one is not having an experience as of a shade of red, how can one continue to hold that one's experience has the phenomenal character common to all and only token experiences as of red? Any subject who took such a view would be deeply irrational.

Once it is acknowledged that visual experience is transparent, there is reason to hold that the phenomenal character of the experience as of red cannot come apart from the color red.[19] But if this is so—if it is possible to over- or under-extend the concept *red*, as one applies it perceptually— then it must also be possible to over- or under-extend the corresponding general concept one has via introspection of the phenomenal character of the experience of red.

Here is another example: Consider the experience of pain, and imagine certain other experiences on the border between the experience of pain and the experience of pressure. Such experiences sometimes occur during dental work. The person feeling such an experience might well classify it as painful. But he or she might also be willing to accept correction from an expert who says that the experience is really a borderline case of pain and pressure. In such a situation, the concept being applied is a deferential one. It is a concept the possession of which enables its subject to form a conception of what it is like for her, but a conception that is not quite right. Nonetheless, this in no way shows that the subject does not really possess the concept. There is partial understanding of it.

Suppose it is replied that when it comes to phenomenal character the subject is the ultimate authority—that experts can correct us about some things, but we are perfectly within our rights to reject their corrections insofar as they pertain directly or indirectly to the subjective character of our experiences.

There is something right in this reply, it seems to me. When I introspect an experience, I do know what it is like for me. There is real knowledge here that cannot be impugned by others. But to the extent that the knowledge I have is factual, there will be cases in which I am prepared to accept correction. Witness the cases just presented. Here it is not that there could not be a general concept whose application conditions are determined by my non-deferential dispositions. The point is simply that this is not how the general concepts we apply to our experiences via introspection typically work.

The situation parallels the one that obtains in Burge's well-known arthritis example (1979). The man who goes to the doctor and complains of having arthritis in his thigh could refuse to accept the doctor's correction and insist that, whatever the doctor may think, he really does have arthritis in his thigh. Such a person would be highly atypical. The usual response would be to accept the doctor's correction, thereby indicating that there is a shared concept in play about whose applications conditions the doctor knows more. One who rejects the doctor's claim that arthritis is found only in the joints is operating with another concept—the concept *tharthritis*, as we may call it. And that concept is non-deferential. Burge, I take it, would not contest any of this. His point is that in actual fact, for most concepts, this is not how things actually work. My point is that the same holds true for the general concepts we apply to our experiences via introspection.

Admittedly, some philosophers reply to Burge that the patient, when he says "I have arthritis in my thigh," has a false meta-linguistic belief. What he really believes is that he has tharthritis in his thigh (which is true, since tharthritis is any condition that feels like arthritis) and further that 'arthritis' in English stands for tharthritis (which is false). But this will not do, for several reasons. First, it entails that a monolingual French speaker cannot believe what the English speaker believes when he says "I have arthritis in my thigh." This seems totally implausible. Second, it entails that the doctor and the patient cannot agree as to whether the patient has arthritis in his ankles. But surely they can so agree. Finally, when the doctor tells the patient that he cannot have arthritis in his thigh, the patient, except in extraordinary circumstances, will not insist that the doctor is wrong and that he does have arthritis in his thigh. But on the meta-linguistic proposal, this is how he should respond.

If the general concepts we apply via introspection to our phenomenal states are deferential, they can be possessed even if they are only partially understood. If this is the case, it is not necessary to have undergone the relevant experiences in order to possess such concepts, any more than it is necessary to have undergone certain experiences in order to possess such concepts as the concept *gold* or the concept *beech*.

Consider now the fact that someone who has never experienced pain (perhaps because of some rare neurological abnormality) can surely know quite a lot about pain and indeed about what it is like to feel pain. For example, someone who has never experienced pain can know the following truths:

(6) what it is like to experience pain is unpleasant

(7) what it is like to experience pain is more similar to what it is like to experience pressure than it is to what it is like to experience the sound of gently running water

(8) someone who has experienced pain knows more about what it is like to experience pain than someone who hasn't

(9) this is not what it is like to experience pain (where 'this' refers to a phenomenal character of which the speaker is presently aware)

(10) bodily damage typically causes the phenomenal experience of pain.

Such a person can surely disagree with someone who has experienced pain about just how bad the experience is—for example, whether what it is like to feel pain for one minute is worse than what it is like to be tickled for a minute. How is such disagreement possible unless there is a shared concept of what it is like to experience pain?

Similarly, one who has never experienced red can still know truths such as the following:

(11) what it is like to experience red is more similar to what it is like to experience orange than what it is like to experience green

(12) someone who has experienced red knows more about what it is like to experience red than someone who hasn't

(13) red things such as fire engines typically cause the experience of red

(14) this is not what it is like to experience red (where 'this' refers to a phenomenal character of which the speaker is aware).

Again, disagreement is possible between one who knows these truths but who has not experienced red and one who has experienced red—about whether, for example, what it is like to experience red is more pleasing than what it is like to experience purple. The very possibility of such a disagreement demands a shared concept.

Of course, it could be replied that all that the truth of (6)–(14) shows is that there is *a* concept of the phenomenal character of pain and *a* concept of the phenomenal character of red, the possession of which does not demand that one have undergone the relevant experiences. In addition to these concepts, there are the special, phenomenal concepts possessed only by subjects who have the right experiential perspective. But this raises some puzzling questions. For example, if I have the right experiential perspective, can I always tell which concept I am applying? It would seem not. At least in my own case, as I reflect on various situations and thoughts about the experience of red occasioned by them, I find that I haven't a clue *which* concept of the experience of red I am employing in my descriptions of the situations, if it is indeed the case that I employ two different concepts of such.

The double-concept line also fails to account for cases such as the following: Suppose that Frank Jackson's Mary, in a pessimistic mood one day, thinks to herself in her black-and-white room:

I'll never know what it is like to experience red.

Upon her release, and staring at a ripe tomato, she thinks to herself

I now know what it is like to experience red.

Prima facie, these thoughts have contradictory contents. But if the latter exercises a phenomenal concept for what it is like to experience red and the former exercises a non-phenomenal concept for the same, then they are not contradictory, any more than are thoughts with the following contents:

I know that Cicero was an orator

I do not know that Tully was an orator.[20]

Here is one further argument: Consider the conceptual possibility that there are zombies among us. Pre-theoretically, surely the natural view to take of zombies in our midst is that when they say such things as "I know what it is like to experience red" they say something false. And likewise if they add "I acquired this knowledge by experience," for they are members of our linguistic community and yet all is dark within for them. There is no technicolor phenomenology. They do not have and have never had any experiences. But if there genuinely are phenomenal concepts we deploy in forming conceptions of our experiences, the acquisition of which demands the appropriate experiences, what grounds are there for saying that the zombies are making false statements here?

Under the phenomenal-concept strategy, zombies among us cannot mean what the rest of us mean by 'experience' or 'what it is like to experience red'.[21] Our concepts here supposedly require experiences; and zombies have no experiences. So why suppose that they say anything *false*? No reason, so far as I can see. If they are employing concepts for ersatz pain, ersatz experience of red, and so on (where these are states in them playing the functional roles of their counterpart experiences but lacking phenomenal character), then what they say is true. But that intuitively is wrong.

If you are not immediately convinced by this, ask yourself how a zombie among us would react if, one day upon waking, he found himself subject to experiences of just the same sort as the rest of us. What would he say about the transformation? Surely, once he had calmed himself down, if he were somehow to be brought to the realization that he was now undergoing what the rest of us were undergoing all along, he would react in the same way as Burge's arthritis man. He would remark "I used to think that I had experiences, but now I realize that I was wrong." He might even then wonder whether others among us are as he was—whether others are zombies and thus lack experiences.

Of course, there is a meta-linguistic interpretation of the zombie's remark. Maybe what he means (and believes) is that he used to think that he was subject to states properly called "experiences" (in English) but now he realizes that this earlier view was wrong. But this is no more plausible than are meta-linguistic construals of the remarks of arthritis man, and for the same reasons.

The right view to take, then, is that zombies in our midst express the very same concepts as we do with their 'what it is like' and other phenomenal vocabulary. These zombies know many things about color experiences generally and about the experience of red in particular, just as the rest of us do. They have a partial understanding of what the experience of red is like, for example. Since they possess the same concepts, what the zombies say when they I utter such sentences as "I know what it is like to experience red" is false.

It follows that the concepts we express in our 'what it is like' (and other phenomenal) vocabulary—the concepts we apply introspectively to what it is like for us—do not require for their possession that we have undergone the relevant experiences. Such concepts are not experientially perspectival in the way that physicalists standardly assume.

It is a consequence of this position that any zombies among us do not have privileged access to their inner states in the following way: Even when their faculty of introspection is working properly, they can firmly believe that they are subject to such-and-such an experience, and yet be wrong. This would be worrisome if privileged access of the sort zombies in our midst lack were held to be something any conceptually possible being equipped with the appropriate concepts has. But why hold that? Some conceptually possible beings are metaphysically impossible, and zombies, as I shall argue later, are among them. Furthermore, for reasons that will become clear in chapter 8, I hold that even *we* lack privileged access to our experiences, under one standard understanding of the thesis of privileged access. Thus, the fact that any zombies in our community lack privileged access cuts no ice against my position.

Suppose it is now objected that my various arguments above assume that phenomenal concepts are expressible in ordinary English words (for example, 'pain') or expressions (for example, 'what it is like to experience red'). However, on the most plausible view, words such as 'pain' have a partly functional connotation and thus do not express purely phenomenal concepts. Further, on the most plausible view, the concept expressed by (for example) 'what it is like to experience red' is complex, whereas the phenomenal concept used to classify the phenomenal character common to experiences of red is simple.

My reply is that this does not undercut my position even if it is the case. English allows for the introduction of new terms, and we could easily introduce '*P*' as a name for the phenomenal character of the experience of pain and '*R*' as a name for the phenomenal character of the experience of red. My claim is now that the concepts '*P*' and '*R*' express do not *require* for their possession that their users have undergone the relevant experiences. Mary in her room can interact via her computers with someone who has introduced the term '*R*', for example, and she can thereby acquire the concept '*R*' expresses.[22] She can think to herself that she will never be in a state with phenomenal character *R*, and later, when finally she experiences *R*, she can think to herself that she is now in the state having R. The content of her later thought contradicts the content of her earlier thought.[23]

The terms 'P' and 'R' can be over- and under-extended in their application, as can the phenomenal concepts they express. Further, generalizing from the example just given, where there is disagreement about the relevant phenomenal characters among speakers who use the terms 'P' and 'R', this disagreement is to be understood in terms of shared concepts whether or not the speakers have undergone experiences having those phenomenal characters. Finally, under the conceptually possible scenario that there are zombies in our midst, the phenomenal concepts 'P' and 'R' express are also ones that such zombies exercise when they use sentences employing these terms (as well as on some other occasions) for essentially the same reasons as those already offered.

Cumulatively, these reflections seem to me to put the phenomenal-concept strategy for defending physicalism under considerable pressure. Leaving theoretical necessities to one side, the simplest and most straightforward reaction to the above considerations is simply to give up the view that there are *special* phenomenal concepts deployed in introspecting phenomenal character.

There is one further suggestion I want to discuss briefly. It is due to Chalmers.[24] This suggestion does not directly place an experience constraint on the possession of phenomenal concepts. Instead, the thought is that what marks out phenomenal concepts as belonging to a special class of concepts is that they are transparent: possessing such a concept puts one in a position to know what its referent is. A non-phenomenal example of a transparent concept, according to Chalmers, is the concept *friend*. On this view, supposedly, phenomenal terms are not "Twin Earthable." Opaque terms such as 'water' are.

To see what is wrong with this suggestion, consider the example of the concept *friend*. Suppose you find out that the word 'friend' does not mean quite what you previously thought. You discover that other people standardly use the word 'friend' so that not only people with whom an individual has ties of trust and affection are classified as friends of that individual but so too are people with whom the individual is on polite and considerate terms, so long as they have had such a relationship for at least five years. You might then say that you used to believe that a friend was someone you regarded well and felt affection for and further someone whom you could trust whereas now you realize that in some cases a friend can meet somewhat weaker conditions. The possibility of deference here shows that the word 'friend' is Twin Earthable: there is a coherent scenario in which you have an intrinsic duplicate who uses 'friend' with a different extension than you do in actual fact. What goes for 'friend' goes for phenomenal terms. In this way, they are Twin Earthable too.

Suppose it is now replied that one who has full understanding of the concept *friend* won't use it deferentially. For such a person, the term 'friend' is not Twin Earthable. What matters, on this view, as far as delineating the class of transparent concepts is concerned, is Twin Earthability under conditions of full understanding.

The immediate difficulty here is that even experts—people who have complete or full understanding in the relevant domain—are prepared to defer to other experts who know more.[25] Thus, full understanding does not entail non-deferential usage.

It does not help to revise the proposal further so that a term counts as transparent just in case it is Twin Earthable under conditions of *non-deferential usage*. Now the term 'arthritis', as used by the individual in Burge's example who refuses to defer to his doctor, is not Twin Earthable in the relevant way. But this shows nothing about the concept *arthritis*. The individual here is using the term 'arthritis' to express a different concept (the concept *tharthritis*). So, the Twin Earthability of a term, as it is now being understood, shows nothing about the character of the concept the term expresses, as it is standardly used, in the case that the standard usage is deferential.

It is interesting to note that Burge is not inclined to adopt the view for which I am arguing. Burge says:

It is obvious that at a certain level, the psychological abilities of the blind person and of the normally sighted person differ in the representation of the redness of a flower. They have different concepts of redness, inasmuch as some of the sighted person's concepts are associated with recognitional abilities through perception. But there remains a sense in which the two can share a thought that the flower is red. In this case, there is a concept of red that does not depend on a visual phenomenal character at all, shareable by different individuals. The relevant shared psychological abilities are associated with a complex of shared background information about red things.... But the blind person lacks the sighted person's perceptual ability to recognize red things. So, there remains an intentional content, or better an array of intentional contents, that they do not share. (Hahn and Ramberg 2003, pp. 413–414)

Harman makes some related remarks about the concept of red possessed by a blind person. His position is slightly different, however:

I am supposing that the person blind from birth . . . has no concept of something's being red that could be immediately brought into service in visual representations of the environment if the person were suddenly to acquire sight. (1998, p. 671)

A little later, Harman adds:

The person blind from birth fails to know what it is like to see something red because he or she does not fully understand what it is for something to be red, that is, because he or she does not have the full concept of something's being red. (ibid., p. 671)

Similarly, Peacocke remarks:

Someone does not know what it is for something to be red and does not fully understand the predicate 'is red' unless he knows what it is like to have a visual experience as of a red object. . . . (1983, p. 24)

Such a person, in Peacocke's view, does not possess the perceptual concept *red*.

It seems to me obviously correct to say that one cannot *fully* understand the term 'red' unless one grasps what it is like to experience red. But it does not follow from this that one does not possess the concept *red*. Concepts can be possessed and exercised in thought in the absence of full understanding. Indeed, partial understanding is the rule not the exception; and in many cases the understanding can be minimal. As I noted earlier, one can possess the concept *fortnight* without knowing much more than that a fortnight is a period of time. One can mistakenly believe that a fortnight is ten days, for example. Likewise, one can possess the concept *elm* even though one cannot tell an elm tree from a beech tree and one knows only that, or little more than that, elms are trees. Ignorance of many of the facts about elms does not prevent one from meaning *elm* by 'elm' or from believing that elms are trees.

Of course, a blind person lacks the ability to recognize red things as red by sight. Burge takes this as a reason to hold that the blind person's concept of red is not the same as that of a normal sighted person. The latter, in Burge's view, has two concepts of red, one perceptual and one not; and the blind person only possesses one of these. But why take this position? An expert can be very good at recognizing elm trees by sight; I am not. Thus, the expert has a perceptual, recognitional ability I lack. Does it follow from this that the expert has two concepts of elm, one that he shares with me and one that he has and I lack? Surely not. There is no reason to multiply concepts in this way.

The expert has certain recognitional abilities I lack. He knows much more than me about elm trees—his conception of elms (that is, the cluster of beliefs he associates with the concept *elm*) is much richer than mine. But intuitively we both share a thought with the same content when we say "That is an elm" on the basis of our respective perceptual experiences.

Why, then, insist that the blind person lacks a concept of red simply because he cannot recognize red things by sight? Suppose someone blind from birth becomes an expert on elm trees. Such a person is not able to recognize elm trees by sight. Does he lack a concept that the sighted expert possesses? Both can think that elms are trees. When the blind person mistakenly says "There's an elm tree on the right" (perhaps he misremembers the location of the elm) and the sighted expert says "No, that tree is not an elm," surely the latter corrects the former. How can this be, if the concepts they express by 'elm' are different? Surely both people are exercising the concept *elm* in their thoughts. Surely both mean *elm* by 'elm'.

Now consider the case of Mary once again. If she leaves her black-and-white room and she is shown into a room on the wall of which is a red patch, she will not be able to recognize the patch as red by sight. Why not? She will be able to work out that the patch is red, of course, given that she has exhaustive physical knowledge and thus knowledge that the patch has such and such a reflectance, etc. But she will not know this on the basis of sight. Again, why not? Well, one obvious explanation is that she lacks a stored memory representation derived from perceptual experience of the color red. Lacking such a representation, she cannot generate a match with her color perceptual input, as she views the patch. So she fails to recognize the patch as red. This explanation, it might well be urged, requires the admission that Mary *lacks* a certain concept of red notwithstanding all that she knows.

My reply is that Mary *does* have a stored memory representation of red. She acquired this representation by reading her books. The representation does not have associated with it an image of red or phenomenal information about red of a sort that could only be gleaned by seeing red things. Thus, Mary cannot use this representation in the way that you and I can use our stored representations of red to recognize red things as red by sight. Still, possession of this representation suffices for Mary to have the same concept of red as the rest of us. She simply has a less rich understanding of red than we do. Her situation with respect to the rest of us is not different in kind from that of the expert on elms to that of the layman. The difference is merely one of degree. There is a single shared concept in both cases.

There is one further objection I want to discuss. Consider Inverted Mary. Suppose that she comes out of the black-and-white room, views a red patch, and says "So this is what it is like to experience red." Does she say something false? My view is that she does. She mistakenly classifies the phenomenal character of her experience as being what it is like to experience red when it is really what it is like to experience green. Inverts, upon viewing red objects, do not experience red. They misrepresent the objects' color. In a standard 180° inversion, they experience green. What it is like for them, on such occasions, is *not* what it is like to experience red. As for how the inverts are to be picked out in the general population, there need be no simple test. Functionally, there are subtle differences between inverts and normals, however, and these differences reveal themselves in the appropriate circumstances.[26]

To repudiate the view for which I have been arguing and to suppose that there are additional, special phenomenal concepts that can only be acquired through experience and that do not give rise to the phenomenon of partial understanding is, I maintain, to take a position that runs into all sorts of difficulties and implausibilities. Better, then, to jettison such concepts. They are not needed anyway to do the work required of them by physicalists. An alternative strategy is available that eschews these concepts and that can handle the deepest puzzles of consciousness.

3.7   Consequences for *A Priori* Physicalism

If the arguments of the preceding section are correct, *a priori* physicalism cannot succeed. There is simply no hope of *a priori* deducing all the truths from the microphysical truths and the indexical truths specified in chapter 2. Of course, *a priori* physicalism does not quite claim that this is possible. The claim is, rather, that the conjunction of the microphysical truths together with the relevant indexical truths and a further "That's all" statement (*T*) *a priori* entail all truths. The addition of *T* amounts to an *a priori* way of capturing the minimality constraint on possible worlds that are microphysical duplicates of the actual world on the physicalist's view.

Recall that, for the physicalist, any possible world that is a microphysical duplicate of the actual world and that contains no more than it must to duplicate the actual world microphysically is a duplicate *simpliciter*. It is this claim that the *a priori* physicalist tries to reconstruct in terms of *a priori* entailment using *T* along with the conjunction of the microphysical and the allowed indexical truths. The thought is that once *T* is added, it will follow from the truth of physicalism that, for example, there are no angels, since the conjunction of the microphysical truths, the allowed indexical truths and T *a priori* entail that there are no angels.

Let us leave T to one side for the moment. One very serious difficulty for the *a priori* physicalist, not yet brought out, concerns which indexical truths are allowed in the base set. Chalmers and Jackson (2001) propose that all that is needed is a statement of the form 'I am A' along with a statement of the form 'Now is B', where 'A' and 'B' are identifying descriptions of the relevant person and time which are themselves *a priori* entailed by the microphysical truths plus T. This will not suffice, however, as the following case (derived from Austin 1990) makes clear.

Suppose that there is a person (call him 'Smith') who is capable of focusing his eyes independently and who looks with each eye through a small hole in a vertical board. Attached to the other side of the board are two separate tubes. Each tube extends away from one of the holes to a vertical screen on which there is a red, circular spot. Smith cannot tell how the tubes are oriented. In fact, the two tubes collapse into one as they get close to the screen, with the result that Smith is seeing just a single red spot.

Smith believes that his eyes may be subject to a complex medical condition, the effect of which is that he cannot tell reliably on the basis of his visual and bodily experiences where objects are located or indeed which eye he is using to see which object. He asks himself whether *that* (referring to the red, circular spot he is actually seeing with his left eye) is identical with *that* (referring to the red, circular spot he is actually seeing with his right eye). How is the truth, "That is identical with that," to be deduced *a priori* from the microphysical truths and the two statements of the form "I am A" and "B is now" for the given subject (along with T)? The short answer is that it cannot be so deduced. Since Smith cannot tell *a priori* where the spot he is viewing with his left eye is located, and similarly for the spot he is viewing with his right eye, he has no *a priori* way of connecting that spot with that one, and so he cannot deduce *a priori* that "That is that" is true.[27]

Chalmers and Jackson suggest that, to deal with this case, the statement of *a priori* physicalism needs to expand the indexical base to include further indexical information "such as information about the referent of certain special demonstratives" (2001, p. 318, n. 4). But this seems *ad hoc*. Further, *prima facie* there is nothing *special* about the demonstratives in the two tubes case. It is also very unclear, once the indexical base is enlarged, where the expansion is to end.

Returning now to T, there is a question as to exactly how T is to be understood on the *a priori* physicalist's position. The 'that's all' statement is a statement to the effect that our world is a *minimal world* satisfying the microphysical truths (P) that are true at our world. Chalmers and Jackson comment:

> Intuitively, this statement says that our world contains what is implied by P and *only* what is implied by P. More formally, we can say that a world W_1 outstrips world W_2 if W_1 contains a qualitative duplicate as a proper part and the reverse is not the case. Then a minimal P-world is a world that outstrips no other P-world. It is plausible that no world containing angels is a minimal P-world: for any P-world containing angels, there is an angel-free P-world that it outstrips. So $P\&T$ implies that there are no angels. (2001, p. 318)

The first sentence of this passage is curious, since presumably what is implied by P is a truth or set of truths but our world does not contain truths. Our world contains various entities the actual truths are about. As for what Chalmers and Jackson mean by 'implied', they make it clear that they mean *a priori entailed*. They thus opt for an epistemic characterization of minimality. The actual world, if physicalism is true, is "minimal among the class of *epistemic* possibilities satisfying P, where an epistemic possibility corresponds intuitively to a maximally specific hypothesis that is not ruled out *a priori*" (ibid., p. 318, note 3).

On the above understanding of T, it follows, as Chalmers and Jackson note, that *a priori* physicalism rules out angels since $P\&T$ *a priori* entails that there are no angels.[28]

However, it is patently obvious that the addition of T is not going to make truths such as

Water covers most of the Earth

any easier to deduce *a priori* from the microphysical and the permitted indexical truths. Thus, *a priori* physicalism is in very bad shape. The attempt to elaborate a version of physicalism that is *a priori* is simply misguided.

4   The Admissible Contents of Visual Experience

One thought that has motivated disjunctivist theories of experience (Hinton 1973; Snowdon 1990; Martin 2002, 2006) has been that in cases of veridical perception, the subject is directly in contact with the perceived object. When I perceive a tomato, for example, there is no tomato-like sense impression that stands as an intermediary between the tomato and me. Nor am I related to the tomato as I am to a deer when I see its footprint in the snow. I do not experience the tomato by experiencing something *else* over and above the tomato and its facing surface. I see the facing surface of the tomato *directly*.

This, of course, is the view of naive realism. And it seems as good a starting point as any for further theorizing about the nature of perception. Some disjunctivists have suggested that to do proper justice to the above thought, we need to suppose that the objects we perceive are *components* of the contents of our perceptual experiences in veridical cases. This supposition is supported further by the simple observation that if I see an object, it must look some way to me. But if an object looks some way to me, then intuitively it must be experienced *as* being some way. And if experience is representational at all, how can the object be experienced as being some way unless the object itself figures in the content of the experience?

A related consideration is that in cases of illusion, the perceived object appears other than it is. In such cases, intuitively, the perceptual experience is inaccurate.[1] And it is so precisely because the object is not as it appears to be. This strongly suggests that, at least in those cases where there is a perceived object, a perceptual experience has a content into which the perceived object enters along with its apparent properties.[2] The experience, then, is accurate if and only if the object *has* those apparent properties.

Once it is acknowledged that the content of visual experience is singular in veridical cases, it must also be acknowledged that in cases of hallucination the content (if there is one) is not singular,[3] for in these cases there is no object with which the subject is in perceptual contact. This has led disjunctivists to conclude that there is no shared mental state common to veridical and hallucinatory visual experiences.[4] The class of such experiences is not like, say, the class of beliefs. Instead, the former class is more like the class of tigers or tables.

This is not to say that to their subjects veridical and hallucinatory experiences never *seem* the same. Occasionally the former may be introspectively indistinguishable from the latter. But when this happens, the veridical experience and the hallucinatory experience are no more closely related than a lemon and a bar of soap that looks just like a lemon (Austin 1962). The one experience is indistinguishable from the other via introspection, just as the lemon and the soap are indistinguishable from one another perceptually. Even so, the two are very different kinds of thing.

The purpose of this chapter is to take a close look at the nature of perceptual content. This discussion is necessary for at least two reasons. First, it is needed to defend some claims I made about visual content in chapter 1. Second, a proper understanding of visual content is essential to understanding the position developed in the next chapter and applied thereafter.

4.1 The Existential Thesis

The thesis that experiences do not have singular contents into which their experienced objects enter is endorsed by Colin McGinn in the following passage:

> ... the content of experience is not to be specified by using any terms that refer to the object of experience, on pain of denying that distinct objects can seem precisely the same.... We are to say that a given experience is as of *a* book that is brown, thick, and has the words 'The Bible' inscribed upon it; we are not to say, when giving the content of the experience *which* book it is that is seen. (McGinn 1982, p. 39)

David Lewis (1980) and Alan Millar (1991) take a similar view.

In a later passage (p. 42), McGinn qualifies the remarks quoted above by saying that the concepts used to characterize the content of visual experience should be restricted to concepts of "colour, superficial texture, shape, etc." Concepts such as the concept *book*, in his view, really only enter into associated beliefs.

It is clear that McGinn supposes that experiences can have the same content but different objects. What is not so clear is why he supposes this. He says in the passage quoted that to hold that particular objects enter into the content of experience is to be compelled to deny that distinct objects can seem precisely the same.[5] This seems too hasty. Singular contents that include different experienced objects are certainly different contents, but why should this be taken to show that the way one object seems to a given perceiver cannot be precisely the same as the way another object seems? Perhaps McGinn's thought is that when the singular contents are different, the *total* 'seemings' cannot be the same. However, if one total 'seeming' is the same as another just in case the two experiences have the same phenomenal character, the fact that the two experiences have different singular contents clearly does not show that the total 'seemings' must be different.[6]

The positive thesis that experiences have only existential contents is embraced by Martin Davies:

... we can take perceptual content to be existentially quantified content. A visual experience may present the world as containing an object of a certain size and shape, in a certain direction, at a certain distance from the subject. (1992, p. 26)

Davies's reason for adopting this view is essentially the same as the reason McGinn offers for his position. One immediate objection to the Existential Thesis, then, is that, as yet, it lacks a clear motivation. For present purposes, I shall put this to one side. The objection to the Existential Thesis I want to develop in this section is that it yields an unequivocal result of veridicality in certain cases in which such a result is not warranted. Thus, the Existential Thesis should be rejected.

Suppose that I am looking directly ahead and that, unknown to me, there is a mirror in front of me placed at a 45° angle, and behind which there is a yellow cube.[7] Off to the right of the mirror, and reflected in it, is a white cube. Through special lighting conditions, this cube appears yellow to me. In these circumstances, according to the Existential Thesis, my experience is accurate or veridical. It 'says' that there is a yellow cube located in front of me, and there is such a cube. But I do not see that cube. I see something else—something that does *not* have the properties in question. *That* cube looks to me other than it really is. My experience misrepresents its color. Thus, my visual experience cannot be counted as accurate *simpliciter*, as the Existential Thesis requires. It follows that the Existential Thesis should be rejected.

One way to try to defend the Existential Thesis against this objection is to make the existential content more elaborate. For example, it might be held that my experience represents that there is a yellow cube that stands in such-and-such a causal/contextual relation to this very experience, where the relevant causal/contextual relation is the one needed for seeing the relevant cube.[8] Now my experience is inaccurate, since the object causing it is *not* yellow.

This proposal does not do full justice to the thought that the cube I see looks to me other than it is. Intuitively, I misperceive *that cube*. My experience misrepresents *it*. This is possible only if the cube I see is itself a component of the content of my experience. Furthermore, the proposal that experiences, in part, refer to themselves is not easy to swallow. Intuitively, when I see a tomato, for example, my visual experience is directed upon the tomato. It is not about *itself* in addition to the tomato.

A third difficulty is that if deviant causal chain counter-examples are to be avoided, it will have to be stipulated that the relevant causal chain is not deviant. But the conditions needed to spell out non-deviance are surely not ones that are *perceptually* available.

A fourth problem can be brought out by considering the case of memory. For me to remember that *p*, there must be a causal connection between the historical event that makes '*p*' true and my current memory state, or so it is usually supposed. But patently that causal connection is not part of the content of the memory. To think otherwise is to confuse the satisfaction conditions for '*X* remembers that *p*' with those for '*p*'. It is also standardly held that truly believing that *p* is not enough for knowing that *p*. In addition, the belief must be appropriately caused. This fits with the causal requirement on memory, given that memory is a species of knowledge. But again, it would clearly be silly to hold that the relevant causal connection must be in the known content. That isn't what is known, although its existence is a necessary condition of the subjects' knowing what she knows. And correspondingly in the case of perception and perceptual experience.[9,10]

The upshot is that the Existential Thesis is in trouble.

4.2 The Singular (When Filled) Thesis

Consider the china frog that is sitting by one of my house plants. As I view it, I think to myself that *that* is a china frog. A little later, I look up from the book I am reading and again think to myself that *that* is a china frog. Unknown to me, a mischievous demon has made the frog disappear in the intervening time period while making it appear to me that the frog is still present. In the second case, then, there is no frog for my thought to be about. Even so, I did think something in the second case, just as I did in the first. According to one standard use of the term 'content', what I thought was the content of my thought. Thus, in the second case my thought has a content, just as in the first.

My first thought, as I looked at the china frog, had a singular content, into which the china frog entered. The second thought did not have a singular content—not, at least, on the usual use of the term 'singular content'. How, then, are we to conceive of the content of the second thought?

The natural proposal, I suggest, is that the second content is just like the first except that where the first has a concrete object in it, the second has a gap. The two contents, thus, have a common structure. This structure may be conceived of as having a slot in it for an object. In the case of the first content, the slot is filled by the china frog. In the case of the second content, the slot is empty. I shall call such structures *content schemas*.

Some may be disinclined to count the second content as a content at all. But, as I noted above, I am certainly thinking something in the above case.[11] Furthermore, there are other, independently plausible examples of thoughts with gappy contents. Consider, for example, the thought that Vulcan does not exist. Here, what is thought is true. But with the demise of descriptivist theories of proper names, arguably the best account of the content of this thought is that it is gappy.

Now let us return to the first thought that that is a china frog. This thought is true: the object in the content has the property in it. What of the second thought? Well, the second thought that that is a china frog is true if and only if that is a china frog. Since there is no object picked out by the demonstrative 'that' on the right-hand side of this bi-conditional, there is no demonstrated object to have the property of being a china frog. Thus, the sentence on the right-hand side of the bi-conditional is naturally classified as false. Correspondingly, then, given the truth of the bi-conditional, the thought is naturally classified as false too.[12]

Hereafter, I shall call content schemas of the above sort *SWF content schemas*, meaning schemas yielding singular contents when their slots are filled. With the failure of the Existential Thesis, it might now be suggested that the general line sketched above for singular (or putatively singular) thoughts can be applied to perceptual experiences.[13]

Whether one is undergoing a veridical visual experience, an illusory experience, or a hallucinatory experience, one experiences *something*. One's
experience has a content, or so it seems very reasonable to suppose. The
Singular (When Filled) Thesis, as I shall call it, holds that in the case that
a visual experience is veridical it has a content that is an instance of an
SWF content schema, the slot in which is filled by the seen object, where
the properties attributed in the content are properties the seen object
has.[14] In the case that an illusion is present, the experience again has a
content that is an instance of an *SWF* content schema, the slot in which
is filled by the seen object, but now the seen object lacks one or more of
the properties attributed in the content. In the case of a hallucination, the
experience has a content that is an instance of an *SWF* content schema,
the slot in which is empty.[15]

One natural way to conceive of the relevant *SWF* schemas is on the
model of Russellian singular propositions having slots in place of
objects.[16] When the slot is filled by a seen object, a Russellian singular
proposition results. In other cases, when the slot is empty there is a gappy
proposition. This, of course, is not the only way to view the *SWF*
schemas.

Since it is often the case that we see multiple things at the same time,
the relevant *SWF* schemas can have multiple filled slots. In cases of hallucinating multiple things, there are multiple empty slots. Exactly how the
metaphysics of empty slots (and correspondingly gappy propositions) is
to be elaborated deserves further discussion, but I take no position on it
here.

It may be replied that what I am calling "gappy propositions" or
"gappy contents" for cases of hallucination are not really contents at all,
on the grounds that they are not truth-evaluable or accuracy-evaluable.
But this would be too hasty. As I noted earlier, the thought that this is a
china frog is plausibly classified as false in the case that there is no china
frog even though it has a gappy content. Why not take the same view for
hallucinatory experiences (and for essentially the same reasons)? This also
fits with the intuitive idea that hallucinatory experiences are inaccurate:
the world is not as it seems to the person who is hallucinating.

Perhaps it will be objected that this view is committed to the implausible claim that there are un-instantiated properties (for example, redness)
in cases of hallucination. To this I reply that the claim is not in the least
implausible. On the contrary, it is part of naive commonsense.[17] Suppose
that you had never seen any red things and then, one day, you halluci-

nated a red car. Did you not then encounter redness in your experience? Did you not then "get a good look" at redness (Hawthorne and Kovakovitch 2006)—a look that enabled you then and there to know what it is like to experience red?

Here is a serious worry for the Singular (When Filled) Thesis. Consider again the mirror case from the preceding section. The present thesis yields the *unequivocal* result that my visual experience is inaccurate, since the cube I am seeing enters into the content of my experience, as does the color property it appears to have, and the latter is a property it actually lacks. But this does not seem the right thing to say. After all, it certainly *appears* to me that there is a yellow cube in front of me; and there is such a cube. The world is as it appears in this respect.

A further problem for the Singular (When Filled) Thesis is this: In front of me, there is a blue, bouncing ball. Unknown to me, the information in the light reflected from the ball and reaching my retina is not processed any further. An evil neuroscientist has blocked the signals from my retina to my optic nerve while simultaneously and serendipitously activating my visual cortex by means of electrical probes in just the way it would have been activated had the signals got through. In these circumstances, I do not see the bouncing ball. There is no item out there in the world in front of me that causes my visual experience. Nor do I misperceive the bouncing ball for the same reason. I am not subject to an illusory experience. The experience I undergo is hallucinatory. I hallucinate a blue, round, bouncing object before me. Even so, my experience is accurate. The world is just as it appears to me. I am undergoing a veridical hallucination.

It seems, then, that the Singular (When Filled) Thesis cannot accommodate cases of veridical hallucination.[18] According to that thesis, where there is no seen object, the visual experience has a gappy content; and the gappy content is false, or at best neither true nor false.

4.3 Kaplanianism

Indexicals are terms that change their reference from utterance to utterance. Examples are 'I', 'here', 'she', 'that', 'today' and 'here'.

Consider the following two utterances:

Tim: "I am hot."

Tom: "I am hot."

Intuitively these two utterances have the same linguistic meaning, but what Tim says is different from what Tom says. Tim, who (let us suppose) is cold, says something false; but Tom, who is hot, says something true. Thus, the content of Tim's remark is different from the content of Tom's.

On David Kaplan's theory (1989), indexicals have contents with respect to contexts. For example, the content of 'I' with respect to a given context C is the subject or agent of C, the content of 'that' with respect to C is the object demonstrated in C, and the content of 'here' with respect to C is the location of C. The content of a sentence containing an indexical is a structured proposition having as its constituents the content of the indexical (the agent, place, object demonstrated, etc.) and the contents of the other terms, where these contents are taken to be worldly entities: particulars, properties, and relations. Thus, in the case of Tim's utterance of the sentence "I am hot," the content of Tim's remark is a structured proposition containing Tim himself (the subject in this context) and the property of being hot (the content of the predicate 'is hot'). The sentence is false in the context, given that Tim is cold.

On Kaplan's theory, the linguistic meaning of an indexical term is a function that maps contexts onto contents, where the latter are those contents the term has at each context. Kaplan calls this function the term's *character*. Thus, consider the term 'here'. Its character is a function from contexts whose value at each context is the location of that context. Similarly, the character of the term 'that' is a function from contexts to the objects demonstrated in those contexts. In the case of sentences containing indexicals, their characters are functions from contexts to the structured propositions that are the contents of the sentences in those contexts.

One case not explicitly discussed by Kaplan that is relevant to the theory below is the case of demonstratives used in failed demonstrations. Suppose I mistakenly think that I have demonstrated something and that I have used the term 'that' to refer to it. In reality, there is nothing to be demonstrated, no referent for my utterance of 'that'. The content of the term 'that' in any given context, on Kaplan's theory, is the object demonstrated in that context. But what counts as a context here? Each context has associated with it at least an agent or subject, a time, and a location. In the case of 'that', it seems plausible to hold that each context is a context of demonstration, and thus that it also has associated with it a demonstrated object. So where there is no demonstrated object, there is no context.

It follows that, in the case of a failed demonstration, the term 'that' has no content. It does, however, have a linguistic meaning. This is a function that maps contexts (of demonstration) onto the objects demonstrated in those contexts.

Consider now the case of the content of visual experience. Let me begin my development of a Kaplanian approach by saying a little more about the case of illusion. Here there is a seen object. That object appears other than it is. The natural further account of this is that the subject's experience represents the object as having some property that it lacks. The case is one of misrepresentation. Thus, when I see a straight stick in water and it appears bent to me, my experience represents it—the seen object—as bent. The difference between this case and the veridical one is not that in the latter I am in direct contact with an object whereas in the former I am not, but rather that the singular content into which the seen object enters is accurate in the latter case but not in the former.

If it is indeed true that veridical and illusory perceptual experiences have singular contents, then one possible view to take of cases of hallucination is that their phenomenology is misleading. It is for the subject of a hallucination as if the experience has a singular content, but in reality there is no content there at all. Thus, hallucinations are like cases of failed demonstration. Just as a token of 'this' uttered in a failed demonstration has a linguistic meaning but no content, so a token experience occurring in a hallucination has a phenomenal character but no content.

For tokens of 'that', a context, I suggested above, is a context of demonstration. Thus, where there is no object demonstrated, there is no context in the relevant sense. In the case of perceptual experience, what experiences *fundamentally* aim to do is put us in contact with objects around us. Where there is no object, as in the case of hallucination, there is no contact and so (we might say) no context of experiential contact. The experience is a failed experience.

On this view, each token experience has a phenomenal character, but not every token experience has a representational content. However, each token experience is a token of an experiential type for which there is a function having as its arguments contexts of experiential contact in which tokens of that type occur and having as its values the appropriate singular contents of those tokens. Again, the model is that of demonstratives. Each token of 'that' is a token of a linguistic type for which there is a function having as its arguments contexts of demonstration in which tokens of that type occur and having as its values the objects demonstrated via the use of those tokens.

I am disinclined to accept this view, though it does have some appeal. My reasons are two. First, in my discussion of the Singular (When Filled) Thesis in section 4.2, I held that when one has a demonstrative thought for which there is no object, nonetheless one's thought has content, for one certainly does think something in such a case. However, on Kaplan's account there is no *content* in the case of a failed linguistic demonstration. Of course, the Kaplanian could reply that even though there is no linguistic content in this case, the subject is expressing a thought that does have content. But if one takes this view, it is very hard to see why one would not then be prepared to grant that the sentence one utters has content too. And if that is the case, then there no longer seems any reason to deny that visual experiences have content in hallucinatory cases. Second, Kaplanianism requires a rejection of the very intuitive view, noted in 4.2, that hallucinatory experiences are inaccurate—that the world is not as it seems to the subject of the hallucination.

4.4   The Multiple-Contents Thesis

So far it has been assumed that each visual experience has (at most) a single content. It is this assumption that the Multiple-Contents Thesis challenges.

What motivates the Multiple-Contents Thesis is really two thoughts. First, it seems natural to suppose that vision involves direct contact with external things in standard, veridical cases. In those cases, the objects seen are just as they appear. Perhaps the most straightforward explanation of this fact is that visual experiences in such cases have accurate singular contents into which the seen objects enter. Second, it also seems natural to suppose that when something O appears F, even though there isn't really something other than O—an appearance O presents—that is F, as the sense-datum theorists would have us believe, still it surely does *appear* to us that something is F. This, in turn, seems best further understood in terms of the experience representing that something is F. So, experiences have a layer of content that is existential, according to the Multiple-Contents Thesis. This layer is to be found in all perceptual experiences, accurate or not, whereas singular contents are missing in some perceptual experiences (namely the hallucinatory ones). Singular contents, thus, are not *essential* to perceptual experiences, whereas existential contents are.

Obviously there is room for disagreement among those who advocate the Multiple-Contents Thesis about how rich this layer of existential content is and whether it requires the subject of the experience to possess the concepts needed to state the conditions under which it is accurate. However the thesis is developed further to deal with these issues, it has no difficulty either with the mirror case of section 4.1 or with the case of veridical hallucination. In the mirror case, my visual experience is accurate with respect to its existential content and inaccurate with respect to its singular content. It appears to me that there is before me an object of a certain shape and size and color at a certain distance away and in a certain direction, and, as it happens, there is an object with the relevant apparent features, namely the yellow cube hidden behind the mirror. Thus, my experience has an accurate existential content. However, the cube I am actually seeing is *not* as it appears to be. It is white rather than (as I am led to suppose on the basis of my experience) yellow. Thus, my experience has an inaccurate singular content.

In the case of a veridical hallucination, the subject undergoes an experience with an accurate existential content. The world appears to contain a blue, round, bouncing object before the subject, for example, and there is such an object. But the subject does not see the object. She is hallucinating. Thus, there is no singular content.

Must the multiple-contents theorist acknowledge a gappy SWF content in addition to an existential content in the case of hallucinatory experiences? One argument for an affirmative answer is that we must suppose that there is a gappy SWF content for such experiences in order to explain the deceptive nature of hallucinations and further to explain the actions hallucinations generate. Suppose, for example, that Sebastian hallucinates a large, furry spider crawling up his leg. He forms the belief that *that* spider is dangerous. In great fear, he reaches for a nearby book to hit it. That is why he reaches for the book.[19]

The general point that hallucinations are deceptive seems to me unpersuasive, for if hallucinatory experiences have existential contents, then they have false contents (leaving aside those experiences occurring in veridical hallucinations). Unsurprisingly, then, they give rise to false beliefs, and thus they deceive their subjects.

However, it is true that the supposition that some experiences have gappy SWF contents provides a straightforward explanation of the action performed by the victim of the hallucination. Consider again Sebastian. It is the spider he is hallucinating that he intends to squash with a book. He reaches for a book with the aim of killing *that* spider, and not the much smaller, innocuous looking spider on the ground to his left. Sebastian did not want to kill *a* spider. He wanted to kill one particular spider—the spider that, according to his hallucination, was on his leg.

Still, this consideration seems to me indecisive. Suppose I say to you that Winston believes that there is a burglar in the house. I may then continue by remarking that Winston wants to find him and shoot him. That's why Winston is going upstairs with a gun in his hand. Clearly the use of the pronoun 'him' here does not show that the content of Winston's belief is singular. What Winston believes has an existential content. Why not suppose that something of the same sort is going in Sebastian's case? On this view, it is perfectly acceptable to say both that Sebastian has a visual experience of *a* spider on his leg and that he wants to kill it.

Perhaps it will be replied that even if the example does not tell definitely in favor of the admission of gappy contents, it is nonetheless the case that the supposition that there is gappy content in hallucinatory cases preserves as much similarity as can be preserved between those cases and the veridical ones. So, given the overall introspective similarity between the two sets of cases, this is a point in favor of the view that some visual experiences have gappy contents.

4.5   The Existential Thesis Revisited

In the introduction to this chapter, I noted that adherence to naive realism requires us to accept that we see the facing surfaces of common or garden material objects directly. The first point I want to make in this section is that granting this point about what is directly seen does not necessitate that we also accept that ordinary objects enter into the contents of our experiences. Indeed, consistent with this point, we could even deny that perceptual experiences *have* contents (as, for example, adverbial theorists do). The view that perceptual experiences have singular contents into which the seen objects enter is most strongly motivated by the thought that, in seeing those object, they look some way to us, together with the further thought that an object can look a certain way only if it is experienced *as* being that way. This in turn, seems to require that the object be represented as being that way. In the case of an illusion, then, there is misrepresentation, since the seen object is not as it is represented as being. Here the seen object looks other than it is.

One possible response to this line of reasoning—a response consistent with the general view that experiences have representational contents—is to grant that one sees an object just in case it looks some way to one but to deny that the object's looking some way demands that one undergo an experience that represents it as being that way. Thus, one might hold that what it is for an object to look F is for it to cause (in the distinctive way appropriate to seeing) an experience of an F, where the experience so caused has an existential content. If this response is cogent,[20] then the existential theorist has a way of handling the mirror case discussed earlier: she can say that, although it is true that the subject misperceives the white cube on the right, this is because the cube the subject sees *looks* yellow and straight ahead, and its so looking requires only that it cause (in the right way) an experience that represents that there is a yellow cube ahead. Thus, the content is accurate even though the case is one of misperception. What we have here, the existential content theorist may say, is a case of *veridical illusion*. The case, thus, is a counterpart to the earlier case of veridical hallucination. The latter case did not demand an inaccurate or falsidical content, so why suppose that the former does?

Here is an answer. Consider again Sebastian, who is hallucinating a spider crawling up his leg. He tries to grab it. Now suppose that Sebastian's hallucination is veridical: there really is a spider crawling up his leg, so what Sebastian succeeds in grabbing is the real spider. Did Sebastian manage to grab the spider he was hallucinating? It seems not, for that spider is unreal. Nonetheless, *that* is the spider he tried to grab—the one that, *according to his hallucination*, was on his leg. To explain what Sebastian was trying to do in this case and further to explain his failure to do it, it seems, we really must suppose that his experience has a gappy content with a quasi-singular character. That content is inaccurate or falsidical. At any rate, it is not accurate. So the claim that cases of veridical hallucination do not demand inaccurate or falsidical contents is mistaken.

Again, however, the existential theorist has a reply. Consider the case of Winston. He believes that there is a burglar upstairs. He is trying to catch him. That seems a perfectly good explanation of why Winston is running up the stairs, gun in hand, even if it turns out that there is no burglar. But Winston's belief certainly does not have a gappy content.

Now admittedly, in the case of veridical illusions, some of the beliefs formed directly on the basis of experience are singular. For example, in the mirror case, I believe falsely that *that* cube is yellow, where that cube is the one I am seeing located off to the right. The most straightforward account of the formation of beliefs with singular contents in such cases, it might be insisted, is that the experiences have singular contents too.

Once again, this point does not refute the existential theory. Consider Winston once again. Winston believes that there is a burglar upstairs. Given the direction of the noise, Winston forms the belief that *he* is in the red room. Even so, Winston's initial belief has an existential content.

It seems, then, that the above considerations do *not* refute the view that visual experiences have existential contents (and only such contents), although they do put pressure on it. The point I wish to establish next is that even if there are existential experiential contents, they are not pure (that is, without any constituent particulars).

Suppose that I am seeing a tomato at 2 p.m. and then I close my eyes for 10 seconds, after which I view it again. How is this to be captured in terms of existential content? The obvious answer is that in both cases my experience represents that there is something red, round, and bulgy. But this will not do. Suppose that at 2 p.m. there was something red, round, and bulgy before me, whereas at 2:00:10 p.m. there is nothing red, round, and bulgy in the world at all, notwithstanding how things then seem to me. In this case, intuitively my later experience is inaccurate. However, its existential content is correct (on the assumption that 'there is' is tenseless).

The obvious response to this difficulty is to say that my experience at 2 p.m. represents that there is something red, round, and bulgy at 2 p.m., whereas my experience at 2:00:10 p.m. represents that there is something red, round, and bulgy at the later time. The difficulty now is that the existential content of my experience at 2 p.m. is no longer pure: it includes a particular time.

One way around this problem is to say that the relevant existential content is that there is *presently* something red, round, and bulgy. The question now becomes how to understand 'presently'. If 'presently' means *at the present time* (that is, at the time of occurrence of the relevant token experience), then the above difficulty recurs. In the case of the experience at 2 p.m., the content involves a different token experience from the content of the experience at 2:00:10 p.m. Let us suppose, then, that 'presently' picks out a way or mode of being. If clear sense can be made of this, the immediate difficulty dissolves.

Another difficulty is not far behind, however. Suppose that there is presently something red, round, and bulgy in front of a perceiver in Lithuania even though there is nothing red, round, and bulgy anywhere else. Intuitively, my visual experience of a tomato, occurring in Texas, is inaccurate. Unfortunately, its existential content is accurate if we suppose that its content is just that there is something red, round, and bulgy. It is also accurate if we suppose that the content is that there is presently something red, round, and bulgy in front of some perceiver.

Some might be inclined to bite the bullet here and allow that experiences need not have the same accuracy or correctness conditions as their contents. But those who value their teeth should pause. After all, if what you believe is true, then your belief is true. Why should the situation be any different for experiences? Furthermore, on a causal covariational account of experiential representation, if the content of my experience, as I view the tomato, is (simply) that there is presently something red, round, and bulgy, then my experience is of the type that, under Normal conditions, is tokened if and only if and because there is presently something red, round, and bulgy. But patently no visual experience is of this type; to suppose otherwise is like supposing that the height of a mercury column in a thermometer Normally tracks the temperature of air *somewhere or other* rather than the temperature of the *surrounding* air.

One simple way to handle the above difficulty is to introduce the subject of the experience into the content. What my experience at 2 p.m. represents is that there is presently something red, round, and bulgy in front of *me*. But again the existential content is not pure: the subject of the experience now enters into it.

It does not help, of course, to remove the subject from the content and replace him or her with an objective place, for again the existential content is not pure. Likewise, if we say that the relevant existential content is one that brings in a causal relationship with the appropriate token experience, even if we set aside the earlier objections to this proposal.

The conclusion I draw is that if it is supposed that visual experiences have existential contents, these contents had better be *partly* singular.[21] The seen object does not itself enter into the content, but other objects do—such objects as particular times or particular places or subjects of experiences or particular experiences themselves. This does not refute the existential view, of course, but it does naturally lead us to ask why, once *some* singularity is admitted, it is necessary to insist, as do both the existential theorist and the multiple-contents theorist, that the seen object in particular does *not* enter into the relevant existential content.

4.6 Still More on Existential Contents

In section 4.2, I urged against the Singular (When Filled) Thesis that it must at least be admitted that there is a layer of existential content in order to account for cases of veridical hallucination. The thought was that without such a layer of content, we cannot understand how it can be true that it appears to me that there is something blue, round, and bouncing ahead (or before me) in the case that there is such an object even though I am not seeing it.

I want now to suggest that there is another explanation available: My visual experience has a gappy content—a content with a gap in it where a seen object should go along with such properties as blueness, roundness and bounciness. But this gappy content disposes me to believe that there is something blue, round and bouncing. This is what makes it the case that it appears to me that there is something blue, round, and bouncing. Cases of veridical hallucination are veridical, then, only to the extent that the visual experiences they involve dispose their subjects to form true beliefs. The experiences themselves, however, are falsidical, or at best neither true nor false.

Note that this proposal does not entail that when it appears to me that *P*, I do actually believe that *P*. Evidently that would be too strong. In the case of the Müller-Lyer illusion, for example, it appears to me that the lines are of different lengths, but I do not believe this. Still I am disposed to believe this if I go by the content of my experience alone. Note further that the proposal does not assume any specific account of how the relevant disposition is to be cashed out. Consistent with this proposal, it could be denied that there is any straightforward further analysis of the relevant disposition. And certainly there is reason to resist any account of the disposition in simple if-then terms, as is shown by counterexamples of the sort proposed by C. B. Martin (1994) to straightforward if-then analyses of dispositions.

Another virtue of the above proposal is that it allows it to be true that, say, it visually appears to me that there are more than three red objects before me, that there are fewer than 100 such objects, that there are more than seven red objects before me, that there are fewer than 300, that there are at least twice as many red objects as green ones, and so on indefinitely, even though I am not subject to any occurrent thought with any of these contents. Nor in this case need any of the given contents attach to my visual experience. I need not see the scene before me as having more than three red objects and so on in order for it to visually appear to me that it is so. It suffices that my visual experience have a content that disposes me to believe that there are more than three red objects before me, fewer than 100, and so on, if I go by the content of the experience alone. The relevant contents, thus, are *potential* cognitive contents and not actual visual contents of my experience. And what goes for these contents is plausibly held to go for *all* contents expressible via sentences of the form "It visually appears to me that *P*."

Where does this leave us? Even though no knockdown argument has emerged against the view that visual experiences have impure existential contents, there is no strong reason left for adopting the view. Neither veridical hallucinations nor veridical illusions provide any strong support. Admittedly, McGinn, in the passage quoted at the beginning, did offer an additional reason, namely that we must suppose that the seen object does not enter into the content of experience "on pain of denying that seen objects can seem precisely the same." And this reason has not yet been discussed, but patently it is not compelling. Different objects seem the same, it is natural to suppose, if they are visually represented as having the same properties. Their being so represented does not preclude them from entering into the contents of the relevant experiences. Indeed, it seems that they must so enter in order for *them* to be represented at all.

This brings us back to the suggestion, made earlier on behalf of the existential theorist, that what is it for an object O to look F is for O to cause (in the way involved in seeing O) an experience of an F. To accept this proposal is to be committed to denying that if O looks F then O is visually experienced as being F, for O cannot be experienced as being F unless the relevant experience represents O as F (assuming that experience is representational at all). But there seems to me a very strong intuitive pull to the thought that if O looks F, O is represented as F; and this is lost on the existential proposal. Furthermore, if experience is representational, then how can O *itself* be visually experienced if O is not in the content of the experience? But if it now conceded that, strictly speaking, O is not visually experienced on the Existential Thesis, then surely O is not seen.

There is an additional difficulty lurking for the above account by the existential theorist of what it is for O to look F—a difficulty I have so far ignored. Suppose that I am seeing two objects, a and b, such that a looks green to me and b looks red to me. Object a causes my experience of something green, and it does so in the way involved in seeing a. But equally so does object b. On the existential proposal, in seeing both a and b, I undergo an experience that represents something green. This experience, however, also represents something red. Thus, b not only causes my experience of something red; it also causes my experience of something green, and it does so in the way involved in seeing b. Thus, b looks red, but it also looks green. Clearly something has gone wrong. The obvious diagnosis of the trouble is that the proposed account by the existential theorist of what it is for an object to look a certain way makes the mistake of removing the seen object from the content of the experience involved in seeing it.[22]

A related thought counting against the existential view is that, intuitively, visual experiences have a singular content or at least a putatively

singular content. They simply do not present the world to us in the way
the Existential Thesis requires. There is a particularity in our experience
which the existential thesis fails to capture fully.

4.7 Conclusion

The Existential Thesis is to be rejected. The Multiple-Contents Thesis is
in somewhat better shape, but it is unnecessarily complicated: there is no
need to suppose that in cases of veridical visual experience there is an
additional existential content over and above the singular content. To
respond that such a content is needed in order to capture the common
factor between veridical and hallucinatory experiences is to forget that
the relevant content must be impure and, being impure, it is different for
different perceivers (and/or different times). Furthermore, the Multiple-
Contents Thesis offers a less than fully persuasive account of veridical
hallucinations.

What remains is the Singular (When Filled) Thesis, and that is the thesis I embrace.[23] It is a form of disjunctivism in that it concedes that the
content of visual experience in the hallucinatory case is different from
the content of visual experience in the veridical case.[24] At the level of
content itself, there is indeed no common factor.[25] For each experience,
there is but a single admissible content, but this content is different in
veridical and in hallucinatory cases. These views on content have important consequences for how to think about consciousness.

5 Consciousness, Seeing, and Knowing

In ordinary English, we use the term 'see' both with respect to objects and with respect to facts. We talk of seeing tables, chairs, trees, stars, and people, for example. We also describe one another as seeing that the table is covered with books, that the chair is made of wood, that the tree has acorns on it, and so on. Chisholm (1957), Drestske (1969), Jackson (1977), and I (1982), among others, have argued that there is a genuine distinction reflected in our talk here: seeing things is not reducible to seeing that things are thus-and-so. To see a thing, it suffices that the thing look some way to the perceiver; and something can look some way without the perceiver's noticing that it is that way and thus without the perceiver's seeing that it is that way.

Suppose, for example, a white cube is bathed in red light and that it looks red to Paul, who is viewing it. Paul cannot see that the cube is red, for the cube is white. Perhaps the cube also looks straight ahead when in reality it is off to the right and Paul is seeing it in a mirror placed at a 45° orientation in front of Paul. Perhaps the cube looks irregular in its shape in virtue of an apparent shape distortion brought about by the mirror. Paul does not see that the cube is off to the right, nor does he see that the object he is viewing has a cubical shape. Still, Paul does see the cube.

The general point here is that one can see an object O without there being any property P such that one sees that O has P, or without there being any property P such that one sees with respect to O that it has P. This is indicated by the cube example and other such cases of ubiquitous error. These points about seeing and seeing-that, I now want to argue, apply to knowing and knowing-that.

5.1 Knowing Things and Knowing Facts

In ordinary English we talk of knowing things and knowing facts. I know Brian McLaughlin, for example. I know the city of Athens. I know the joy of victory and I also know the thrill of driving very fast. I know the feeling of anger. I do not know the city of Istanbul, however. Nor do I know the pain of childbirth.

I know *of* the city of Istanbul. And I know *of* the pain of childbirth, for I know truths about these things. I know that Istanbul is located in Turkey. I know that the pain of childbirth is sometimes difficult to bear. I know also that the Earth is 93 million miles from the sun, that hydrogen is the first element of the periodic table, and that AIDS is rampant in Africa. Philosophers have typically supposed that knowing things is to be understood in terms of knowing facts—that in the end all knowing is knowing-that. But there have been notable exceptions—for example, Bertrand Russell:

> Knowledge of things, when it is of the kind we call knowledge by *acquaintance*, is essentially simpler than any knowledge of truths and logically independent of knowledge of truths, though it would be rash to assume that human beings ever, in fact, have acquaintance with things without at the same time knowing some truth about them. (1912, p. 46)

Here Russell is not claiming that all knowledge of things is separable from knowledge of truths. Obviously that would be too strong. Clearly there is a familiar sense of 'know' under which I would not count as knowing Brian McLaughlin if I did not know *any* truths about him. Furthermore, in one sense I do not know the thrill of driving very fast unless I know with respect to some thrill I have experienced *that* it is the thrill of driving very fast. Russell's thought is that knowing a thing *can* occur without knowing any truth about it simply in virtue of being acquainted with the thing. The corresponding claim about seeing is that one can see a thing without seeing that it is thus and so simply in virtue of its looking some way to one. A stronger but no less plausible thesis is that, just as there is a sense of 'see' such that one sees an object if and only if it looks some way to one, so there is a sense of 'know' such one knows a thing if and only if one is acquainted with that thing.

By 'acquaintance', Russell himself had in mind acquaintance of the sort that is provided by *direct* awareness, not the sort of acquaintance I have with, say, the city of London. According to Russell, when I see a table, I am directly acquainted with the sense data the table presents, not with the table itself or its facing surface. I know the table indirectly, in Russell's view, *as* the physical object that causes certain sense data. Thus, I know it by description. Russell puts it this way:

> All our knowledge of the table is really knowledge of *truths*, and the actual thing which is the table is not, strictly speaking, known to us at all. We know a

description and we know that there is just one object to which this description applies, though the object itself is not directly known to us at all. In such a case, we say that our knowledge of the object is knowledge by description. (1912, pp. 47–48)

In Russell's view, we are not only directly acquainted with particulars such as sense data; we are also directly acquainted with some properties. For example, as I view the table, I am directly aware of a particular shade of color, and in being so aware of it, I know it, according to Russell:

The particular shade of colour that I am seeing may have many things said about it—I may say that it is brown, that it is rather dark, and so on. But such statements, though they may make me know truths *about* the colour, do not make me know the color itself any better than I did before: so far as concerns knowledge of the colour itself, as opposed to knowledge of truths about it, I know the colour perfectly and completely when I see it, and no further knowledge of it itself is even theoretically possible. (ibid., pp. 46–47)

In this passage Russell seems to be accepting what is often called "the thesis of revelation"—the thesis that colors have no hidden nature.[1] There is, however, a weaker interpretation of the passage: that knowledge of a particular shade of brown via direct awareness of it is knowledge of a sort that cannot *itself* be improved or deepened by knowing truths about that shade of brown (which is not to say that one cannot add to such knowledge a further kind of knowledge of the given shade). In this way, knowledge by acquaintance of the color is complete and perfect.

On this interpretation, Russell, in the above passage, has not yet said anything that automatically commits him to denying that the color has an inner nature. Consistent with these remarks, it could be held simply that knowledge of what that nature is, knowledge that the given shade of brown has a certain nature is not knowledge that one can glean by direct awareness. The latter is knowledge by description. Elsewhere, Russell makes claims that fit with the stronger interpretation. For example, immediately after the above remarks he says that sense data are "things with which we have acquaintance, things known to us *just as they are*" (1912, p. 47, emphasis added). My point for present purposes is simply that drawing a distinction between knowledge by acquaintance of the colors and knowledge by description of them does not require us to endorse the thesis of revelation.

According to Russell, then, the primary suggestion is that, just as one can see an object without seeing that it is any particular way simply via its looking some way to one, so one can a know an item without knowing any truth about it simply via direct awareness or consciousness of that item. Here, as I noted above, one's consciousness of an item, or equivalently one's awareness of it, is taken to be direct if and only if there is no other item such that by being conscious or aware of the latter item one is aware of the former.

Russell assumed that indirect awareness involves inference, and this is why he insisted that things known through such awareness are known by description. But the account of directness I have just given does not entail that indirect consciousness is inferential. And to the extent that it is not, as (I would say) in the case of the awareness of a material object via awareness of its facing surface, there seems no clear reason to deny that indirect awareness of a thing yields knowledge of it of a sort that can occur without knowledge of truths about that thing.

There is another aspect of Russell's view on acquaintance from which I wish to distance myself. Russell held that "every proposition which we can understand must be composed wholly of constituents with which we are acquainted" (1912, p. 5). This is sometimes called "the principle of acquaintance." On Russell's view, then, Frank Jackson's Mary cannot entertain propositions having redness as a constituent while she is in her black-and-white room. Thus, Russell is committed to accepting a version of the phenomenal-concept strategy I have already rejected.

Still, why should consciousness of something, direct or indirect, yield knowledge of that thing? One partial answer is that such consciousness is undeniably epistemically enabling; via consciousness of a thing, one is put in a position to know facts about the thing. A more direct answer is that it is simply incoherent to suppose that one might be genuinely (non-inferentially) conscious of an entity and yet not know it *at all*.[2] In being conscious of a particular shade of red at a particular moment, say, I know that shade of red. How could I not? I know it just by being conscious of it. I may not know that shade of red a few moments later, after turning away; I may not know any truths about that shade of red; but, as I view the shade, know it I do in some ordinary, basic sense of the term 'know'.

Perhaps it will be replied that, in every such case, while it is true that I know the thing of which I am directly (that is, non-inferentially) conscious I always know some truth about it. Such knowledge is really factual knowledge. But what could the fact be in the case that I am conscious of a particular shade of red? That this is what I am seeing (or of which I am conscious), where the demonstrative 'this' refers to the relevant shade? That cannot be right. First, intuitively it is a precondition of my knowing the above perceptual fact that I know the relevant shade. If I didn't know the shade at all, how could I know that this (the given shade) is what I am seeing? My knowing the shade, then, cannot *consist* in my knowing the above fact. Second, small children are conscious of determinate shades of color, and in being so conscious they know the shades while they are conscious of them, but they are not capable of higher-order consciousness and thus knowledge of such facts as the fact that this is what I am seeing until they are about 3–4 years of age.

Suppose it is now said that the relevant fact one knows in knowing the given shade is simply that this belongs to a surface before me, where this is the shade and I am the relevant perceiver. But again this cannot be right. Maybe I am misperceiving. Maybe the surface I am seeing appears to have the given shade but in reality it does not; maybe the surface isn't before me but is off to the side, being reflected in a mirror that I have failed to notice; maybe I am hallucinating and there is no surface before me at all.

What about the fact that this is a shade of red, or simply that this is a shade? In the former case, one might easily be conscious of a particular shade of red without realizing that it is a shade of red. Imagine a previously blind person seeing the shade of red for the first time and not realizing that the relevant shade is a shade of red. In the latter case, surely one can be conscious of a shade of color without having the concept *shade*.

The fact is that there need be no fact I know in knowing the color. I can know a thing simply by being conscious of it.[3] In taking this view, I am not denying that I may sometimes be said to know a thing without ever being conscious of it. There are things with which I am familiar and which I thereby count as knowing even though they are not things I have encountered in experience. Consider, for example, Julius Caesar. But in knowing this individual what I really know are truths about him. In each such case, my knowing the thing amounts to knowing *of* it. But when I know a given shade of red simply by being conscious of it, at the time at which I am so conscious I do not know of it. I know it, period.

I suspect that some philosophers will respond to the general claim that not all knowing is knowing-that by saying that "If it ain't propositional, it ain't knowledge." But some seeing ain't seeing-that, as I have already noted, and the case of seeing is hardly special on this count. For example, not all liking is liking-that, not all loving is loving-that, and not all fearing is fearing-that. In ordinary English, we talk of liking, loving, and fearing *things*. I like the songs of Neil Young, for example. My mother loves me. My great aunt used to fear spiders. It is not in the least obvious that in *any* of these cases the mental state is one that relates its subject via the liking, loving, or fearing relation to the content of a 'that' clause, where the content involves the relevant object or is about that object—which is not to say that typically when one likes, loves, or fears some thing one does not like that, love that, or fear that so-and-so is the case with respect to the thing.[4]

Still, might one not be conscious of a thing and yet not know it at all? Suppose, for example, that on a black curtain there is a black crayon mark. I do not know where it is. I do not know that there is any black crayon mark on the curtain. I can't pick it out from the background. Still, I see it, and thus I am conscious of it.

The reply I gave to this sort of case in chapter 1 is that I am not conscious of the crayon mark. My general suggestion in the earlier discussion was that I am conscious of a given entity only if my conscious state is so situated that it enables me to ask "What is that?" with respect to that entity (and it does so solely on the basis of its phenomenology). In the case of the crayon mark, then, since my experience does not enable me directly to ask "What is that?" I am not conscious of it.

It is important to realize that, on the proposal I am making, one can know something without actually bringing it under a concept at all, even merely a demonstrative one, for a sufficient condition for knowledge by acquaintance, I claim, in the perceptual case, is that one's experience or conscious state *enable* one to produce a conceptual, propositional response with respect to the relevant entity (and to do so non-inferentially).[5] One need not *actually* produce such a response.

This is not to suppose or imply that one can know a certain item by being non-inferentially conscious of it without having *any* representation of it. If the item is so known, then it enters into the content of one's conscious state. The relevant state, in my view, is a *nonconceptual* state. (I will discuss this familiar idea further in the next section.)

Perhaps it will be said that the notion of acquaintance to which I am appealing is insufficiently clear. This charge seems to me unwarranted. It is certainly true that the notion of acquaintance has been understood in different ways, as has the notion of direct acquaintance. On one standard usage, a person P is acquainted with an object O if and only if P has the ability to have *de re* mental states about O (Burge 1977; Evans 1982; Pryor forthcoming). Sometimes it is supposed that this requirement is too demanding, and that the ability to have *de dicto* mental states about an object suffices (pretty much) for acquaintance with it (Jeshion 2002). Sometimes it is held that there can be indirect testimonial acquaintance. As I use the term 'acquaintance', the requirement that one have the ability to have *de re* mental states about the relevant object is not demanding enough.[6]

My notion of acquaintance can be illustrated by example. I am acquainted with the color red, the city of Athens, the Apple computer at which I am now typing, the feeling of pain, the urge to gamble a large sum of money, and the feeling of jealousy. I have encountered (or am now encountering) all these things in experience.[7] Where I have not encountered a thing in experience, as is the case with the city of Istanbul and the shape of a chiliagon, I am not acquainted with it in the relevant sense of 'acquaintance'. In such cases, I may have some familiarity with the thing, and thereby have knowledge *of* it. But familiarity of this sort essentially involves knowing (or at least believing) truths about the thing, whereas acquaintance with a thing, as I understand it, does not. One can be acquainted with a thing (in my sense, following Russell) without knowing any truths about it.

Still, there are limits on just how minimal an encounter in experience can be yet count as acquaintance with a thing. For example, what if the thing one experiences is seen in very poor light or is located on the other side of thick, distorting glass? It seems plausible to say that in these cases one isn't properly acquainted with the thing and thus one does not know it by acquaintance. Genuine acquaintance in the visual case requires an encounter in experience of a sort that allows for a good look at the thing. Corresponding requirements seem appropriate for non-visual cases of acquaintance.

Suppose that I am acquainted with the statue of David in a museum but I don't realize that I am, failing to appreciate that the statue I am seeing is a statue of him. Do I know the statue of David? My answer is that in one sense of 'know' I do know the statue: I know it by acquaintance. Of course, I do not know *that* I know the statue of David, and relatedly I do not know the fact that the statue before me is of David, but still I know the statue of David.

Knowledge by acquaintance of a thing stands to certain kinds of factual knowledge in something like the relationship in which seeing a thing stands to certain kinds of seeing-that. I can see that the gas tank is empty by taking off the cap, directing my flashlight, and peering inside. In this case, I see the gas tank. But I can also see that the gas tank is empty by viewing the pointer on the gauge. Similarly, I can see that the door has been forced by seeing the marks on it. I do not see the gas tank or the forcing of the door. In these cases, my seeing-that is secondary or displaced. I am not aware—not conscious—of either the gas tank or the forcing of the door, nor am I aware of their qualities. I see something else—the gas gauge or the marks on the door—and by seeing this other thing, I see *that* so-and-so is the case. Secondary seeing-that, or more generally secondary perceiving-that, is a partly experiential state, for it is part and parcel of such a state that something is experienced.

Correspondingly, as I view a tomato, I know that the facing surface of the tomato is red in part by knowing the tomato by acquaintance. I know that Julius Caesar was a Roman emperor in part by knowing the page in the history book I am reading. In the latter case, my knowledge is secondary: here I know a fact about a thing even though I do not know that thing by acquaintance. Still, such secondary knowledge-that involves knowing *some* thing by acquaintance.

One general worry that might be raised for the overall position I am adopting is that it leaves no room for animals to see things, for seeing something, on my proposal, requires consciousness of it, and that requires the capacity to wonder about it or to form other *de re* conceptual attitudes about it. Many non-human animals lack concepts, so they cannot form such attitudes. It follows, on my account, that such animals do not see things. And that is absurd.

In chapter 1, I said that I was offering a test for consciousness in creatures capable of undergoing propositional attitudes. This provides a way to sidestep the above worry. But I am prepared to meet the concern head on. Consider my dog, Quigley. I show him a bone, and then I pretend to bury it in the ground in a corner of the garden. Quigley watches me do this from a distance. When I have finished, I release him and he rushes over to where I was and he begins digging. Quigley saw the bone. He wants it. He believes that it is in the ground. As he digs deeper, he fails to find it. Eventually he gives up. Evidently, Quigley here has *de re* propositional attitudes with respect to the bone. To the extent that it is agreed that such attitudes require concepts, Quigley has concepts. To be sure, Quigley does not have the concept *bone*, for he cannot draw any distinction between bones and fool's bones. Thus, Quigley's concepts need not be the same as ours. Nor is this needed for us to correctly ascribe attitudes to Quigley using concepts he lacks. It suffices for such ascriptions to be true that Quigley's concepts be sufficiently like ours. Furthermore, for Quigley to wonder where *that* is, where that is the bone, his conceptual resources can be slim indeed.

What goes for Quigley goes for many other non-human animals. There is no obvious general difficulty with the requirement that the possession of some concepts is necessary to see things.

5.2   Nonconceptual Content

Thoughts are composed of concepts, and the contents of concepts individuate in a fine-grained way. Concepts that refer to the same entities can differ in their content. Indeed, I said earlier that concepts can differ in their content even if they refer to the same entity in all possible worlds.

What is it for a given concept to be a concept of mine? What is it for me to possess a concept? I noted in chapter 3 that a very straightforward answer is that I possess a concept C if and only if I am able to exercise C in my thoughts. To this one might object that I can possess concepts that are available only for use in experience (on a conceptualist view of experience), and so not all my concepts need be concepts I am capable of exercising in thoughts. But if experience is conceptual then it must be capable of standing as a reason for belief, and the subject of each experience must be capable of appreciating its justificatory role, of inferring the content of the belief from the content of the experience. Thus, the subject must indeed be capable of exercising concepts in thought that are deployed in experience. With these largely terminological matters out of the way, we are now ready to take up the thesis of nonconceptual content for experiences.

On the usual understanding of this thesis, a visual experience E has a nonconceptual content if and only if (i) E has correctness conditions; (ii) the subject of E need not possess the concepts used in a canonical specification of E's correctness conditions. The first point to note here is that the thesis, as just stated, does not preclude the nonconceptual content of a visual experience from being the content of a thought of another subject, for what makes the content nonconceptual for subject S is simply the fact that S need not herself have the relevant concepts and thus need not herself be in a position to form the relevant thought. Moreover, given the above thesis, the nonconceptual content of an experience E of a subject S can even be the content of a thought of S. All that is required in such a case is that S need not possess the pertinent concepts to undergo the experience: thus, were S to lose the concepts and with them the capacity to have such a thought, that would not preclude her from having the experience if the content of the experience is nonconceptual.

It appears, then, that, given the usual understanding of the thesis of nonconceptual content, as far as the nature of content itself goes, there need be no distinction between conceptual and nonconceptual content. All the thesis, as usually stated, requires, as far as visual experiences go, is that visual experiences be contentful, nonconceptual states, where a contentful, nonconceptual state is a contentful state the tokening of which does not involve the exercise of concepts.

We see, therefore, that the original thesis of nonconceptual content for visual experiences leaves open three possibilities: (1) that such experiences are nonconceptual states having conceptual contents (and thus are the same as thoughts along the content dimension only), (2) that such experiences are nonconceptual states having fine-grained nonconceptual contents (and thus are similar to thoughts along the content dimension), and (3) that such experiences are nonconceptual states having coarse-grained contents (robustly nonconceptual contents, as I shall call them).

Since conceptual contents have fine-grained individuation conditions, those philosophers who embrace nonconceptualism for visual experience and who opt for alternative 1 above face the following very awkward question: How can an experience E of a subject S have a fine-grained content without being built from concepts? Those philosophers who embrace nonconceptualism and who opt for alternative 2 face the same awkward question and a further one: How can an experience E of a subject S have a fine-grained content without that content's being conceptual?[8] Perhaps these questions can be answered adequately, but I am skeptical. Accordingly, in my view, the advocate of nonconceptual content should embrace alternative 3.

But what is the robustly nonconceptual content of an experience? One answer is that such a content is a set of possible worlds. Another answer is that each robustly nonconceptual content is a possible state of affairs built out of worldly entities. The structured account delivers coarse-grained contents in that representations with such contents (unlike representations having conceptual contents) cannot represent the same entities arranged in the same possible states of affairs and yet differ in content. On the unstructured account, coarseness of grain follows from the fact that sameness of content is guaranteed by sameness of correctness conditions in all possible worlds. Of these two accounts, I prefer the second, as should be clear from my comments in the preceding chapter about the content of experience. In my view, objects and properties enter into the contents of visual experience.

The two accounts do not yield the same degree of coarseness of grain in robustly nonconceptual contents. For one thing, some people may wish to deny that necessarily co-instantiated properties (and relations) are identical, and this view generates differences in content on the structured account that do not exist on the unstructured one. For another, on the structured account, some necessarily co-obtaining states of affairs can differ even if necessarily co-instantiated properties (and relations) are identical. Consider, for example, the object-involving state of affairs of X's being red and the necessarily co-obtaining state of affairs of there being exactly one actual F that is red, where 'actual' is understood as a rigidifier and X is the actual F. These states of affairs differ in their structure and thus are different possible contents (on the structured account), but there is no difference in content on the unstructured alternative. The upshot is that the unstructured account is more coarse-grained than the structured one.

The claim that there is a fineness of grain in visual experience that cannot be captured by the concepts possessed by the subject of the experience (or at least any ordinary subject) dates back to Gareth Evans's book *The Varieties of Reference* (1982, p. 229). John McDowell puts Evans's underlying thought as follows:

Think of ordinary color concepts such as those expressed in 'red', 'green', 'blue' as concepts of bands on the spectrum. Evans' point is then that color experiences present properties that correspond to something like lines on the spectrum, namely minimal shades of red, blue, green, etc. (where a minimal shade is one for which there is no other shade that is a shade of it). (1994, p. 56)

Here are some further representative quotations from philosophers who are on Evans's side of the fence. First, Chris Peacocke:

If you are looking at a range of mountains, it may be correct to say that you see some of them as rounded, some as jagged. But the content of your visual experience in respect of the shape of the mountains is far more specific than that description indicates. The description involving the concepts round and jagged would cover many different fine-grained contents which your experience could have, contents which are discriminably different from one another. (1992, p. 111)

Second, Richard Heck:

Before me now, for example, are arranged various objects with various shapes and colors, of which, it might seem, I have no concept. My desk exhibits a whole host of shades of brown, for which I have no names. The speakers to the sides of my computer are not quite flat, but have curved faces; I could not begin to describe their shape in anything like adequate terms. The leaves on the tree outside my window are fluttering back and forth, randomly, as it seems to me, as the wind passes over them—Yet my experience of these things represents them far more precisely than that, far more distinctively, it would seem, than any characterization I could hope to formulate, for myself or for others, in terms of the concepts I presently possess. The problem is not lack of time, but lack of descriptive resources, that is, lack of the appropriate concepts. (2001, pp. 489–490)

Some philosophers claim that the determinacy of detail in visual experience can be captured by concepts at play in the experiences. The onus is on such philosophers to spell out how the determinacy of detail in visual experience is represented conceptually. What is needed, according to the first view I shall consider, is simply the acknowledgment, in the case of color experience, that some of our color concepts pick out minimal shades of color. This is one view[9] adopted by McDowell in his book *Mind and World*:

What is in play here is a recognitional capacity, possibly quite short-lived.... (1994, p. 57)

McDowell's thought, elucidated more clearly in a subsequent symposium on *Mind and World*,[10] is that there is a recognitional capacity that persists for a little while after an experience of the shade recognized, and thus a recognitional concept is exercised. More specifically, according to McDowell, the conceptual content *This is colored (with) S* is in the content of the experience, where *S* is a general recognitional concept of a fine-sliced shade.

This is not convincing. Human memory is limited. We abstract away from details to avoid information overload. We have recognitional concepts (such as red, green, and blue), and we have more specific ones (such as scarlet and bright scarlet). But we do not have recognitional concepts for minimal shades. The recognitional capacities to which McDowell adverts simply do not exist. The ordinary person cannot recognize red_{27}, even having just seen it. People who are shown a patch of color and then very shortly afterward are asked whether a second patch has the same shade of color or a minimally different one do not do well at the task.[11] Of course, if the original patch is re-presented before the original experience is over, the match will be made successfully. But this does not show a recognitional capacity, for that requires the capacity to recognize the given hue when it comes again after the initial experience ends.[12]

A second reply the conceptualist might make to the alleged fineness of grain in visual experience is to allow that the subject of an experience of a minimal shade lacks a general recognitional concept of that shade, but to insist that it does not follow that the experience has a nonconceptual content, since the subject can conceptualize the given shade in the experience by means of a general, fine-grained perceptual concept that the subject is hard-wired to exercise in the given situation. Such a 'concept' is one that never enters memory. It is automatically manufactured on the spot, as the subject undergoes the experience; the concept is then lost as soon as the experience is over. The obvious trouble with this view is that if such concepts occur in the subject's experiences, they must be concepts the subject possesses and hence concepts that the subject is capable of exercising in thought. But if these concepts can occur in the subject's thoughts as well as in her experiences, and they really are general concepts, then the subject should be able to think thoughts that use the concepts even when the experiences are not present; and this conflicts with the hypothesis that the relevant concepts are lost once the experiences end.

Here is another problem. Suppose that I am viewing a colored patch and that my visual experience conceptually represents this patch as red_{25}. Suppose further that my experience is not fleeting: I am staring at the patch for a considerable length of time. While my experience lasts, can I think to myself a thought that exercises this concept—for example, the thought that I am seeing something with shade red_{25}? It seems to me that the only thoughts I can form at such a time about red_{25} have a demonstrative content. I can mentally 'point' at the shade I am experiencing. I can think of it as *that shade* or *that shade of red* or perhaps just *that*. But if my thoughts here seem to me to have a demonstrative content, then, given that I have privileged access to the contents of my thoughts (that I can know via introspection alone what I am thinking[13]), they do have such content. It seems, then, that I cannot think the thought that I am seeing red_{25}, from which it follows that I do not possess the general concept red_{25}. And if I do not possess this concept, then I cannot exercise it in my visual experience.

This brings me to the third reply that the conceptualist might make, namely to suggest that the concept for a shade employed by visual experience is indeed demonstrative. The obvious immediate question for this reply is "What form does the demonstrative concept in the experience take?" McDowell, also in *Mind and World*, appeals to the demonstrative *that shade*. To experience a particular shade (say, red_{27}) is to have an experience of something as being of that shade, where the latter is to be understood as involving the application of the concept *that shade* to red_{27}. On this view, seeing a shade is the same as (or at least is to be modeled on) seeing something as having that shade. The difference between seeing red_{27} and red_{28}, then, is the difference between applying the concept *that shade* to red_{27} and applying it to red_{28}. The concept *that shade*, in the context of the one experience, refers to red_{27}; the concept *that shade*, in the context of the other experience, refers to red_{28}. The two experiences thereby have different correctness conditions and thus different contents.

This is problematic, as has been noted by several philosophers, most forcefully by Peacocke (1998, 2001). First, exactly which concept is exercised in the experience of a particular shade of red? The concept McDowell appeals to is the concept *that shade*. But why not *that shade of red*, or *that color*, or *that red*? There seems no non-arbitrary way of deciding between these candidates—they all seem equally eligible—and thus no fact of the matter as to which one is applied in the experience. It appears, then, that the problem of differences of grain between conceptual resources and experience of shades is genuine but opposite to that envisaged by Evans, for now we have too many available concepts for each shade rather than too many shade experiences for each available concept. Second, what is the referent of the demonstrative in the color case? The obvious answer is "the particular shade." Which shade? Suppose I am viewing a color patch with the shade red$_{18}$. Pointing at the patch and the shade, I say, on the basis of my experience, "That has that shade." Should we suppose that the concept *that*, exercised in the experience with respect to a shade, refers via a sample of the shade, namely the shade of the patch the subject is viewing? Then, on the sample view, both my remark and my experience are accurate. However, if I am misperceiving the patch and experiencing it as having a shade different from the one it actually has, then my experience will not represent the patch as having *that* (understood as the actual shade of the patch) at all. Thus, the content of my experience cannot be demonstrative.

The conceptualist might respond that, whatever may be the case for the demonstrative expression 'that shade', the demonstrative concept exercised in the experience is a concept of the shade the given surface appears to have. But now, in the case of misperception, there is no sample of the color in the relevant part of the world. So how is the referent of the concept fixed? The obvious reply is that it is fixed by the content of the subject's experience: the concept refers to the shade the given experience represents the surface as having. However, this reply is not available to the conceptualist about the content of visual experience, for the content of the demonstrative concept is supposed to be part of the content of the experience and so the concept cannot have its referent fixed by that content (Heck 2000, p. 496).[14]

The picture of visual experience I wish to recommend, then, is one under which the content of visual experience is robustly nonconceptual.[15] If the experience involved in seeing things is veridical or illusory, the content is also singular. In the case that the experience is hallucinatory, it is gappy. Even though the entities entering into the content of visual experi-

ence are represented nonconceptually, for creatures capable of propositional attitudes, a condition of their so entering is that they enable the
subject of the experience to form *de re* conceptual attitudes about them
and to do so non-inferentially. These attitudes can be very minimal. The
subject may simply be put in a position to wonder "What is that?" Furthermore, the subject need not actually undergo any such attitude in having a visual experience.

5.3   Why the Phenomenal Character of an Experience Is Not One of Its Nonrepresentational Properties

The many-property problem was raised by Frank Jackson 33 years ago
for adverbial theories of visual experience. In this section, I am going to
raise a version of this problem for theories that take the phenomenal
character of a visual experience (what it is like to undergo the experience)
to be a nonrepresentational property of the experience. I shall call the
new problem "the phenomenal many-property problem."[16]
  Consider first the following claim:

(1) What it is like for me to have an experience of a red square has
something in common with what is it is like for me to have an experience of a red, round thing.

This surely is true. There is a phenomenal overlap between my experience
of a red square and my experience of something red and round. Another
obvious phenomenological truth is the following:

(2) What it is like for me to have an experience of a red square and a
green triangle is different from what it is like for me to have an experience of green square and a red triangle.

These claims are unproblematic for those who hold that the phenomenal
character of an experience is a structured representational content the experience has into which the experienced qualities enter. In the case of (1),
the representational content that there is a red square is a content into
which the color red enters, as is the representational content that there is
something red and round. In the case of (2), the representational content
that there is a red square and a green triangle is a different content than
the content that there is a green square and a red triangle, even though
the two contents include the same color and shape properties.
  Claims (1) and (2) are also unproblematic for those who hold that the
phenomenal character of an experience is the property of being a sensing

of so-and-so sense datum or sense data. In the case of (1), the property of being a sensing of a red', square' sensum clearly includes the property of being a sensing of a red' sensum. Here I use a prime to indicate a phenomenal property—for (1), phenomenal redness and phenomenal squareness. (I myself do not have any clear grasp on what these phenomenal properties might be if they are not just plain old colors and shapes, but I take it that at least some of those who appeal to sense data would want to distinguish between sensed properties of sensa and properties of material surfaces.)

In the case of (2), the property of being a sensing of a red', square' sensum together with a green', triangular' sensum clearly is not the same as the property of being a sensing of a green', square' sensum together with a red', triangular' sensum.

There is, however, a *big* problem here for those who hold that the phenomenal character of an experience is a nonrepresentational property of the experience and who also eschew the sense-datum theory. To see this, consider my experience of a red square, and suppose that it has the nonrepresentational color and shape qualia Q_r and Q_s. This handles (1) well enough, since my experience of something red will have the quale, Q_r, whatever other shape quale it has. But what now grounds the phenomenal difference in (2)? After all, each experience has the *same* color and shape qualia: Q_r, Q_s, Q_g, and Q_t.

A possible way out for the philosopher who holds that phenomenal character is nonrepresentational and who wishes to avoid the obvious dead end provided by the sense-datum theory is to embrace the adverbial theory. On this view, or at least on any version of this view which does not try to eliminate token experiences altogether in favor of sensing properties of subjects, one who has an experience of red senses redly and one who senses redly undergoes an event having the property of being a red' sensing (just as one who walks slowly undergoes an event which has the property of being a slow walking). Unfortunately, the adverbial theory also encounters immediate difficulty. That was the point of the original many-property problem.

Consider (2) again. Clearly it will not do to try to account for the phenomenal character of the experience of a red square and a green triangle by appealing to the experience having the properties of being a red' sensing, being a square' sensing, being a green' sensing, and being a triangular' sensing, for these properties are possessed by the experience of a green square and a red triangle. Thus, (2) now comes out false.

Nor will it do to appeal to the experience having the property of being a red' and square' and green' and triangular' sensing in the case of the former experience and to the property of being a green' and square' and red' and triangular' sensing in the case of the second experience, for there is no difference in these properties (any more than there is in the case of the property of being a charming and seductive smiling and the property of being a seductive and charming smiling).

It seems, then, that, on an adverbial account, in the case of (1) we need to appeal to the property of being a red-square-thing sensing, where this includes the property of a red-thing sensing. For (2), we need the properties of being a ((red-square-thing) and (green-triangular-thing)) sensing and being a ((green-square-thing) and (red-triangular-thing)) sensing.

This gets very unattractive and highly complicated. How exactly are we to understand such adverbial operators as (red-square-thing)-ly? What are the relevant detachment rules? And the complications created by the above example are just the tip of the iceberg.[17]

A final response the defender of nonrepresentational, phenomenal properties or qualia might make is to propose that experiences have qualia in something like the way that a person who is touching a table has the property of touching a table. Here the person has the property via his having a part (his hand) that has that property. Correspondingly, an experience has the quale Q by its having a part that has Q.

This does not help, however. To see this, consider again the experiences to which (2) adverts. On the above view, the experience of a red square and a green triangle has a part with the conjunctive property, Q_r and Q_s, and a part with the conjunctive property, Q_g and Q_t. Similarly, the experience of a green square and a red triangle has a part with the conjunctive property, Q_g and Q_s, and a part with the conjunctive property, Q_r and Q_t. The former experience, then, has the conjunctive property, Q_r and Q_s, and also the conjuctive property, Q_g and Q_t. The latter experience has the conjunctive properties, Q_g and Q_s, and Q_r and Q_t. But an item has a conjunctive property just in case it has the properties that are its conjuncts. So again (2) comes out false: no relevant difference has been generated at the level of nonrepresentational properties of the experiences.

Furthermore, qualia are now being attributed to parts of experiences as well as to experiences themselves, so that parts of experiences must now be counted as experiences. Thus, it will no longer be true that, in undergoing an experience of a red square and a green triangle, I undergo a single token experience. This seems very counter-intuitive. There is also the question "Just how many experiences do I then undergo?"

Thus, unless we are prepared to make the retrograde move of buying into the sense-datum theory, with all its well-known problems and objections, we are left with the view that the phenomenal character of an experience is *not* a non-representational property of the experience.

5.4   Phenomenal Character and Representational Content: Part I

Strong intentionalism or representationalism is the view that phenomenal character is one and the same as a certain sort of representational content. Weak intentionalism, unlike strong intentionalism, is not an identity thesis. It does not purport to identify phenomenal character with representational content. It is, rather, a supervenience thesis. It asserts that necessarily experiences with the same representational content have the same phenomenal character. This more modest thesis offers no real illumination about the nature of phenomenal character.

Strong intentionalism handles the phenomenal many-property problem in a straightforward way. Unfortunately, it is refuted by the considerations developed in chapter 4 above. In brief, the argument against strong intentionalism is just this:

(3) No veridical and (non-veridical, non *de re*) hallucinatory experiences share the same representational content.

(4) Some veridical and (non-veridical, non *de re*) hallucinatory experiences have the same phenomenal character.

Therefore,

(5) Phenomenal character is not the same as representational content.

Premise (3) is a consequence of the earlier Singular (When Filled) Thesis. In my view, (4) is the best explanation of introspective indiscriminability in many cases.

It may be objected that this is too fast. Consider again the case of the lemon and the bar of soap (Austin 1962). These two very different objects may nonetheless be visually indistinguishable. The best explanation of this fact, it could be urged, is not that the two items are intrinsically the same but rather that they produce experiences that cannot be told apart introspectively.[18] On this view, the visual indistinguishability of the soap and the lemon is grounded upon a relational fact about them: that they cause introspectively indistinguishable experiences.

Likewise, then, perhaps it can be denied that some veridical experiences and some hallucinatory ones have the same phenomenal character. What is really true is merely that these experiences sometimes have indistinguishable phenomenal characters, where this is to be understood in terms of their possession of a common relational property. Now there is no immediate difficulty in identifying phenomenal character with representational content.

The trouble with this retort is that there is no plausible candidate for the relevant relational property. The best alternative seems to be that both the phenomenal character of the veridical experience and the corresponding phenomenal character of the hallucinatory experience cause their subjects to believe, when they introspect, that the two experiences are exactly alike. But alike in which respect? Presumably, phenomenal character. The subjects of the relevant experiences are simply not conscious of any phenomenal difference via introspection.

The question now becomes "*Why* are they not conscious of any such difference?" Surely the most straightforward and natural answer is that in some cases there is no difference; the phenomenal character is the same.

What, then, is phenomenal character? In this section I will explore an attempt to model phenomenal character on Kaplanian character. The resulting account of the nature of phenomenal character, if not fully within the intentionalist camp, is certainly in the general neighborhood.

Let me begin my development of this proposal with some comments on the case of illusion.

Here there is a seen object. That object appears other than it is. The natural further account of this is that the subject's experience represents the object as having some property that it lacks. The case is one of misrepresentation. Thus, when I see a straight stick in water, and it appears bent to me, my experience represents it—the seen object—as bent. The difference between this case and the veridical one is not that in the latter I am in direct contact with an object whereas in the former I am not, but rather that the singular content into which the seen object enters is accurate in the latter case but not in the former.

If it is indeed the case that veridical and illusory perceptual experiences have singular contents, then one possible view to take of cases of hallucination is that their phenomenology is misleading. It is for the subject of a hallucination as if the experience has a singular content, but in reality there is no content there at all. Thus, hallucinations are like cases of failed demonstration. Just as a token of 'this' uttered in a failed demonstration has a linguistic meaning but no content, a token experience occurring in a hallucination has a phenomenal character but no content. This parallelism suggests that we might plausibly take phenomenal character to be modeled on Kaplanian character.[19] In particular, we might take phenomenal character to be a function on contexts of experiential contact whose value at each context is a singular content that meets certain further conditions (for example, that it is nonconceptual and suitably poised to bring about cognitive responses[20]). I call such a view of phenomenal character "Kaplanianism."

The relevant model for contexts of experiential contact is that of demonstratives. For tokens of 'that', a context (I suggested in chapter 4) is a context of demonstration. Thus, where there is no object demonstrated, there is no context in the relevant sense. In the case of perceptual experience, what experiences *fundamentally* aim to do is put us in contact with objects around us. Where there is no object, as in the case of hallucination, there is no contact and so there is no context of experiential contact. The experience is a failed experience.

On this theory, each token experience has a phenomenal character, but not every token experience has a representational content. However, each token experience is a token of an experiential type for which there is a function having as its arguments contexts of experiential contact in which tokens of that type occur and having as its values the appropriate singular contents of those tokens. Again, the model is that of demonstratives. Each token of 'that' is a token of a linguistic type for which there is a function having as its arguments contexts of demonstration in which tokens of that type occur and having as its values the objects demonstrated via the use of those tokens.

The main worry with the above proposal is that it is circular. Phenomenal character is identified with a certain function, the specification of which adverts to an experience type. But the relevant experience type, it seems, is itself phenomenal.

An initial reaction may be that this worry can be overcome. Consider the intentionalist claim that what it is for a token experience to have phenomenal character P is for it to have a representational content, C, that meets certain further conditions. Some intentionalists (see, e.g., Tye 1995) conjoin this claim with the further claim that what is it for a token experience, t, to have a given content is for t to belong to the type of experience that causally covaries with the occurrence of the appropriate external state of affairs under optimal conditions.[21] Patently, if it is now said that the type of experience that so covaries is a phenomenal type, we have a small circle.

The obvious way to handle this problem is to say that t occurs in a particular subject S, and that, in S, t has some property Q (for example, a neurological property) the tokening of which in S causally covaries with the occurrence of a certain state of affairs under optimal conditions. Correspondingly, the Kaplanian can hold that what it is for a token experience to have phenomenal character P is for t to have some property Q and for there to be some function F such that F has as its value in each context C of experiential contact involving the subject of t, the relevant singular content of the token of Q in C. Now the circularity disappears.

This is not persuasive, however. Consider, for example, the case of my hallucinating a ripe tomato. My token experience t has a range of properties, some functional, some neurological, some chemical, and some microphysical. Which of these properties is the relevant property as far as the function goes? Suppose we choose a certain chemical property. There seems no obvious reason why that chemical property of t could not be tokened in me in any number of very different veridical perceptual contexts involving experiences with singular contents into which very different objects enter. However, the phenomenal character in these contexts will vary. To make matters worse, for other properties of my experience, the function could take on different values in the same contexts. So the function is not well defined.

The only way I see out of this problem is to say that the relevant property with regard to defining the function is the phenomenal character of the experience. But this re-introduces the original circularity. We are left, thus, without any substantive account of the nature of phenomenal character. The attempt to stake out a defensible position in the neighborhood of intentionalism has failed.

5.5   Phenomenal Character and Representational Content: Part II

Consider the singular content my experience has as I veridically experience something red, round, and bulgy directly before me and the gappy content your experience has as you hallucinate something red, round, and bulgy directly before you. The contents are different, but they are of the same type. What the two experiences have in common is the possession of an *SWF* content of a certain sort. One way to capture this is to say that the two contents fall under a single *SWF* content schema having a slot in it that is filled by an object in the one case and left empty in the other. Another way to put the point is to say that each experience has an *SWF* content into which all the same (non-object involving) properties enter. This could be used to begin to develop the intentionalist position further without collapsing it into strong intentionalism in the following way: the phenomenal character *P* of a given token experience *E* could be taken to be a matter of *E*'s having within its content a certain cluster of properties.

In my view, for reasons elaborated elsewhere (Tye 1995, 2000), the relevant content should be nonconceptual and should also meet a functional role condition. What emerges from these reflections, thus, is a form of intentionalism that bears the same sort of relationship to strong intentionalism as functionalism bears to the type identity theory. Just as functional properties are multiply physically realizable, so phenomenal properties, on this proposal, are multiple realizable via strong intentional properties of the sort strong intentionalism took to be identical with them. There is no one nonconceptual content that an experience must have in order to possess a given phenomenal character. Instead, its phenomenal character resides in its having *a* nonconceptual content into which a certain cluster of properties enters (and which plays the appropriate functional role). We might call this view "second-order intentionalism."

One objection to this proposal is that it seems somewhat contrived. Can it really be that the phenomenal character of an experience is a *second-order* intentional property? However, in my view, the biggest difficulty this proposal faces is that does not do justice to the phenomenon of transparency. It is to a development of this point and the construction of an alternative proposal that provides for a straightforward and intuitively plausible account of our knowledge of phenomenal character that I turn in the final section.

5.6 Phenomenal Character and Our Knowledge of It

We all know what it is like to feel pain, to have an experience of red, and to feel angry. But what is it to know these things? Some physicalists have said that it is the possession of abilities. David Lewis, for example, remarks:

The Ability Hypothesis says that knowing what an experience is like just **is** the possession of these abilities to remember, imagine, and recognize.... It isn't knowing-that. It's knowing-how. (1990, p. 516)

The reason it is tempting to endorse the Ability Hypothesis, if one is a physicalist, is that it gives a straightforward explanation of how Frank Jackson's Mary can come to know something she didn't know before when she leaves her black-and-white room and sees often red. She doesn't thereby learn a new truth, for (as the reasoning often goes) in her room she knows all the physical and topic-neutral truths, and if physicalism is true there are no non-physical truths. So what does Mary come to know? Answer: She comes to know how to image red, how to recognize red when it comes again, and how to remember what red things look like.

There are well-known difficulties with this view that I shall not rehearse here. I discuss the view further in chapter 6. The point I want to make for present purposes is simply that, whatever position is taken on the adequacy of the ability hypothesis with respect to the analysis of the 'knowing what it is like to experience' construction, the hypothesis intuitively does not come to grips with what it is to know the phenomenal character of an experience. The phenomenal character of the experience of red is a thing (although not a concrete thing). Phenomenal characters can be compared. Some are more similar to one another than they are to others. In talking of my knowing the phenomenal character of a given experience, I am talking of knowing a certain thing—something you too can know. Surely the natural and obvious view to take is that you and I know this thing by being acquainted with it. We experience phenomenal character, and thereby we know it. In so knowing it, we do not know a truth. We do not merely have abilities. We know a thing.

It may seem as if in making these remarks I am endorsing an inner-scanning model of introspection—at least as far as phenomenal character goes. But such is not the case, for I endorse the transparency thesis with respect to introspective awareness.

The thesis that perceptual experience is transparent is quite widely accepted.[22] Here is one way of illustrating the thesis of transparency for the perceptual case: Suppose you are standing before a tapestry in an art gallery. As you take in the rich and varied colors of the cloth, you are told to pay close attention to your visual experience and its phenomenology. What do you do? Those who accept the transparency thesis say that you attend closely to the *tapestry* and details in it. You are aware of something outside you—the tapestry—and of various qualities that you experience as being qualities of parts of the tapestry, and by being aware of these things you are aware of what it is like for you subjectively or phenomenally.

Here is another way to put these points: When you are told to attend closely to your visual experience, what you actually do is attend closely to the tapestry and the various ways it looks to you (or the various ways parts of it look to you). Ways things look to people are typically expressed by predicates (as in 'looks red', 'looks square', and 'looks close'), and predicates express qualities—in this case, qualities represented by the relevant experiences of those people, qualities such that, if the things seen have them, the experiences are veridical or accurate.

In earlier work (Tye 2000), I took the view that it followed from these observations that your awareness of what it is like, of the phenomenology of your experience, cannot be *de re* awareness *of* the experience or its qualities but must instead be *de dicto* awareness *that* you have an experience with a certain phenomenal character or 'feel'. I thus endorsed the displaced perception model of introspective awareness of experience.[23]

According to this model, introspecting an experience and its phenomenal character is like secondary or displaced seeing-that (as discussed in section 5.1). The displaced-perception model of introspection of phenomenal character can allow that there are limitations to the model. For example, my belief that the fuel tank is empty, formed as I read the fuel gauge, is based on a background belief that when the fuel gauge reads zero there is no gas in the tank. Someone who lacked that background belief would not believe, having read the fuel gauge, that the fuel tank was empty. The background belief and the content of the perceptual awareness explain why the other belief state is present. They provide a propositional justification for that state. In the case of introspection of phenomenal character, however, there is no corresponding justification. If I am aware of certain external qualities, I do not need a background belief to be aware that I am undergoing an experience with a certain phenomenal character, once I introspect. The process is automatic. Introspection of phenomenal character, the advocate of the displaced-perception model may say, is a *reliable* process that takes awareness *of* external qualities (in the case of perceptual sensations) as input and yields awareness *that* a state is present with a certain phenomenal character as output. It is the reliability of this process that supposedly underwrites knowledge of phenomenal character.

I still think that there is something right about this view (see below). But it goes wrong in trying to force knowledge of phenomenal character into the box of fact awareness when the natural view is that we have such knowledge via thing awareness. I previously assumed that phenomenal knowledge had to be fact awareness on the ground that if phenomenal character were a thing of which we were conscious or aware, transparency would be violated. That is, I thought that endorsing a thing-awareness view of phenomenal character would commit us to an implausible inner-scanning model of introspection. But I now hold that such is not the case.

To see why, consider again what the thesis of transparency tells us. It tells us that in the case of perceptual experiences, the only qualities of which we are introspectively aware are qualities of external things if they are qualities of anything at all. But intuitively, we are aware of phenomenal character when we introspect. The conclusion to draw is that the phenomenal character of a perceptual experience consists in, and is no more than, the complex of qualities the experience represents. Thus, the phenomenal character of the experience of red just is red. In being aware of red, I am aware of what it is like to experience red, since what it is like to experience red is simply red.

Of course, red is the phenomenal character of the experience of red— red is what it is like to experience red—only if red meets certain further conditions, just as Benjamin Franklin is the inventor of bifocals in the actual world only if he meets the condition of having invented bifocals in the actual world. What are these conditions? My answer draws in part on what I have said in past work on phenomenal character: Red must be nonconceptually represented by a state that plays the appropriate functional role.[24] The relevant state may have a singular content or a gappy one. But on the current proposal there is no need for a common representational content shared by veridical, illusory, and hallucinatory experiences of red, since phenomenal character is not the same as representational content.

What goes for perceptual experiences goes for other experiences too. The phenomenal character of an experience, then, is out there in the world (or in the body, in the case of bodily sensations[25]). It is not a property of the experience at all. It is a complex of properties *represented* by the experience. In being aware of the external qualities, we are aware of phenomenal character. We are confronted by it. When we are told to attend to the phenomenal character of our experience there is nowhere to look other than the external qualities, since the phenomenal character just is the complex of external qualities.[26] This is why necessarily any change in the external qualities with which we are acquainted in undergoing a given experience generates a change in the phenomenal character of the experience.

Phenomenal character is manifest to us in our being aware of the external qualities. We cannot focus on it in any way that separates it from our focus on external things and qualities. Thus, if I say, while viewing a ripe tomato, "*This* is what it is like to experience red," the referent of my demonstrative is simply the color represented by my experience. It is to the color that I attend—and *that* is what it is like for me to experience red. The story could hardly be simpler.

On this view, the phenomenal character of the experience of red in a case of veridical perception is a feature of the surface the perceiver sees. The surface itself has the phenomenal character. This may seem strange; after all, don't *experiences* have phenomenal character? Yes and no. We do talk of experiences having phenomenal character, but this should not be taken to imply that the phenomenal character of the experience of red is a quality the experience has. The phenomenal character is what it is like to experience red, and, intuitively, what it is like to experience red is *not* a quality the experience has. What it is like to experience red is something one confronts in experiencing red. It is the quality one experiences—*that* is what it is like to experience red; and that quality is *represented* by the experience of red. Thus, in the veridical case, what it is like to experience red is indeed a property of the seen surface.

This proposal offers a straightforward explanation of why it is that as soon as we are acquainted with red, we know the phenomenal character of the experience of red. The phenomenal character of the experience of red just is red. So, in being acquainted with red, we are acquainted with the phenomenal character of the experience of red. Thereby, we know the phenomenal character of the experience of red.

It is a consequence of this account that creatures that lack the capacity to form beliefs about their experiences can nonetheless know the phenomenal character of their experiences, for such creatures experience various qualities and in so doing they experience what it is like to undergo those experiences. So, by acquaintance with the relevant qualities, they come know what it is like to experience those qualities. They have "thing knowledge" of them. Intuitively, this seems to me very plausible. When I try to think of the first-person perspective of another creature undergoing the experience of red, say, I think of the creature as experiencing *this*, where *this* is the color my current perceptual or imagistic experience of red represents. But as soon as I do this, it seems to me very hard to deny that the creature, in undergoing the experience, is aware *of* the phenomenal character of the experience of red.

We who have the capacity to form beliefs about our experiences also know the qualities we experience by acquaintance, and thereby we have "thing knowledge" of the phenomenal character of our experiences. But we can go further. On the basis of that "thing knowledge," we can form such beliefs as that we are having an experience of red. This transition is to be understood, in my view, on the model of displaced perception.

There is, then, something (almost) right after all in the self-representational account of phenomenal consciousness that I discussed in chapter 1. That account had it that token experiences not only make us aware of external things and qualities but also make us aware of them-selves. What the self-representation theorists should have said was that token experiences make us aware of external things and qualities and also make us aware of what it is like to undergo those experiences. But, contra self-representation theories, token experiences do not have two contents and do not refer to themselves.

An objection worth briefly mentioning is that if colors such as red are objective, mind-independent entities (as I believe[27]), there can be red sur-faces even if there are no minds. But *prima facie* it is absurd to suppose that there can be red surfaces having the phenomenal character of the ex-perience of red without any minds.

To see what is wrong with this objection, consider the claim that red is the property represented by the experience of red. This claim is true. Fur-thermore, both 'red' and 'the property represented by the experience of red' are rigid designators. Thus, if the claim that red is the property rep-resented by the experience of red is true, it is true in all possible worlds in which both 'red' and 'the property represented by the experience of red' denote something. Consider, then, a possible world in which there are red surfaces but no minds. Arguably, in that world 'the property repre-sented by the experience of red' fails to denote anything since there are no minds and no such thing as the experience of red. So the existence of such a possible world does not undermine the truth of the identity claim.

Suppose, however, that we understand the expression 'the property rep-resented by the experience of red' as follows. Using the abstraction oper-ator "$\lambda(x)(\ldots x \ldots)$" to abbreviate "the property of being an x such that $\ldots x \ldots$," we formalize the expression thus:

$(\lambda x)(y)(y$ is a token experience of red $\rightarrow y$ represents $x)$.

On this reading, 'the property represented by the experience of red' is still a rigid designator, but now any possible world with red surfaces in it and no minds is nonetheless a world with surfaces having the property represented by red, so again there is no difficulty for the truth of the identity claim that red is the property represented by the experience of red.

The expression "the phenomenal character of the experience of red" is also a rigid designator. In my view, in every possible world in which it denotes anything, it picks out the property that is nonconceptually represented by any state that plays the appropriate functional role and that nonconceptually represents red. My response to the objection now runs exactly parallel to that given above in connection with the claim that red is the quality represented by the experience of red.

The position taken in this section on our knowledge of phenomenal character has an interesting epistemological consequence: in a sense to be explained later, it rules out error with respect to phenomenal character.[28]

The view being proposed concerning the nature of phenomenal character is one that is compatible with physicalism provided that the external qualities themselves have a physical nature and a further reductive account can be given both of what it is for a state to nonconceptually represent those qualities and of the role the state plays. The really big general question that remains to be answered is whether *any* physicalist account of phenomenal consciousness can handle the four major puzzles of consciousness I distinguished in chapter 2.

6   Solving the Puzzles

In this chapter, I shall put to work the views developed in previous chapters in an attempt to solve four famous philosophical puzzles: the Puzzle of Mary, the Explanatory Gap, the Hard Problem of Consciousness, and the Possibility of Zombies.

6.1   Mary, Mary, How Does Your Knowledge Grow?

I begin with the case of Mary (Jackson 1982). Mary is locked in her black-and-white room. She has been there all her life, and she has only ever experienced things in black, white, and shades of gray.[1] Using computers (with black-and-white monitor screens) and an extensive library, she comes to know a great deal about color vision. Indeed, she comes to have exhaustive knowledge of the physical facts of color vision. She comes to know all there is to know about, for example, the surfaces of red objects, the way they reflect light, and the subsequent changes in the retina, the optic nerve, and the visual cortex. But there is something she doesn't know; indeed there is something she cannot know while she remains in her room. This is shown by the fact that when she leaves her room and is shown something red for the first time, she makes a significant discovery. She comes to know something she was unable to know before. Since she knows all the physical facts, she must discover a nonphysical fact. Therefore, physicalism is false.

This argument is often called the "Knowledge Argument." One way of regimenting the argument that fits nicely with Jackson's original essay (1982) and also with some more recent statements[2] is as follows:

(1) In her room Mary knows all the physical facts pertaining to color vision.

(2) After Mary leaves her room and she sees something red, she comes to know something new (something she cannot know in her room).

Therefore,

(3) After Mary leaves her room, she comes to know a non-physical fact.

Therefore,

(4) Physicalism is false.

The above statement of the knowledge argument is not the only one to be found in the literature. Sometimes the argument takes a different form that ties it to *a priori* reasoning (see, e.g., Chalmers 1996, 2004; Jackson 2004). Let P be the totality of physical truths and Q be some phenomenal truth about color experience. Now the alternative version of the argument goes as follows:

(5) Mary in her room knows that P and she is an ideal *a priori* reasoner, but still she isn't in a position to know that Q.

(6) If (5) is true, then Q does not follow *a priori* from P.

(7) If $P \rightarrow Q$ is not *a priori*, then physicalism is false.

Therefore,

(8) Physicalism is false.

In this second form, the most obvious premise to contest is (7). And given my earlier discussion of *a priori* physicalism, it should be clear that I reject (7). In this section, I shall focus mainly on the first version of the argument.

It is clear that the physicalist cannot allow that Mary, in coming to know something new when she sees red for the first time, is making a discovery of just the same sort as the discovery that Hesperus is Phosphorus or that Clark Kent is Superman. In these cases, in making the relevant discoveries, one also discovers that properties previously associated (some would say *a priori* associated) with the object or individual under one concept are associated with it or him under the other. Thus, in discovering that Hesperus is Phosphorus one comes to realize, among other things, that Phosphorus has the property of being the evening star. Before the discovery, one associated that property only with the heavenly body conceived of as Hesperus. Similarly, in discovering that Clark Kent is Superman, one finds out (among other things) that Superman has the property of being a mild-mannered newspaper reporter. Before the discovery, one associated that property only with the person conceived of as Clark Kent.

The reason that Mary's discovery cannot be of this sort, at least if physicalism is true, is that it would then be necessary for Mary to associate with color experiences properties she did not associate with them before she left her room. But there are no such properties if physicalism is true, for Mary in her room knows all the physical facts pertaining to color experiences.

One standard physicalist response to the knowledge argument is to say that Mary gains only know-how when she leaves her room (Lewis 1990; Nemirow 1990). She acquires new abilities—for example, the ability to recognize red things by sight, the ability to imagine red, and the ability to say whether she prefers red-colored things to yellow-colored things. But she gains no new factual knowledge. On this proposal, the knowledge argument in its first form fails in the step from (1) and (2) to (3).

One question that arises for this proposal is whether it is really true that Mary, in gaining know-how, does not gain any factual knowledge. Lewis and Nemirow certainly thought so, but Stanley and Williamson (2001) have raised difficulties for this view. Whatever we say about the nature of know-how,[3] it seems clear that Mary makes a genuine discovery about the world when she sees red for the first time. Anyone who has any doubts about this should consider the case of Kevin Staight, who was born with a rare eye defect that resulted in his seeing the world in black and white. As a teenager, Kevin was fitted with revolutionary contact lenses that enabled him to see in color. He commented (in a newspaper article):

> After I put them on I went for a walk and slowly saw the world in color for the first time. Up until then, I didn't have any idea what color was because I couldn't see it. I couldn't stop crying because the world looked so different from what I was used to. The reds just kept on jumping out at me and I had to ask my grandparents which colors were which because I didn't have a clue.
>
> It has opened up a whole new world for me. I never realized just how beautiful things like trees and flowers are.

Patently, Kevin did not *merely* acquire new abilities.

Consider also the case of Mary's experiencing a particular shade of red for the first time. As she attends to that shade, Mary comes to know something new; but she will not be able to remember that particular shade, nor will she be able to recognize that shade, if it comes again, nor will she be able to regenerate her experience of that particular shade imaginatively. Mary here lacks the Lewis-Nemirow abilities, but she comes to know something new nonetheless.[4]

The most popular physicalist reaction to the Puzzle of Mary is to claim that Mary acquires new concepts when she leaves her room: phenomenal concepts.[5] Having acquired these concepts, Mary can come to think thoughts she could not think in her black-and-white room. This being so, Mary is in a position to know facts she did not know previously, namely fine-grained facts built out of physical worldly entities and phenomenal concepts. On this proposal, the facts Mary comes to know are genuinely new facts, but they are not non-physical facts. They involve only physical worldly entities and concepts, themselves *a priori* irreducible to physical concepts, that refer to those physical entities. So, on this view, the knowledge argument again fails in the step from (1) and (2) to (3).

The appeal to phenomenal concepts is part and parcel of the general phenomenal-concept strategy for defending physicalism. And this strategy can also play a role in undermining the second version of the knowledge argument above, for even if Q does follow *a priori* from P (which I deny), if Mary lacks the concepts needed to think that Q she will not be able to deduce Q *a priori* from P and so she will not be in a position to know that Q. Thus, an advocate of the phenomenal-concept strategy can insist that (6) is not true, since its truth demands that Mary possesses the relevant concepts and Mary does not possess those concepts while in her room.

The main difficulty for the phenomenal-concept strategy is that, as I argued in chapter 3, there are no phenomenal concepts in the sense that the strategy requires. To be sure, there are concepts for conceiving of experiences—concepts deployed in forming beliefs on the basis of introspection—but these are concepts Mary had during her period of confinement.

Thus, when released, Mary can certainly think that she is having an experience of red, that what it is like to experience red is wonderful, and so on. But she could think these thoughts in her room, even though she could not then experience red. This is not to say, of course, that Mary in her room ever *believed* that she was having an experience of red. Still, she has no cognitive abnormalities, and in her room she has the relevant concepts. So there is nothing to prevent her from combining these concepts into the above thoughts, if she so chooses.

Another physicalist reaction is to claim is that Mary makes a demonstrative factual discovery when she leaves her room and views something red. As she does so, she discovers that *this* is the experience of red (or that *this* is what it is like to experience red). On this proposal, Mary comes to know a new fine-grained fact, but that fact need not involve any non-physical worldly entities. If physicalism is true, the constituent worldly entities are physical in nature but there is also a component demonstrative concept being exercised in Mary's thought, a concept not before applied by Mary to the experience of red. The fact that Mary comes to know, thus, is again not a non-physical fact.

An obvious objection to this proposal is that we can certainly imagine Mary in her room viewing the brain of someone else experiencing red via a cerebroscope and using the demonstrative concept *this* with respect to the brain state with which, according to some physicalists, the experience of red is identical while also categorizing that brain state as the experience of red. In this event, it may be argued, Mary, upon her release, fails to make a genuine discovery when she says "This is the experience of red" as she undergoes the experience of red herself. However, the situation is more complicated than it first appears.

To appreciate this, consider the thought I express by uttering "That is a coin" as I view a coin before me, and further consider the thought I express by uttering "That is a coin" as I reach out and feel a coin with my hand. Suppose that I am participating in a psychological experiment on visual illusions and, although I can see a hand touching the coin, I wonder to myself whether it is really *my* hand. So wondering, I also wonder whether *that* (the coin I am seeing) is one and the same as *that* (the coin I am feeling). In both cases, I am referring to the same object via the demonstrative concept *that* and I am also using the same general concept: *coin*. Do my two thoughts have the same content? It would seem not, for thoughts (as I noted in section 3.1) have fine-grained contents, and in the given situation it can be a discovery to me that *that* is the same as *that*. The suggestion, thus, is that the demonstrative concept *that*, on these different occasions of its exercise, utilizes different modes of presentation which contribute to its content on those occasions. In the one case, there is a visual mode of presentation; in the other, there is a tactual one. These modes of presentation cannot be generic to the relevant senses, however, for similar cases can be constructed within a sense. For example, I may wonder whether that (seen from one perspective) is the same as that (seen from another). So case-specific, sense-specific modes are needed.

In the case of Mary, then, some physicalists may be inclined to say the following: When she thinks in her room that this is the experience of red, as she views someone else's brain via a cerebroscope, the thought she entertains is different from the thought she entertains when she experiences red for the first time upon her release and says "Aha, so this is the experience of red." It is not that there is any difference in the concept expressed by 'experience of red' or 'red' (at least if the phenomenal-concept strategy fails). It is not that there is one demonstrative concept in the one thought and a different demonstrative concept in the other. It is just that in one case the referent of the demonstrative concept is presented under a different guise than in the other, and this changes both the content of the concept and the content of the thought. On this view, since Mary *can* think a new demonstrative thought about the experience of red upon her release, she can come to make a discovery.[6]

One worry for this line of reasoning is that if the mode of presentation the demonstrative concept supposedly uses is held to consist in properties Mary *a priori* associates with the referent, then Mary will only be in a position to make a genuine discovery if the properties she associates with the experience of red upon her release, as she conceives of it demonstratively, are properties she did not already associate with it in her room. But if she really does have exhaustive knowledge of all the physical facts (past, present, and future), then the only way Mary can associate *new* properties with the experience of red is if those properties are non-physical.

There is also a question as to whether it is at all plausible to suppose that demonstrative concepts get their reference fixed in part via *a priori* associated properties, for the considerations adduced in chapter 3 against such a view in connection with the concept *water* seem to apply equally well here (mutatis mutandis). Moreover, if it is now denied that demonstrative modes of presentation are to be viewed in the above way then some alternative account must be supplied, if the physicalist continues to insist that Mary makes a demonstrative discovery notwithstanding her knowing all the physical facts in her black-and-white room.

In characterizing Mary's discovery above as taking the form "This is the experience of red," I am going along with what some physicalists say. But it should be clear from my comments in chapter 5 that I regard this way of putting things as untenable. When Mary first experiences red, she is not then in a position to refer to the experience of red demonstratively. She has no access to that experience. All she can attend to is the color, red. She can refer to that demonstratively. But red is not the same as the experience of red.

To be sure, Mary can refer to the phenomenal character of the experience of red. But, as I explained in chapter 5, that is because what it is like to experience red is the same as the color red, given that red is what the experience of red represents. Thus, Mary's putative discovery is best expressed via the sentence "Aha, so this is what it is like to experience red," or, more simply, via "Aha, so this is red." Still, there remains the concern that the factual knowledge Mary acquires here does not really capture the nature of her new knowledge—that Mary's discovery is not *just* like the discovery that now is 2 p.m., or the discovery that here is Paris, Texas, or the discovery that this is a frog.

What is it that the demonstrative account is missing? One response not yet considered is to grant that Mary in her room possesses phenomenal concepts (in opposition to the usual phenomenal-concept strategy) and to concede that she has a deferential grasp of them while now holding that it is only the possession of phenomenal concepts under a *non-deferential* grasp that necessitates having undergone the relevant experiences. On this view, when Mary leaves her room she acquires a new way of grasping a fine-grained fact that she already knew in her room. Thereby, it could be held, Mary increases her knowledge.[7]

The trouble with this suggestion is that it entails that what Mary knows later is just the same as what she knew before, for there is no change in the fine-grained facts she knows. So there is no new propositional knowledge. Here is a parallel: Consider my remarking, to a friend of mine who is the world's leading authority on elm trees, "That's an elm over there." I can know that this is the case—perhaps I planted the elm and I recall doing so—but my grasp of the concept *elm* is deferential. My friend also knows that that is an elm over there, but his grasp of the concept *elm* is non-deferential. What he knows is the same as what I know. There is no difference in the fact we know here—we are in agreement—but the way we grasp what we know is different. If later I become the world's leading authority on elm trees, and I repeat my earlier remark in the same situation, what I know is what I knew earlier. I make no discovery. So this strategy seems to me to offer no real progress.

What, then, is it that the demonstrative account (and, for that matter, the account just offered) is missing? Surely the intuitive thought is that Mary in her room really does not know certain things *in the world*: the phenomenal character of the experience of red, the phenomenal character of the experience of green, and so on. When she leaves her room, she comes to know these things. It is not that she merely comes to acquire new ways of thinking about and thus new ways of knowing certain worldly things she knew before in her room in a different way. That does not take the full measure of her discovery. She comes to know new *worldly things*—that is, things she did not know before. And if physicalism denies this, then so much the worse for physicalism.

In saying that Mary comes to know a new thing when she leaves her black-and-white room and sees something red, I am not committed to claiming that *this* new knowledge is clearly well expressed by the following sentence, at least if this sentence is given the semantic treatment usually accorded in linguistics to constructions containing embedded questions (that is, embedded clauses that are interrogatives):

(9) Mary knows what it is like to experience red.

The standard semantics, applied to (9), yields the result that (9) is true if and only if Mary knows some proposition that is a legitimate answer to the question it embeds. Thus, on the standard semantics, (9) expresses a species of propositional or factual knowledge.[8]

There are difficulties for the standard semantics, as applied to (9), on the view that this semantics supplies the only way to understand (9); for what is the proposition Mary knows, when she leaves her room, that is a legitimate answer to the question "What is it like to experience red?" The obvious candidate is the proposition that *this* is what it is like to experience red. This proposal, however, makes Mary's new knowledge demonstrative, and thus it encounters the same difficulties as the demonstrative account above.

There is another difficulty for the standard semantics, as applied to sentences like (9), at least if it is developed in the way just sketched. One can know what it is like to experience a given color at times at which one is not experiencing the color either via the use of one's eyes or via a phenomenal memory image. Right now, for example, I know what it is like to experience teal, but I am not imaging teal and I am not seeing anything teal. So right now I do not know the fact that this is what it is like to experience teal.

One possible reply is that right now I do know the relevant demonstrative fact. Indeed I know that fact even when I am asleep, for I need not be referring to the phenomenal character of the experience of teal via a demonstrative in order to know that this is what it is like to experience teal. The trouble with this very plausible reply is that the conditions on the use of the demonstrative with respect to the phenomenal character of the experience of teal have now been so loosened that there is no obvious reason why Mary in her room should not be truly reported as knowing that this is what it is like to experience teal. After all, we may suppose that, using a cerebroscope, Mary often views in others the brain state that, according to some physicalists, just is what it is like to experience teal.

The only way I see to rule out this objection, consistent with the view that the knowledge Mary gains when she leaves her room is exclusively factual, is to require that the subject of the relevant knowledge have experienced teal and further that the subject be exercising a non-demonstrative concept of the phenomenal character of the experience of teal in her knowledge of the fact reported via the sentence "This is what it is like to experience teal." This effectively is to endorse the phenomenal-concept strategy already rejected.

Interestingly, the standard semantics has an easier time with the sentence

(10) I know what Caligula was like.

For I know that Caligula was a Roman emperor who was perverted, tempestuous, cruel, unstable, and maniacal, and thus I know some proposition that is an answer to the question "What was Caligula like?" I know what Caligula was like simply in knowing various facts about Caligula. Likewise, Mary in her room knows a host of facts about the experience of red even though she does not know what it is like to experience of red. In one weak sense, then, she knows what the experience of red is like and thus what it is like to experience red. But this isn't a sense that is relevant to the Knowledge Argument. Mary in her room does not know what it is like *phenomenally* to experience red. She does not know what the experience of red is like *in its phenomenal character*.

Of course, again, Mary does know various facts about the experience of red and its phenomenal character, for she can "triangulate each color experience exactly in a network of resemblances and differences" (Lewis 1990, p. 502). She knows, for example, the fact that phenomenally the experience of red is more like the experience of orange than the experience of green. But still there remains a sense in which she does not know what the experience of red is like while she remains in her black-and-white room.

So what is the physicalist to say in response to the knowledge argument? Well, the physicalist can begin by pointing to an implicit assumption of the argument: that Mary cannot come to know something new unless she discovers a new fact. The argument thus assumes that all worldly knowledge is knowledge *that*. I now think that this is where the knowledge argument crucially goes wrong.

As we saw in chapter 5, there is knowledge by acquaintance and there is fact knowledge. Mary in her room knows all the physical facts *about* the subjective character of the experience of red. But there is a perfectly ordinary sense of 'know' under which she does not know the thing that is the subjective character of the experience of red. She is not acquainted with that thing. When she leaves the room and becomes acquainted with the phenomenal or subjective character of the experience of red, thereby she knows it. This is genuinely new knowledge, logically distinct from her earlier factual knowledge.

It is important to grasp that Mary, in acquiring this knowledge, is *not* just acquiring a new way of knowing something she knew by other means before. Mary in her room did not know the phenomenal character to the experience of red. She knew *of* it, of course; she knew many truths *about* it; but there remains a sense in which she did not know the phenomenal character itself. And this is the case even if, as physicalists suppose, the phenomenal character has a physical nature.

Mary's situation is anomalous, of course, but it is commonplace to know about something without knowing it. I know of the pope, for example. I know many truths about the pope—that he lives in the Vatican, that he is a Roman Catholic, that his name is Benedict XVI, that he shops at Prada. But in one very ordinary sense of 'know' I do not know the pope.

Perhaps it will be replied that a 22nd-century biographer could know Benedict XVI simply by knowing enough facts about him. Obviously I do not wish to deny that the biographer could come to know a lot about Benedict XVI. She could come to understand his motives for various papal decisions. She could acquire a clear grasp of how his childhood was, why his rulings were conservative, and so on. But armed only with this fact knowledge, there is a clear sense in which the biographer would not know *him*.

This solution to the Puzzle of Mary is so obvious and so natural that it is surprising that it has not occurred to more philosophers. Furthermore, it is the only solution that really does justice to the thought, expressed above, that when Mary experiences red for the first time she comes to know some *thing* she did not know before.

In coming to know a new thing, Mary thereby makes a discovery. It seems infelicitous to say that the new thing she knows just *is* her discovery. What does she discover? What does she learn? The natural answer is that she discovers (learns) what it is like to experience red. This, I now want to suggest, involves a mixture of factual and objectual knowledge.

Stanley and Williamson (2001) propose a version of the standard semantics in linguistics for 'knows how' constructions that appeals to knowing Russellian propositions under a practical mode of presentation. "Jane knows how to ride a bicycle," for example, is true, on their semantics, if and only if there is some contextually relevant way w such that Jane stands in the knowing-that relation to the Russellian proposition that w is a way to ride a bicycle and Jane entertains that proposition under a practical mode of presentation. The relevant mode of presentation is different from the one under which Jane knows the above proposition as someone brings to her attention a nearby cyclist and remarks "That is a way to ride a bicycle." It is also different from the mode of presentation under which Jane knows the above proposition as she reads a book on how to ride a bicycle.

Exactly how practical modes of presentation are to be understood is not fully explained by Stanley and Williamson. Given that 'knows-that' contexts individuate as finely as 'believes-that' contexts, the relevant modes had better be conceptual even if they are different from the conceptual modes at play in the other two cases mentioned above. But do we really have a firm grip on the practical concepts using such modes? And do we really need to multiply concepts in this way?

An alternative proposal suggested by that of Stanley and Williamson, but eschewing additional practical concepts, is that the proposition to which Jane stands in the knowing-that relation is fine-grained, rather than Russellian (for example, that it is the proposition that this is a way to ride a bicycle[9]), and that Jane, in knowing how to ride a bicycle, is in a position to entertain that proposition in a practical way, where this is a way that disposes her to engage in certain sort of behavior on certain occasions.[10]

A corresponding proposal is that Mary, in knowing what it is like to experience red, stands in the knowing-that relation to the fine-grained proposition that this is what it is like to experience red and is in a position to entertain this proposition in a phenomenal way via her acquaintance with the color red.[11] Mary's consciousness of red gives her objectual knowledge by acquaintance of red, and (partly) via that knowledge she knows a certain proposition. On this view, we can say that after she leaves her room Mary knows a certain fact (partly) *by* knowing a certain entity she did not know in her room (namely red or the phenomenal character of the experience of red) and that this combined knowledge is what is needed to know what it is like to experience red.

Note that on the above proposal the following inference is invalid:

(11) Mary knows the phenomenal character of the experience of red.

(12) The phenomenal character of the experience of red = what it is like to experience red.

Therefore,

(13) Mary knows what it is like to experience red.

This is as it should be, for the inference is parallel to the following:

(14) Mary knows the color red.

(15) The color red = my favorite color (what my favorite color is).

Therefore,

(16) Mary knows what my favorite color is.

Furthermore, intuitively, a person blind from birth who suddenly regains his sight and who asks himself "Is this what it is like to experience red?" as he sees a red rose, does not know at that moment what it is like to experience red. (If he did know that, he would not ask himself the above question.) But he surely does then know the phenomenal character of his experience. Thus, assuming that he is experiencing red, he knows the phenomenal character of the experience of red.

The account I am proposing has the resources to handle the following variant on the standard Mary case, which might initially seem to pose a difficulty: Suppose now that while Mary is in her black-and-white room she is shown a splotch of red but the color is not identified for her. After she is released from the room, she sees a ripe tomato and comes to learn something new. How can this be? In each case Mary is acquainted with the phenomenal character of the experience of red, and in each case she knows the fine-grained demonstrative fact that this is what it is like to experience red.

In my view, what changes for Experienced Mary[12] is not her factual knowledge, nor is it her knowledge by acquaintance; it is her 'what it is like' knowledge. She comes to know what it is like to experience red. In the room, she does not know what it is like to experience red, since her factual knowledge that this is what it is like to experience red is not *based on* her knowledge by acquaintance of the phenomenal character of the experience of red. Rather, the former knowledge is based on Mary's cerebroscope reading of the brain of someone who is seeing something red, or perhaps it is based indirectly on Mary's believing truly and justifiably of some one else's experience that *that* must be (and so is) what it is like to experience red, as she looks at a black-and-white monitor on which is displayed a picture of someone outside the room looking at a ripe tomato. Once Experienced Mary steps outside and makes the connection between the phenomenal character of her experience and the color red, she knows what it is like to experience red. Thereby she learns something.

A further objection that might be raised to my view is that it entails that Mary in her room is able to think the very same thoughts she thinks outside the room. But if this is the case, why is it that when she sees a red thing for the first time, she can truly say not just "I never *knew* that this would be what it is like to experience red" but also "I never even *thought* that this is what it would be like"?[13]

My reply is that in the case of the latter report, what is being reported is the absence of a past actual occurrent thought and also arguably the absence of a belief, not the absence of an *ability* to think the relevant thought. Compare with the case in which, upon meeting you, I (having heard some negative comments about you from others) say "I never thought that you would be so charming." Clearly I am not reporting the absence of an ability to entertain such a thought. Mary *can* think the relevant thought, on my view. It is just that if she makes the above report, she has not actually thought the relevant thought, and she certainly has not endorsed the thought in belief.

Perhaps it will now be objected that Mary in her room *can* know the experience of red itself, since she can be acquainted with the physical state that is the experience of red in other people via the cerebroscope. In reply, let me say first that I deny that it is possible for Mary in her room to be non-inferentially conscious of the brain state that partly realizes the experience of red. To be sure, she can be non-inferentially conscious of a token brain state. But I deny that she can be so conscious of the neurological type that token instantiates. In my view, the types of which she is directly visually conscious are at the level of color and shape (for example).

Leaving this to one side, the point I want to emphasize is that when Mary sees something red for the first time, she comes to be acquainted with *red* and thus with the phenomenal character of the experience of red. She does not come to be acquainted with the *experience of red.* Thus, what she knows when she sees something red is not a brain state, even if the experience of red *is* a brain state. So there is no threat here to my claim that, on my proposal, in seeing red things Mary genuinely makes a significant discovery.

What about Zombie Mary when she leaves her black-and-white room? Does *she* come to know something new? If she doesn't, how can this be? After all, if physicalism is true, there is no difference between Mary and Zombie Mary.[14] If Zombie Mary comes to know something new, how does she come to know it, given that she is a zombie and thus does not experience it?

It is conceptually possible for there to be a creature who physically replicates Mary but who lacks phenomenal consciousness. Such a creature does not know what it is like to experience red when she sees red for the first time. She never knows what it is like to see red. Furthermore, when, upon leaving her room and being shown something red, she says "Aha, so that is what it is like to experience red," she says something false (or at least neither true nor false). For the reasons elaborated in chapter 3, Zombie Mary possesses the same color and color experience concepts as Mary, but she does not undergo experiences.[15] This would be a threat to physicalism if Zombie Mary were a genuine metaphysical possibility instead of just a conceptual one. But she is not.

To my knowledge, the proposal closest to my own in connection with Mary is the one made by Earl Conee in his insightful 1994 essay.[16] Conee asserts that Mary comes to know the phenomenal character of the experience of red by attentively experiencing it. Attentively experiencing a thing is one way of being acquainted with it. But what does Conee have in mind by attentive experience? It is clear that he takes attentive experience to be the same as noticing. He comments:

> The acquaintance hypothesis under consideration is the view that coming to know what an experience is like requires only noticing the experience as it is undergone. (1994, p. 143)

Unfortunately, this further step seems to me to place the acquaintance hypothesis on potentially shaky ground. For one thing, at least under one standard usage of 'notice', noticing is inherently conceptual: one cannot notice something without applying a concept to the thing noticed. On this view, one cannot notice the color red without thinking of the experienced color as red. To be sure, one can notice *that* color, where that color is red, without thinking of the experienced color as red, but now one thinks of the experienced color as that color. However, one can know something by acquaintance without subsuming it under a concept at all.

Suppose I am conscious of a particular shade of red—say, red_{29}. My consciousness of that shade allows me to get a good look at it. Even so, my consciousness of red_{29} does not require that I subsume it under the concept red_{29}, for the concept red_{29} is not one I possess. Nor can my consciousness of the shade itself involve the application of a demonstrative concept to the shade, since a condition of applying such a concept via experience is that one be conscious of the shade. Thus, applying the concept cannot be part and parcel of being conscious of the shade.

What needs to be appreciated is that knowledge by acquaintance of an entity is a kind of non-conceptual, non-propositional thing knowledge. I know the shade red_{29} simply by being directly acquainted with it via my consciousness of it. In the case of the phenomenal character of the experience of that shade, I know it in just the same way—by acquaintance. Our consciousness of things, both particular and general, enables us to come to have factual knowledge of them, but that consciousness is not itself a form of factual knowledge at all. It serves as the ground or warrant for beliefs about what we experience, but it is not itself a kind of belief. Knowledge by acquaintance is the foundation for knowledge by description, but it is a completely different kind of knowledge.

A second worry for Conee's proposal is that zombies can properly be said to notice things, but they have no experiences. Thus, noticing something is not to be identified (*a priori*) with attentively experiencing that thing.[17]

6.2   The Explanatory Gap

We all know what it is like to undergo the visual experience of bright purple, the feeling of fear, or the sensation of being tickled. We also have an admittedly incomplete grasp of what goes on objectively in the brain and the body. But there is, it seems, a huge chasm between the two. Presented with the current physical story of the objective changes that occur when a certain subjective feeling is experienced, we have the strong sense that the former does not fully explain the latter, that the phenomenology has been left out. We naturally ask "What is so special about *those* physical goings-on? Why do they feel like this instead of like that?" We think that, as far as our understanding goes, something important is missing. This is the famous Explanatory Gap for consciousness.

Some respond to the Explanatory Gap by saying that it is unbridgeable and that the proper conclusion to draw from it is that there is a corresponding gap in the world (Chalmers 1996, 2005). Experiences and feelings have irreducibly subjective, non-physical qualities over and above whatever physical qualities they have. The physical story is incomplete. Others take essentially the same position on the gap while urging that being objective is not a necessary condition of being physical (Searle 1992). Thus, it is claimed that there is nothing in the gap that detracts from a purely physicalist worldview. Experiences and feelings have introspectible, phenomenal qualities, and these qualities are indeed irreducibly subjective, but this is compatible with their being physical. Others hold that the Explanatory Gap may one day be bridged but that we currently lack the concepts to bring the subjective and objective perspectives together (Nagel 1974). On this view, it may turn out that phenomenal states are physical, but we currently have no clear conception as to how they could be. Still others adamantly insist that experiences and feelings are as much a part of the physical, natural world as life, aging, photosynthesis, or lightning. It is just that with the concepts we have and the concepts we are capable of forming, we are cognitively closed to a full bridging explanation by the very structure of our minds (McGinn 1991). There is such an explanation, but it is necessarily beyond our cognitive grasp.

My previous view on the Explanatory Gap appealed to phenomenal concepts (Tye 1999). I held that there is nothing in the Explanatory Gap that should lead us to any bifurcation in the world between experiences and feelings on the one hand and physical phenomena on the other. There aren't two sorts of natural phenomena: the irreducibly subjective and the objective. The so-called Explanatory Gap, I claimed, derives largely from a failure to recognize the special features of phenomenal concepts. These concepts, I argued, have a character that not only explains why we have the intuition that something important is left out by the physical story, but also explains why this intuition is not to be trusted.

Since I no longer believe that there are any phenomenal concepts (conceived of as concepts having special features applied via introspection), this proposal with respect to the Explanatory Gap is no longer available.

To illustrate what I now take to be the correct response to the Explanatory Gap, let me focus on the case of color experience. Given the thesis of transparency, I am aware of the phenomenal character of the experience of red, for example, by being aware of red. When I introspect, my attention goes to the external quality red, and thereby I am aware of the phenomenal character of the experience of red. On the proposal made in chapter 5, this connection between red and the phenomenal character of the experience of red is very straightforward. Red is the phenomenal character of the experience of red. Thus, that very phenomenal character, the one possessed by experiences of red, could not be a character of which I am made aware via introspection by being conscious of a different external quality (for example, the color green).

There will be an explanatory gap, then with respect to phenomenal character just in case there is such a gap with respect to the qualities *experienced*. On this interpretation, the gap really amounts to our sense that something significant is missing with respect to *these* qualities and our experience of them—something that is naturally expressed by our asking, and failing to come up with a satisfying answer to, questions such as "Why is it that I am experiencing *this* quality, red, rather than *that* one, green, when so-and-so physical facts obtain?"

The first point to make by way of reply is that our sense that something significant is left out from our account of the underlying physical facts can be explained at least in part by means of the distinction between knowledge by description and knowledge by acquaintance. There is a kind of knowledge of the color red that is not given to us by our knowledge of all the relevant physical facts. The knowledge we get by acquaintance with red is *logically* independent of our knowledge of truths. Indeed, it is *physically* possible for someone (for example, Mary in her black-and-white room) to know all the physical facts pertaining to the experience of red and not know red (in the relevant sense of 'know'). Thus, knowing the relevant *facts* does not in itself enable us to know red rather than green. Of course, if physicalism is true, the relevant physical facts with respect to my own experiences of red-involving facts necessitate that I know red (although they do not necessitate this *a priori*). The point is that it is not my reflecting on the physical facts and thus my knowing them that accounts for my knowing red (in one important sense of 'knowing red'). Knowledge of the latter sort is not part and parcel of knowledge of the former sort. This is why I have the sense that I do not know everything there is to know as I ponder the physical story. There really are things I do not know *in* knowing the physical facts.

The physicalist can combine this response to the gap by claiming that, as far as the gap questions go (e.g., the question as to why I am experiencing this quality, red, rather than that one, green), *a posteriori* answers can be given even if we do not yet know those answers, for the physicalist can maintain that there are true *a posteriori* identities of the following sort:

(17) Red = physical property R (for example, so-and-so reflectance).

(18) Experiencing red = standing in physical relation M to physical property R.

On this view, *a priori* reflection on the concepts involved and the physical facts will not enable us to deduce that we are experiencing so-and-so. Thus, the gap questions are perfectly coherent questions for us to ask. Even so, they have *a posteriori* answers.

Some philosophers balk at the above identities, however. One objection that has been raised to phenomenal-physical identities of the type given in (18) is that they are epistemically primitive and therefore they commit the materialist to the acceptance of brute facts that are inimical to her position. In order for us to evaluate this objection, we need to know how the expression 'epistemically primitive' is to be understood. On one way of

140																																																									Chapter 6

interpreting this expression, a hypothesis is epistemically primitive if and only if it cannot be deduced *a priori* from the microphysical facts (supplemented with some indexical information, as explained in chapter 2, and the 'that's all' qualifier).

This places too heavy a burden on the materialist. As should be clear from the discussion in chapter 3, it is simply wishful thinking to suppose that even the claim that water is H_2O is deducible *a priori* from the microphysical truths (with or without the 'that's all' qualifier and permissible indexical information). But water certainly is identical with H_2O, and this is no brute fact.

In the case of identities of the sort in (17) and (18), there is no reason why empirical justifications cannot be provided without *a priori* deductions.[18] In the case of (17), for example, we might amass evidence that red is always correlated with physical property R, and then we might justify the identity in (17) on the grounds that it provides the best explanation of these correlations by appealing to considerations of simplicity and causal role. In the case of (18), we might appeal to the causal efficacy of the property of experiencing red together with the empirically based general hypothesis that there are no non-physical causes and a further claim to the effect that the preferred physical candidate for identification with this property is the best candidate, all things considered. So, the physicalist may insist, identities of the sort in (17) and (18) are certainly not epistemically primitive.

There is an alternative way of understanding the claim that phenomenal-physical identity claims are epistemically primitive. According to Chalmers and Jackson (2001, p. 354), these identity statements are primitive in that their truth cannot be deduced *a priori* by persons having all the relevant concepts from the microphysical truths (P), the 'that's all' statement (T), the locating information of an indexical sort that amounts to a "you are here" marker added to the objective map provided by PT (I), *and* the phenomenal truths (Q). The phenomenal truths, we are told, specify "the phenomenal states and properties instantiated by every subject bearing such states and properties at every time" (ibid., p. 319). These truths use terms that express phenomenal concepts.

The claim that Chalmers and Jackson make (albeit tentatively) is that all macroscopic truths, including truths of identity about macroscopic phenomena, can be so deduced. Thus, the putative phenomenal-physical identities are anomalous and this counts against them. Chalmers and Jackson comment:

It is sometimes held that "identities do not need to be explained" (for example, Papineau 1993). Block and Stalnaker say something similar ("Identities don't have explanations"). But this seems to conflate ontological and epistemological matters. Identities are ontologically primitive, but they are not epistemically primitive. Identities are typically implied by underlying truths that do not involve identities. The identity between genes and DNA, or between water and H_2O, is implied by the underlying truths in $PQTI$, for example. Once a subject knows all the truths about DNA and its role in reproduction and development, for example, the subject will be in a position to deduce that genes are DNA. So this identity is not epistemically primitive.

Of course, just as with other truths involving macroscopic phenomena, subjects do not typically come to know these identities by deducing them from the microscopic truths. But the identities are so deducible all the same, and their deducibility is what makes the phenomena in question reductively explainable. (ibid., p. 354)

One worry that immediately arises for the claim that a truth is epistemically primitive just in case it is not *a priori* deducible from $PQTI$ is that T itself (the "That's all" statement) is so deducible. Yet it is epistemically primitive, or so it seems. But suppose for the moment that Chalmers and Jackson are right at least to the extent that phenomenal-physical identities are not *a priori* deducible from $PQTI$ whereas macroscopic truths generally are. Then we should agree that there is a sense in which phenomenal-physical identities are epistemically *anomalous*. In *this* respect, such identities are like the fundamental psycho-physical laws, if property dualism is true. But it does not follow from the epistemic anomaly of the identities that they are epistemically *primitive*, for they can be justified empirically in the manner suggested earlier.

Is it true anyway that macroscopic truths generally are *a priori* deducible from $PQTI$? It is very hard to evaluate the claim that they are, in part because it is not clear what exactly goes into Q. The truths in Q are supposed to employ only phenomenal concepts. Presumably, then, they do not include terms for individual persons, even though they cover the experiences of all persons. "Michael Tye is now experiencing red," for example, will not count as a phenomenal truth. So what form exactly do these truths take? Perhaps the idea is that they are existential: they assert that there is an individual x such that, for every time t at which x exists, if x is experiencing anything at t, x is experiencing so-and-so at t and there is an individual y such that, for every time t' at which y exists, if y is experiencing anything at t', y is experiencing such-and-such at t', and so on, where the experiences are characterized in purely phenomenal language. But it is radically unclear how adding such general truths to PTI is going to get us *a priori* to truths about macroscopic particulars not implied by *PTI* alone, especially given the possibility—not to be ruled out *a priori*—that some different individuals have phenomenally identical experiences throughout their lifetimes.

Leaving this point to one side, as Chalmers and Jackson note, we might well worry whether mental truths about subjects' propositional attitudes are *a priori* deducible from *PQTI*; likewise with respect to truths involving social concepts or terms "used deferentially (for example, 'arthritis' used by a non-expert)" (ibid., p. 336, note 19). If, as was suggested earlier, nearly all concepts are deferential, this should make us wonder whether phenomenal-physical identity truths really are anomalous at all.

There is a deeper concern about the proposed identities. How *could* any such identities be true? For example, how could *this* quality, experienced redness, just be a certain reflectance profile? Isn't redness wholly given to me in my experience of it? How could red have a *hidden* nature? Lying *behind* redness, there could be a quality with a hidden nature. In this way, the thing I experience, redness, could have something on its other side, so to speak, that has a nature to be discovered. But how could red *itself* be such a quality? It is here that the Explanatory Gap fundamentally resides.

Those who raise these questions would agree with the following comment by Mark Johnston:

The intrinsic nature of canary yellow is fully revealed by a standard visual experience as of a canary yellow thing. (1992, p. 138)

Johnston calls this view "Revelation."

Why should we accept Revelation? Presumably the thought is that our experience itself reveals red or canary yellow as simple, as not having a hidden nature. That is why the physicalist's view that red is so-and-so reflectance, to take one example, generates an incredulous stare. Our experience itself goes against such a view. Given that experience, how could red just be so-and-so reflectance? It defies credulity.

The mistake in these reflections lies in the idea that our awareness of red in color experience is an awareness of it as simple, as not having a hidden nature. It is certainly true that we are not aware of red *as* having a hidden nature, but it does not follow from this that we are aware of red as *not* having such a nature. Those who think otherwise are effectively assuming that all awareness is fact awareness, and that we must be aware of red *as* something or other if we are aware of it at all. But if we are not aware of red as having a hidden nature, then how are we aware of it? "Surely as simple," those who take this view say.

This is to ignore the point (which I have been hammering) that there is genuine, knowledge-giving awareness of things that is not awareness of them *as* anything at all. Not all awareness is fact awareness. Those who suppose otherwise over-intellectualize consciousness and knowledge. There is non-conceptual awareness and non-conceptual knowledge. When we and other sentient creatures are conscious of red, we are conscious of it, period. We do not need to know any truths about it to be so conscious. We need not even know that the color before us *is* red.

Furthermore, there is a sense in which our knowledge of the color red via acquaintance is complete as soon as we have it, for *that* knowledge cannot be improved or deepened by knowing truths about red. It is tempting to infer from this that red cannot have a hidden nature, that there is no more to the color than is revealed to us in our consciousness of it. But this does not follow. It trades on different senses of 'completeness'. The *nature* of the color red is not completely known to us in acquaintance. Acquaintance does not tell us what that nature is. To know the nature of red, we need to know *that* the nature is so-and-so. And knowledge by acquaintance does not issue in knowledge of this sort. Nonetheless, we know the color red completely via acquaintance in that once we are acquainted with it, we know *it*, and that knowledge cannot *itself* be improved or deepened. All we can subsequently discover are *truths* or *facts* about the color red, including facts about its nature.[19]

As for providing reasons for accepting *a posteriori* identities of the sort that must be true if physicalism is true, this surely is not problematic once we have convinced ourselves that there is no barrier to supposing that the relevant identities *can* be true. The form that such reasons can take was presented a little earlier. But suppose it is said by way of reply that even once such a story is in place, we will *still* be able to ask. What is so special about those physical goings-on? Why do they 'feel' the way they do? So, the gap question remains.

My answer, again, is as follows: To the extent that it is felt that something important has been left out, this derives from a failure to appreciate that there is thing knowledge over and above fact knowledge and/or an uncritical acceptance of the thesis of Revelation. Of course, if Revelation is true there is no further story as to the nature of experienced qualities such as red and thus any proposal as to their nature will be met by questions of the gap sort just presented. But there is a clear diagnosis available to the physicalist as to why some philosophers have wrongly *thought* that Revelation is true. The physicalist can also note that there is independent reason to resist Revelation anyway—namely that, once Revelation is accepted, the causal efficacy of experienced qualities (and relatedly phenomenal states) becomes a mystery.

6.3 The Hard Problem

The Hard Problem (Chalmers 1995) is an extension of the Explanatory Gap. Just as we can coherently wonder why we are experiencing *this* quality (red) rather than *that* one (green), and relatedly why our experience has this particular phenomenal character even after we understand the relevant underlying physical processes, so we can coherently wonder why we have any experiences at all—that is, why there is any phenomenal consciousness associated with the given physical goings-on. How is this possible?

My reply rests, in part, again on the distinction between knowledge by acquaintance and knowledge by description. Given the epistemic gap between the latter and the former, it is possible to know all the relevant physical facts and not know *any* quality by acquaintance. Thus, I do not know any phenomenal character simply in knowing the physical facts. Since, intuitively, fully knowing phenomenal consciousness demands knowing some phenomenal character or other, I cannot fully know phenomenal consciousness in knowing the physical facts. Thus, I may have the sense that, as far as phenomenal consciousness goes, something significant is missing from the physicalist story.

To the question "Why, once so-and-so physical facts are in place, am I experiencing anything?" the physicalist can appeal again to an *a posteriori* identity—this time of the following sort:

(19) Having an experience (being in a state that is phenomenally conscious) = having physical property *P*.

Given this identity, the question just raised has an answer, though not one that can be deduced by *a priori* reflection on the concepts involved and the physical facts.

Of course, as before, there are those who will reply that all we have here is another epistemically primitive identity and such identities are unacceptable. Here I have nothing to add to what I said about such identities in connection with the Explanatory Gap. Others will respond "How *could* phenomenal consciousness just be a certain physical property?" Surely phenomenal consciousness wears its nature on its sleeve. If something *seems* phenomenally conscious, it *is* phenomenally conscious. There is no further story to tell.

This is the thesis of Revelation once more, though now at a more general level than in the preceding section. In reply, I concede that we are not aware of phenomenal consciousness as having a hidden nature, but it doesn't follow from this that we are aware of it as not having such a nature. Indeed, in my view, we are not aware *of* phenomenal consciousness at all. What we are aware of are the qualities of which phenomenally conscious states make us aware.

Since the bearers of phenomenal consciousness are experiences and we are not aware of our experiences, nothing *seems* phenomenally conscious to us. Hence, the idea that if something seems phenomenally conscious it is phenomenally conscious rests on a false presupposition. Of course, we are often aware *that* we are undergoing an experience of a certain sort, but obviously this fact cannot be used to support the thesis of Revelation.

One worry that might be raised for my treatment of the Hard Problem is that it leaves unclear how it is that I can know that I am not a zombie. If I am not aware of phenomenal consciousness—if I am only aware of the qualities phenomenally conscious states represent—how can I know that I have phenomenally conscious states? In section 8.5, I will address this worry in the context of my discussion of privileged access and the impossibility of error.

A related worry that might be raised both for my treatment of the Explanatory Gap and for my treatment of the Hard Problem is that, since they allow that explanations can be offered in physicalistic terms of why certain phenomenally conscious states are present, given certain physical states, these explanations have as a consequence that my zombie replica is phenomenally conscious, for my zombie replica is physically identical with me. But zombies *lack* phenomenal consciousness. The conclusion to draw is that the proposed treatments are unacceptable.

That zombies present problems generally for physicalist responses to the Explanatory Gap has been argued by Chalmers (2005). The physicalist can reply that zombies are not metaphysically possible. In the final section of this chapter, we will look more closely at the case of zombies and the relationship between conceptual and metaphysical possibility.

6.4 The Possibility of Zombies

Zombies are conceptually possible. One can conceive of a world, just like our world physically in every respect, in which there is no 'technicolor' phenomenology. If a zombie replica of the actual world really is possible, then there can be a minimal, physical duplicate of the actual world that is not also a mental duplicate, and thus physicalism is false. Or so the familiar argument goes. There is trouble for physicalism here, however, only if a zombie replica of the actual world is *metaphysically* possible. The mere *conceptual* possibility of such a replica is not enough, for, as is well known, conceptual possibility does not suffice for metaphysical possibility. For example, one can conceive of water in the absence of H_2O, but it is still metaphysically necessary that water is H_2O.

Those who try to use zombies against physicalism typically acknowledge that there are conceptual possible scenarios that are not metaphysically possible. But they insist that the zombie case is one of the "good" cases. Here, conceptual possibility can be trusted.

Why should we believe these philosophers? One response appeals to a distinction between "illusory conceivability" and "veridical conceivability." Illusory conceivability occurs just in case we are under the illusion that we are conceiving of something (S) when in reality we are conceiving of something else (S′). Veridical conceivability is conceivability that is not illusory. The suggestion here is that, just as we can be under the illusion that we are seeing a headless woman on the stage before us, when we are really seeing a woman with her head in a black bag, so we can be under an illusion with respect to what we are conceiving. Illusory conceivability occurs with respect to situations that are metaphysically impossible.

Consider, for example, the case of water and H_2O. It is metaphysically necessary that water is H_2O, but we can conceive of water in the absence of H_2O. This is an example of illusory conceivability. What is *really* being conceived is a world lacking H_2O in which there is a colorless, odorless liquid that comes out of taps and fills lakes.

But what is the relationship between the thing we *are* genuinely conceiving as possible (S′) and the thing we are illusorily conceiving (S)? The view associated with Saul Kripke (1980/1972) is that S′ is the way S is presented in thought. When we think of water, for example, we think of it as the colorless, odorless liquid that comes out of taps and fills lakes (or the watery stuff, for short). And so when we illusorily conceive of water without H_2O, we are really conceiving of there being a unique watery stuff without H_2O.

The general proposal, then, is that conceivability suffices for metaphysical possibility except in those cases in which the world we think we are conceiving is different from the world we are conceiving. In such cases, we are in the grip of an illusion. The world we are conceiving is presented to us in thought (in part) via a contingent reference fixer (e.g., the concept *the watery stuff*) whose satisfaction in the conceived world misleads us into supposing that the thing satisfying the reference fixer in the actual world (water) is thereby present in the conceived world.

In the case of phenomenal consciousness, it seems plausible to hold that there is no distinction between the thing thought about and the way it is presented to us in thought. Consider, for example, the feeling of pain. Pain is presented to us in thought as painful. Given this, when we think that we are conceiving of a world W that is just like our world microphysically but lacking pain, we are conceiving of a world W' that is just like our world microphysically but lacking painfulness. There is no difference between W and W', however. Thus, here conceivability suffices for possibility, and zombies are metaphysically possible. Thus, physicalism is false after all.

The zombie argument, as it is presently being understood, can be reconstructed as follows:

(20) A zombie replica of the actual world is conceptually possible.

(21) If a situation S is conceptually possible then S is conceivable.

(22) If a situation S is conceivable in a non-illusory way then it is metaphysically possible.

(23) A situation S is illusorily conceivable just in case some other situation S' is conceivable that is as much like S as possible consistent with its failing to contain some entity E in S but instead containing some other entity E' that is the way E is presented in thought.

(24) There is no distinction between pain and the way pain is presented in thought (and likewise for other experiences).

Thus,

(25) A zombie replica of the actual world is not illusorily conceivable (from (23) and (24)).

Thus,

(26) A zombie replica of the actual world is conceivable in a non-illusory way (from (20), (21), and (25)).

Thus,

(27) A zombie replica of the actual world is metaphysically possible (from (22) and (26)).

But

(28) If a zombie replica of the actual world is metaphysically possible then physicalism is false.

Therefore,

(29) Physicalism is false.

The most straightforward way for the physicalist can respond to this argument is to reject premise (22). To see this, consider first the hypothesis that every even number is the sum of two prime numbers. I can certainly conceive of that hypothesis being false. But when I conceive of its falsity, there are no contingent reference-fixing concepts I am deploying in thought. I am not under any illusion with respect to what I am conceiving. Even so, if the hypothesis is true, it is necessarily true. Second, consider the claim that there is a being whose essence includes existence. This claim, which has been advanced by those theists who take necessary existence to be part of supreme perfection, is necessarily true if is true at all. But surely it is conceivable that there is no such being. And this is the case even though there is no term in the sentence "There is a being whose essence includes existence" whose reference is fixed by a contingent reference fixer (Yablo 1999). So again the relevant conceivability is non-illusory and (22) is in trouble. Third, the appeal to contingent reference-fixing concepts or terms presupposes that it is *a priori* that the thing denoted by the expression or concept whose reference is fixed by a contingent reference fixer has the properties attributed in it. In the case of water, for example, the idea is that water is presented to us in thought as the watery stuff, and this could not be the case if it were not *a priori* that water is the watery stuff. If it were merely an *a posteriori* discovery that water is the watery stuff, it would be possible for us to think of water as something other than the watery stuff, and thus it could not be true that for us water is always presented in thought as the watery stuff. Where it is not so presented, no explanation would be forthcoming of the conceptual illusion we are allegedly under when we claim to be able to conceive of water in the absence of H_2O.

The difficulty here is that it is not *a priori* that water is the watery stuff. Indeed, it is not even *a priori* that water is *a* watery stuff. This was established in chapter 3, and I shall not repeat the arguments here.

In my view, I am not under any sort of illusion when I conceive of water in the absence of H_2O. I am not really conceiving of there being watery stuff without H_2O. I am simply conceiving of water without H_2O. The thought I have in this case is one that no amount of *a priori* reflection on the concepts involved will show to be false. Still, it is metaphysically impossible that water is not H_2O. Yet again, (22) is in trouble.

The conclusion I draw is that the zombie argument, as reconstructed above, is unsuccessful. Suppose that now it is replied that the argument should take a much simpler form. Instead of being viewed as a proof that physicalism is false, it should be viewed as providing good grounds for rejecting physicalism by appealing to conceptual possibility as a guide to metaphysical possibility in something like the way that how things perceptually seem to us is a guide to how they really are. In the latter case, the existence of illusions does not lead us to deny that the perceptual appearances are a good *guide* to reality. Why treat the former case differently?

The new argument can be stated as follows:

(30) A zombie replica of the actual world is conceptually possible.

(31) If a zombie replica of the actual world is conceptually possible then it is conceivable.

(32) Conceivability, notwithstanding the existence of illusory conceivability, is generally a good guide to metaphysical possibility.

Thus, we are warranted in concluding that

(33) A zombie replica of the actual world is metaphysically possible

even though (33) is not entailed by (30)–(32). Viewed in this way, the zombie argument is intended to provide warrant for rejecting physicalism without refuting it conclusively.

The trouble with this argument is that it is now being conceded (implicitly, at least) that conceivability fails in some cases other than illusory conceivability, for (32) is stated as it is in order to accommodate other "odd" or "bad" cases such as the ones already adumbrated. But once these cases are allowed, what warrants supposing that the zombie replica scenario is not itself also "odd" or "bad"? The anti-physicalist surely needs to say more here. Furthermore, as I noted in chapter 2, there is strong general evidence for physicalism. This evidence may be taken to defeat the presumption that the non-illusory conceivability of a zombie replica warrants the conclusion that such a replica is metaphysically possible.

It might be replied at this stage that the emphasis on conceivability in the appeal to zombies is misguided. Instead, we should appeal to intuition. The argument now is as follows:

(34) We have the intuition that zombies are metaphysically possible.

(35) Intuitions generally are a good, though not infallible, guide to how things are.

Thus, we are justified in concluding (though not with certainty) that

(36) Zombies are metaphysically possible.

Do we really have the intuition that zombies are metaphysically possible? The natural reply is that intuitions differ here. Some people may have such an intuition, but others do not. What is common currency is the intuition that zombies are *conceptually* possible. Thus, the appeal to conceivability cannot be avoided after all.

David Chalmers has recently tried to resuscitate the appeal to conceptual possibility by placing three constraints on the relevant kind of conceivability. First, according to Chalmers, the conceivability should be ideal, where a statement S "is ideally conceivable if an ideal reasoner would find it to pass the relevant tests (if an ideal reasoner could not rule out the hypothesis expressed by S a priori, for example)" (2002, p. 148). As Chalmers is aware, there is potentially trouble for ideal conceivability, so understood, for if an ideal reasoner is one whose reasoning perfectly tracks possibility, the connection between conceptual possibility and metaphysical possibility is trivialized.

If conceivability is understood in the above ideal way, mathematical hypotheses whose truth value is currently unknown but which are true, will not count as having denials that are conceivable, since those denials can be shown to be false by ideal *a priori* reflection.

A second constraint on the relevant kind of conceivability is that it be positive. Some situations are negatively conceivable in that their obtaining cannot be ruled out *a priori*. Likewise, some statements are negatively conceivable in that their truth cannot be ruled out *a priori*. But, according to Chalmers, this is not the sort of conceivability that is needed in the zombie argument. What is needed is imaginability: "... to positively conceive of a situation is in some sense to imagine a specific configuration of objects and properties" (ibid., p. 150). Further, the imagining must be coherent and modal, where one coherently modally imagines a statement S just in case (i) one imagines a situation as possible that verifies S and (ii) reasoning about the imagined situation reveals it as a situation that verifies S.

In order to understand positive conceivability as presented above, we need to understand the notion of verification that is being employed. Chalmers says:

On my usage, verification is an (idealized) epistemic relation. A scenario verifies P when consideration of the scenario can reveal it to be a scenario in which P. On the other side, verification is stronger than a mere evidential relation. One can consider a scenario in which one has strong evidence that P, but such that the scenario is epistemically compatible with not-P.... (1999, p. 3)

The final constraint is that the conceivability be primary, where a situation is primarily conceivable just in case it is conceivable that it is *actually* the case. Chalmers comments:

Primary conceivability is grounded in the idea that for all we know *a priori*, there are many ways the world might be. The oceans might contain H_2O or they might contain XYZ; the evening star and the morning star might be the same or distinct; and so on. We can think of these ways the world might be as *epistemic possibilities*, in a broad sense according to which it is epistemically possible that *S* if the hypothesis that *S* is not ruled out *a priori*. When *S* is epistemically possible, there are usually a number of imaginable situations such that if they actually obtain *S* will be the case. These situations can be taken to verify *S*, when they are considered as actual. (2002, p. 157)

The argument from zombies against materialism can now be restated as follows:

Let *P* be the conjunction of physical truths about the world, and let *Q* be "Someone is conscious."

Then

(37) P & ~Q is ideally primarily positively conceivable.

(38) If P & ~Q is ideally primarily positively conceivable then P & ~Q is metaphysically possible.

(39) If P & ~Q is metaphysically possible, materialism is false.

Therefore,

(40) Materialism is false.[20]

This argument handles some of the worries raised for the first zombie argument I considered. But it does not handle all of them. In particular, it appears that if the above argument is counted as sound, so too should be the following argument:

Where *Q'* is "There is a being whose essence includes existence,"

(41) Q' (~Q') is ideally primarily positively conceivable.[21]

(42) If Q' (~Q') is ideally primarily positively conceivable, then Q' (~Q') is metaphysically possible.

(43) If Q' (∼Q') is metaphysically possible, then Q' (∼Q') is true.[22]

Therefore,

(44) Q' (∼Q') is true.

But it cannot be the case that Q' and $\sim Q'$ are both true. Clearly something has gone very wrong.

The natural reply to this argument is to say that, although Q' and $\sim Q'$ are negatively conceivable (no amount of *a priori* reflection will show either to be false), at least one of the two is not *positively* conceivable. Likewise, the natural reply for the materialist to Chalmers's zombie argument is to deny that P & $\sim Q$ is positively conceivable.

Recall that for Chalmers positive conceivability is a kind of imaginability. One does not positively conceive that S unless one imagines a situation such that reflection on it can reveal it as a situation in which S. If reflection merely reveals the situation as one in which there is good evidence for the claim that S, one has not positively conceived that S. Understood in this way, it is not in the least obvious that P & $\sim Q$ is positively conceivable—just as it is not in the least obvious that Q' is positively conceivable.

Here is another example: Consider the thesis, T, that the only entities that have being are those that exist. Ontic pluralists deny this thesis, but its advocates take it to be a necessary truth. Is $\sim T$ positively conceivable? Is T positively conceivable? My reaction is to say that it isn't clear. If the best theory with respect to the nature of being and existence is one that holds that to be is to exist, then we should embrace it and accept, *as a consequence*, that T is positively conceivable whereas $\sim T$ is not. But before we decide whether T is superior to $\sim T$, we cannot decide which of the two is positively conceivable.

In general, if we believe that we can genuinely imagine something, we have a warrant for believing that the thing in question is metaphysically possible. But we can revise our beliefs about what is imaginable, or form beliefs where before we had none, in light of theories we develop about the nature of reality, for these theories will issue in metaphysical necessities that may conflict with our earlier beliefs concerning what is imaginable or may cause us to take a position on imaginability where before we had none. In such a case, if there is a conflict, we should be guided about what we can really imagine from what our theory tells us is metaphysically possible, not the other way around.

Thus, in the case of a zombie replica of the actual world, if the best theory with respect to the nature of mentality is the physicalist thesis, as

I maintain, we should deny that a zombie replica is positively conceivable. What is true instead in this case is that such a replica is negatively conceivable. No amount of *a priori* reflection rules out the possibility of a zombie replica of the actual world. Even so, it is metaphysically impossible.[23]

The conclusion I draw is that physicalists can happily accept both that zombies are conceptually possible and that they are not conceptually possible (though not in the same breath). Either way, there is nothing for the physicalist to fear from zombies.

7   Change Blindness and the Refrigerator Light Illusion

Recent psychological experiments (Simons 1997) have shown that very large changes can be made in pictures without viewers' being conscious of them. This phenomenon is known as *change blindness*. In the initial experiments, the phenomenon was found to occur when the changes were synchronized with eye movements. As one views a picture, one's eyes move around in quick, jerky ways. These movements, which are known as saccades, last from 25 to 200 milliseconds. During saccades, the visual system does not respond to the incoming light; thus, changes that occur at such times are not processed. Visual information generally is processed only during eye fixations.

Subsequent experiments showed that change blindness can occur without there being synchronization of the change with eye movements. One important method that was used is known as the *flicker technique*. Here a brief flicker is presented between successive pictures. The flicker masks the change. Eye blinks have also been used to trigger changes. (See figure 7.1.)

In further experiments, large changes were made during camera cuts of which subjects in the experiments were entirely unconscious. Another important technique involves "mudsplashes" (five or six small, localized disturbances). These mudsplashes occur in parts of the picture distinct from the part in which the change occurs, so it cannot be supposed that the reason that the subjects fail to register any change is that it is occluded by the mudsplashes.

Various hypotheses have been forward on the basis of the change-blindness experiments. The most important of these are the following:

(1) We do not see the changes.

(2) We are under the impression that we see everything in the visual field, but this is an illusion.

(a)

(b)

(c)

(3) Our visual experience is much sparser than is commonly supposed.

Among those who have endorsed these claims are both philosophers (Dennett (1991) and Noe (2001)) and psychologists (O'Regan (1996, 2001), Blackmore (2003), Rensink, O'Regan, and Clark (1997), and Simons and Levin (1997)).

Why, then, do we (commonly) think that we see everything in the visual field?

The standard answer given by those who accept the above hypotheses is that if we "so much as faintly wonder whether we're actually seeing something," we "turn our eye (and our attention) to that thing, and it becomes available for processing" (O'Regan 2000/2001). It's like the refrigerator light. Whenever we open the door, the light is on. This may give rise to the illusion that the light is on all the time. In reality, the light is only potentially on all the time. Likewise, we are under an illusion that we see (and experience) everything in the visual field. In reality, we see things only if we attend to them. Things to which we do not attend are only potentially seen.

These claims, interesting in their own right, are of special significance to philosophical (and psychological) theories of the nature of perception and consciousness. For example, some have supposed that the experiments provide support for doxastic theories of visual perception, according to which one sees an object just in case one forms a belief about it on the basis of the information contained in the light striking the eyes; for if one fails to see the changes in the change-blindness experiments, a simple explanation of why one fails to see them is that, given how one's attention is directed, one fails to form any beliefs about them. One's cognitive processes are at work elsewhere. On this view, seeing is just a form of believing (Armstrong 1968; Pitcher 1971; Dennett 1991).

The hypotheses are also relevant to philosophical theories of the nature of consciousness. For one thing, they force us to reflect on a very basic question about consciousness which has occupied us in earlier chapters: "What conditions must obtain for us to be conscious of some thing?" For another, a common initial response to the experiments was to say

Figure 7.1
a: the first of two pictures, presented with a flicker between them. In the second picture (not shown), the bush to the left of the sphinx's head is missing. b: the first of two pictures; in the second (not shown), the aircraft engine under the wing is missing. c: one of two pictures, the other of which (not shown) lacks the box sitting on the boat.

that they provide support for the view that consciousness is just a form of cognitive access.

Recently some philosophers have argued that none of the hypotheses allegedly supported by the experiments are really supported by them at all (Dretske 2004 and forthcoming; Block 2007b). And even some psychologists who have been advocates of these hypotheses have backed away from their initial positions. For example, Daniel Simons and Ronald Rensink (2005) recently made the following comments:

> We and others found the 'sparse representations' view appealing (and still do), and initially made the overly strong claim that change blindness supports the conclusion of sparse representations (Rensink 1997, Simons 1997). We wrote our article because change blindness continues to be taken as evidence for sparse—or even absent—representations, and we used O'Regan and Noe's influential paper (O'Regan and Noe, 2001) as an example. However, as has been noted for some time ... this conclusion is logically flawed. (2005, p. 219)

In this chapter, I shall argue that a significant (and suitably qualified) part of what was initially claimed by change-blindness theorists is correct or at least very plausible.

7.1   A Closer Look at the Change-Blindness Hypotheses

Consider first the claim that we do not see the changes. The changes here are the differences. It is not that the one picture itself suddenly changes so that there is a sudden change event. Rather, there is one picture and then another, and the second picture differs from the first. Now, everyone will agree that we do not see *that* there is any difference between the two pictures. This is a failure to see a factive difference. We do not see the fact that the one picture differs from the other. We do not notice any difference.

What about the things that are the differences? In typical examples of change blindness, there is a spatio-temporal thing that is present in one picture but missing in the other—for example, the clump of bushes to the side of the sphinx's head in figure 7.1a, the aircraft engines in figure 7.1b, the box on the boat in figure 7.1c. Do we see such things? Here is an argument that we do not, drawing on considerations developed earlier:

(4) I see an object if and only if it looks some way to me.

(5) An object looks some way to me if and only if it is experienced as being that way.

(6) If I experience an object at all then I am conscious of it.

Thus,

(7) If I see an object then I am conscious of it.

But

(8) Subjects are not conscious of the things that are the differences.

Thus,

(9) Subjects do not see the things that are the differences.

This argument, in my view, stands or falls with premise (8). Consider again the case of the perfectly camouflaged moth resting on a tree trunk. In chapter 1, I held that we are not conscious of the moth and thus we do not see it. We are not conscious of the moth, I claimed, since the moth does not enter into the content of our experience. This is reflected in the fact that our experience, on its own, does not enable us even to ask ourselves "What is that?" with respect the moth. Thus, the moth is hidden from us. It seems to me plausible that, at least in some cases of change blindness, we are correspondingly blind to the spatio-temporal things that are the differences in the two pictures. We are not conscious of these things, so we do not see them.

Now consider the example illustrated in figure 7.2a. As you fixate on the plus sign, you see the bars on the right. But you do not see the fourth bar away from the plus sign.[1] That bar is certainly large enough to see, but, given your fixation point, you do not see it. We have here further support for the view that we do not always see each thing in the field of view that is large enough for us to see.

Now consider figure 7.2b. As you move your eyes from the top black dot to the plus sign to each of the lower two black dots, there are particular bars on the right you do not see. Of course, you would have seen each of those bars, had your eye movements been suitably different. But in that event, your experience would have been different; as I noted in chapter 1, shifting the focus of your eyes changes the phenomenology of your experience somewhat.

Some cases of change blindness are like this, it seems to me. Consider a case involving a real scene rather than a picture. Your friend Bill is in the crowd before you. You do not notice him. A moment later he leaves, and you do not notice any difference. Did you see Bill before his departure?

Change detection requires an explicit comparison. Where such comparisons fail, change blindness occurs. Furthermore, explicit comparisons demand that one attend to the part of the picture or scene where there is a change both before and after the change takes place (Mitroff et al. 2002).

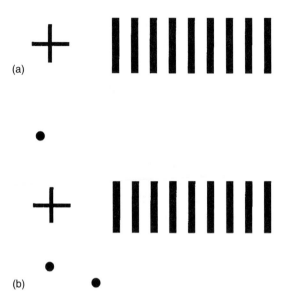

Figure 7.2
a: Fixate on the cross. You see the bars on the right, but you do not see the fourth bar away from the plus sign. b: Fixate on the top black dot and then move your eyes down to the cross and from there to the two lower black dots, one after the other. As you do so, there are particular bars on the right you do not see.

In the above example, you certainly do not see that Bill was present and is now missing. Still, did you see Bill? A plausible view is that you may well *not* have. Bill's status is like one of the bars in the middle of the group of bars in figure 7.2b as you move your fixation point from the top black dot to the plus sign to the lower two black dots. Bill is then only potentially seen. You would have seen him if your eye movements had been different.

Consider next figure 7.1a. After the flicker, the bush directly to the left of the sphinx's head is missing. Do you see that particular bush in the picture in which it is present while you are a victim of change blindness? You certainly see the trees in the background. For example, if asked immediately afterward, you will respond affirmatively to the questions "Were there trees in the background?" and "Were they palms?" Your experience enables you to believe of the bushes in the background that they are palms (for example). You see *them* collectively. But your experience may not enable you to say directly whether there is a bush immediately to the left of the sphinx's head. It may not enable you to discriminate that bush *in particular* from the background at all. In that case, you do not see the bush.

Quite often, when we suddenly notice the difference between two pictures, it is as if something that was hidden has suddenly come into view (as with the box on the boat shown in figure 7.1c). With the shift in the focal point of our eyes, our experience seems to change. Its phenomenology now includes a colored shape marked out from the background. The shape "pops out at us." As this happens, we suddenly become visually conscious of the thing. The change here is phenomenologically similar to that which would occur were we to be viewing a nearby table with several objects on it to which a further easily noticed object was added while we blinked. With the extra object in place, our experience is different. The new experience enables us to pick out the object, to identify it (typically), and to relate it to other items in the field of view. We are thus visually conscious of the object. Before blinking, given the absence of the object, we were not.

Again, let me emphasize that I am not claiming that in *all* cases of change blindness involving a difference in the presence of some spatio-temporal thing we fail to see the thing. In some cases, especially those involving changes that take longer, there may simply be a failure of memory. In others, we may see the thing and then fail to notice its absence. In these cases, when we finally notice the difference in the pictures, the phenomenology at the moment of discovery is one of *removal*. It is for us phenomenally much as it would be if a large object among four or five such objects on a table directly before us were suddenly to vanish while we blinked. My claim is simply that quite often when we notice the difference, the phenomenology at the moment of discovery is one of *addition*. We have the strong sense that something new is marked out in our experience—something that wasn't there as an individual item before. When this happens, it is not as if our experience has suddenly become *sparser*. Nor is it as if we are suddenly conscious of details in the relevant thing that had escaped us before, even though we were conscious of the thing all along. Rather, it is as if the thing has suddenly been marked out in our experience, just as the fourth bar away from the plus sign in figure 7.2a is suddenly marked out when we switch our fixation point from the plus sign to the first bar. To insist otherwise is to fail to do justice to the phenomenology—or so it seems to me.

Not all cases of change blindness involve a difference in spatio-temporal things. In some cases, one picture differs from the other in some feature that changes. In figure 7.3 it is the position of the bar behind

Figure 7.3
Two pictures of a couple having lunch. Note the difference in the position of the bar.

the couple having lunch that is altered. Ned Block (2007a) remarks that the view that we do not see the features that change "strains credulity." I disagree.

To begin with, strictly speaking, no features are ever seen. For an entity to be seen, it must look some way, and no feature ever looks any way. Red, for example, does not look red (or green), though a red surface may. Similarly, squareness does not look square. Still, in seeing things, we are, of course, conscious of various features which we experience the things as having. The interesting question, thus, is whether in the change-blindness cases involving a feature change we are conscious of the relevant feature. For example, are we conscious of the exact position of the horizontal bar in each of the two pictures in figure 7.3?

It seems clear that we are conscious of the bar in both pictures. If asked "Was there a horizontal bar behind the couple in both pictures?" we would respond affirmatively. But it is not at all clear that we are conscious of the exact position of the bar relative to the couple in either the first picture or the second. There is nothing that strains credulity in the idea that we are not so conscious. What *may* strain credulity is the thought that there is no difference in visual representation of the position of the bar between the first and the second picture. But that is a separate issue, and one about which I shall have something more to say of a general sort later in this chapter.

In the case of feature change blindness, the delicate question to be answered is whether the experience we undergo enables us to form any *de re* conceptual attitudes with respect to the relevant feature. I regard this question as currently open. It may well be that in some cases of feature change blindness we are conscious of the feature that changes but in others we are not.

In the above example (figure 7.3), my experience of the first picture clearly does put me in a position to ask "What is the position of that bar?" Thus, I am conscious of the bar. But it is not so clear whether my experience enables me to ask "What is that position?" with respect to the exact position of the bar. If you do not appreciate the difference between these two questions, consider "What is the shape of that thing?" versus "What is that shape?" (where that shape is the shape of the thing in question). One's experience of the relevant object might enable one to ask the first question without enabling one to ask the second. Suppose, for example, that one is seeing the thing from a great distance and one cannot make out its shape at all. Or suppose one is viewing the thing through strongly distorting lenses.

Figure 7.4
If you fixate on the cross and close one eye, at a distance away of roughly ten inches, one of the smiley faces should disappear. That smiley face will then be in the blind spot for your open eye.

Whatever the final account of feature change-blindness cases, the view to which I am attracted—that, in at least some such cases, subjects are *not* conscious of the feature that changes—deserves to be taken seriously. In the next section, I put the feature cases to one side and concentrate on the cases involving spatio-temporal thing change. I return to the issue of consciousness of features that change in 7.3.

7.2 The "No-See-Um" View

One worry for the "No-See-Um" view, as we might call it, is that it leads to gaps in the visual field, where the unseen objects are located. This is not a genuine consequence of the view, however, as I shall now try to show.

Consider first the case of the blind spot. This is the spot on the retina where the optic nerve joins it. At this spot, there is no sensitivity to incoming light.

The existence of a blind spot can be demonstrated very easily by means of a diagram such as figure 7.4. To uncover one of your two blind spots, stare fixedly at the cross in the middle and close one eye while holding the page just a few inches away. As you slowly move the page further from the eyes, you will find that suddenly, at a certain distance away, one of the smiley faces disappears. The no longer visible smiley face is then in the blind spot for the open eye. At that moment, you do not see the smiley face. Even so, there is no gap in your experience. It seems to you that the relevant portion of the page is uniformly white. In reality a smiley face is located there. Your experience is in error. It "fills in" incorrectly. You are conscious of white throughout the blind spot, but there is no whiteness in that location.

Writing of the blind spot and the phenomenon of filling in, Sir David Brewster remarked:

We should expect, whether we use one eye or both, to see a black or dark spot upon every landscape within 15 degrees of the point which most particularly

Figure 7.5
The Kanizsa triangle.

attracts our notice. The Divine Artificer, however, has not left his work thus imperfect.... This spot, in place of being black, has always the same colour as the ground. (1832)

Filling in is not restricted to the blind spot. Consider the Kanizsa triangle (figure 7.5). Here there is no triangle, but the brain fills in the sides of a triangle on the basis of the information with which it is provided. Again, the resultant experience is in error. It represents that there is a triangle when in reality there is not.

Dennett has objected to the description of such cases as examples of filling in on the grounds that the brain does not really add anything. Instead it ignores the absence of information from the relevant regions of the visual field. Dennett says that to talk of filling in "suggests that the brain is *providing* something when in fact the brain is ignoring something; it mistakes the omission of a representation for the representation of presence" (1992, p. 48). This is confused. Where there is filling in, the resultant experience is a *mis*-representation. It is not an *under*-representation. The experience misinforms its subject about the relevant spatial regions. It does not *fail* to represent them. The experience in such cases does not under-represent the relevant spatial regions relative to elsewhere in the field of view.

Here is one more example: King Charles II used to amuse himself by positioning a courtier so that his head was in his blind spot. He then 'decapitated' the chosen courtier by closing one eye. King Charles's visual experience, with one eye shut, represented the courtier as being without a head. That is how it appeared to him, and that is why he was amused.

One possible hypothesis with respect to change blindness, then, is as follows: In at least some cases, at a conscious level, there is filling in with respect to the regions occupied by the things that are the differences in the two pictures, assuming that the subject is not conscious of these things.

Another possible hypothesis is that some regions in the field of view are not represented at all at the conscious level, so that there is under-representation instead of misrepresentation. Think of a partially colored sketch of a scene in which parts of the scene are left out. Such a sketch, by not depicting parts of the scene, does not depict the scene as having holes or gaps in it. The absence of a representation is not the same as the representation of an absence.

One objection to these two hypotheses is that they conflict with the empirical data. Consider the fact that, when presented with a forced choice task, subjects are able to select pairs of pictures where there is change at above chance levels even when they report being unaware of any change. Moreover, given a forced choice task of saying which of two block figures in a picture of sixteen such figures is more likely to have changed in a second picture of the figures, subjects are faster at selecting the changed figure than the unchanged one, even if they have reported being unaware of any change in the pictures.[2]

It seems, then, that there is evidence that the visual representation generated in viewing the second picture is not the same as the visual representation generated in viewing the first. And one natural explanation for the difference in visual representation is that some thing is seen while viewing one of the pictures but not seen while viewing the other. This is not the only explanation, however. Why not grant the point about visual representation while insisting that the information is not present at a conscious level? Still, on either explanation the above evidence counts against the filling-in model for cases of change blindness, for where there is filling in of a sort that hides a thing, there is no visual representation of the thing. There is no information *about* the thing available to the visual system. The smiley face in the blind spot, for example, is not visually represented at all, and there is no information about it at a conscious or an unconscious level.

However, the evidence does not count against the drawn-picture model, viewed as a model for understanding what the vehicles of conscious awareness of things are like. Consistent with that model, it can be held that the visual representations of the two pictures differ; but sometimes there is no difference in representations *at a conscious level*.

What I am suggesting, then, is this. We do not always see everything that is large enough for us to see in the field of view. We are not conscious of the things that are the differences in at least some cases of change blindness. We do not see these things. Even so, our visual fields do not have gaps in them; however, they are somewhat sparser than we ordinarily suppose, in that some of the things we would ordinarily take to be represented at a conscious level are not. At a conscious level, a constructive process operates that is something like drawing a picture. This drawing process does not fill in all the details. It is not like taking a clear, color photograph. It leaves things out. Allowing for some poetic license, seeing things is like drawing pictures of them with the eyes. Still, the underlying non-conscious or pre-conscious representations are not sparse. Thus, there is some truth in the claims of the original change-blindness theorists. But they went too far with the *unqualified* claim of sparse representations.

It may seem that the view I am proposing fails to do adequate justice to the determinacy of detail in our experience. Relatedly, talk of seeing as a constructive process may seem to suggest that seeing things involves bringing them under concepts.

Appearances can be deceptive. I am not denying that *with respect to* the things that we see there is typically (though not always) a real richness and determinacy of detail in our experience of them. Consider, for example, the content of my current visual experience as I stare at the sea and the old port on the island of Mykonos. I cannot hope to capture the richness of my experience in words. The blues of the ocean and the sky are deeper and more intense than any I have ever encountered before. The flowers have colors that are shades of purple and pink and red, and they form clusters that are large and irregular in shape. As far as my current visual experience goes, there are *many* shapes and determinate shades of color for which I lack general concepts, but these shapes and colors certainly contribute to the phenomenology. Nor, for reasons I gave in chapter 5, are these shapes and colors represented demonstratively in my experience. They are represented nonconceptually.

My actual visual experience, as I stare out the window, enables me to wonder about, ask questions about, and form *de re* beliefs and judgments about many (but not all) the concrete things before me in the old port of Mykonos. These things I see, and my seeing of them, at least to the extent that they are things to which I am attending, involve my visually representing them in my experience in great detail.

Even though my visual experience nonconceptually represents the things I see, my conceptualization of the scene and of things in it may guide how my eyes move with respect to the scene. This, in turn, can causally affect further beliefs I form about what is before me. Further, my conceptualization of a scene can itself causally influence how the scene is segmented into parts in my experience (and likewise individual objects and their parts).[3] Thus, I accept that both the focal point of my eyes and my conceptualization can influence the character of my experience.

Think about an artist drawing a picture of a scene. He begins by fixating on some part of the scene. As his eyes move around, they are guided in part by his conception of the scene. The picture he draws will be rich in detail with respect to some parts of the scene and not so rich with respect to others. Some things in the scene will be left out of his picture altogether. We might be a bit like such an artist as we see the things around us.

The idea that seeing is like drawing pictures is reminiscent of Stephen Kosslyn's view of mental image generation (1980, 1994). Kosslyn takes vision and imagery to share a medium he calls "the visual buffer." This buffer, according to Kosslyn, is filled in the case of vision using information provided by the eyes and in the case of imagery using information in long-term memory. Kosslyn argues that generating an image is not like retrieving a clear photograph from memory. Rather, it is best taken to be a constructive process similar in certain ways to drawing a picture. I am proposing that the best explanation of the data in the case of vision likens seeing things to drawing pictures too.

7.3   Sperling and the Refrigerator Light

What about the supposed refrigerator light illusion? The claim here is that we do not see things to which we are not attending, that such things are only potentially seen. Again, in this case, the original change-blindness theorists went too far. As a way of getting at how they went wrong, let me begin with a discussion of George Sperling's classic experiment on sensory memory (1960).

Sperling presented subjects with a 3×4 array of 12 letters for 50 milliseconds in the center of their field of view followed by a blank field (figure 7.6). Subjects were asked to report what they saw under two sets of conditions. In condition 1, they were asked to identify as many letters as possible. In condition 2, they were asked to identify letters in a single row. The chosen row was identified by a tone (either high, medium, or low) whose use had been explained in advance. The tone was not played until immediately after the display had been extinguished. Sperling found that

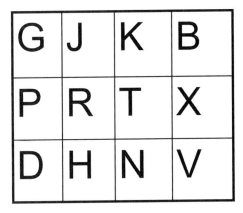

Figure 7.6
In Sperling's experiment, an array like the one shown was displayed for 50 milliseconds.

in condition 1 subjects were able to identify only about one-third of the twelve letters. In condition 2, they were typically able to identify three or four of the letters in the relevant row. Sperling also found that the accuracy of the subjects' reports in condition 2 about the content of the row diminished as the time of presentation of the tone from the disappearance of the array was delayed.

In response to these results, Sperling hypothesized that there is a visual sensory memory that fades away very quickly and is entirely gone after about 300 milliseconds. In ordinary language, Sperling's claim is that the array *appears* still to be displayed for some 300 milliseconds. He reasoned that in condition 1 the act of reporting all the letters takes too long, and that the sensory memory has faded away by the time the subjects have reported three or four letters. In the case of subjects in condition 2, however, the sensory memory is still available when the tone sounds, and it persists long enough for the subjects to identify three or four of the letters in the relevant row. Since in condition 2 the subjects do not know until the tone sounds which row to report on and the tone does not occur until the array display is turned off, the fact that the subjects successfully report at least three of the four letters shows that all (or nearly all) of the letters in the array appear to be present.

So do the subjects see all the letters after the array has gone? If indeed all the letters appear to be present, as Sperling hypothesizes, they do. Furthermore, the subjects certainly believe that they see each individual letter (just ask them), and while, of course this isn't conclusive, there is no clear reason not to take their reports at face value. However, in condition 2 the subjects attend to letters in only one of the rows. Thus, Sperling's experiment provides strong evidence that we can see and thus be conscious of things to which we are not attending.

So there is no general refrigerator light illusion. The truth is that *some* of things to which we do not attend and which are large enough for us to see, we do not see even if they are in plain view. But others we do. Still, we are under a kind of illusion in that some of the things that we would ordinarily, pre-theoretically suppose that we see we do not see.

The connection between seeing a thing and attending to it, in my view, is just this: Each individual thing we see is such that we *can* attend to it (in the sense that we *can* mentally focus on it[4]) without altering the fixation point of our eyes.

In closing this section, it is worth mentioning a fascinating experiment (by Richard Wiseman) that involves inattentional blindness and color change.[5] Subjects are shown a video, the title of which is "The Color Changing Card Trick." They attend closely, expecting to see a color change involving the cards. One of the cards does change color. The subjects are then told that the video is not about the color of the cards, and that there were four other color changes—one involving the color of the tablecloth upon which the cards were resting, one involving the color of the backdrop, and two involving the shirts of the experimenters. This is shocking news to nearly all subjects. When the video is played again, the color changes are obvious.

Having seen this video, I can tell you that I was not conscious of any of the four color changes, even though they were dramatic. The question I want to raise is whether I was conscious of the colors of the tablecloth, the backdrop, and the shirts before or after the changes.

Given the empirical evidence from the change-blindness cases about the visual representations involved, it seems plausible to suppose that there are changes in the visual representations of the four colors. What is much less clear is whether, given how attention is allocated, the relevant colors are all ones of which the subjects are conscious.

Think about the drawn-picture model again. An artist drawing a partial picture of a scene may ignore certain parts of the scene and may, further, leave parts of her picture in which she does not have a central interest uncolored. Or perhaps initially some parts are colored in and later they lose their color: imagine that the crayons the artist is using are special ones that have disappearing colors. It is not that the information isn't there for her to use; it is just that, for one reason or another, she does not use it. Likewise, our eyes take in a huge amount of information about the surfaces before us. That information is there for us to use, but we do not use all of it at a conscious level. We draw pictures that are very detailed in some respects but less detailed in others; as our eyes move around, these pictures change. Some things get dropped out; others get added. Where we fixate, our pictures are most detailed; in these regions, the things we see are typically represented at a conscious level in great detail. But the detail is lost at that level as our eyes move and our attention and interest shift. Thus, colors that are initially consciously represented may not be so represented a little later.

7.4 Phenomenology and Cognitive Accessibility

In his 2007a paper, Ned Block argues that the results of the Sperling experiment lend support to the view that phenomenology outstrips or overflows cognitive accessibility. In this section, I shall show that Block fails to make a compelling case for this claim, understood without further restriction, on the basis of Sperling's data.[6]

As should be clear from my remarks in the preceding section, I agree with Block that the subjects in the Sperling experiment see all twelve letters in the array even though they can accurately report only three or four. I also agree that each individual letter is such that the subjects see it. The first point I want to make here is that there is an important sense in which each of the twelve letters is cognitively accessible notwithstanding the subjects' inability to identify two-thirds of them, for with respect to each letter in the array the subjects' experiences enable them at least to wonder "What is that letter?" Their experiences thus put them in a position to bring each letter under the demonstrative concept *that*. The content of the concept varies with the putative query. Were a subject to wonder "What is that letter?" with respect to the letter 'B' in the top right corner of the array, say, the cognitive content of the query would be different from the content of the query, expressible in the same sentence, with respect to the letter 'H' in the middle of the bottom row. Of course, subjects do not typically so wonder with respect to each letter in the array. They may not so wonder with respect to any letter. The point is that their experiences *enable* them to wonder "What is that?" with respect to each letter, whether or not they actually wonder anything, and the content of this possible cognitive response varies with the letter. Thus, each letter that is phenomenally registered is cognitively *accessible* via a cognitive act, the content of which is distinctive to that letter.

This brings me to Block's claim that phenomenology outstrips cognitive accessibility. Let us look more closely at how this is supposed to be the case. One way of understanding Block's claim in a particular instance is that the subjects' phenomenal consciousness of, say, the letter 'B' in the top row is different from the subjects' phenomenal consciousness of, say, the letter 'H' in the bottom row, even under the condition that the middle tone is heard and subjects are attending to the central row. But this does not show that phenomenology outstrips cognitive accessibility, since the possible act of demonstrative wondering with respect to the former letter has a different content from the possible act of demonstrative wondering with respect to the latter.

What happens when the middle tone sounds? One possibility is that there is no change in phenomenology as the subjects attend to the letters in the central row. The subjects simply focus their attention on the row and report what the letters look like. This is Block's position. (See his 2007b.) But patently this does not show that phenomenology outstrips cognitive accessibility. I am happy to allow, of course, that when one focuses on a given letter, one is then put in a position by one's experience to identify the letter as being the letter so-and-so and thus to cognitively classify the letter in a way that one could not before. With the shift in attention, then, one's cognitive possibilities are enriched—one goes from possibly wondering "What is that?" to actually thinking that *that* is the letter 'P', for example—even though (I am now supposing) the phenomenology stays the same. But this is not to the point. It shows that cognitive accessibility, content-wise, outstrips phenomenology, not the other way around.

Is it true anyway that when one shifts the focus of one's eyes to a particular row there is *no* change in the appearance of the letters? I think not. Granted, there is no dramatic or big change, but the situation seems to me similar to the following: Focus on an object—a watch, say—lying on a magazine in the middle of your field of view. There will likely be letters on the magazine's cover close to the watch that you will not be able to identify even if you try, given your focus of attention. It is not that the letters are fuzzy or obscure; it is just that they are insufficiently determinate in your experience. Now switch your attention slightly from the watch to the letters. With the new focus for your eyes, you will be able to identify them, but there will be no marked or sudden change in the phenomenology. The letters will not sharply change in their appearance. Still, the phenomenology does change a little. At a conscious level, there is a detail in the letters that simply was not there before—a detail that now enables you to identify them. Subtle changes of this sort happen all the time as we move our eyes around. But these changes are not dramatic or pre-reflectively obvious.

In taking this view, I am not claiming that when one shifts one's attention to a particular row the letters suddenly "pop out" in the phenomenology, or that there is a shift in kind at the phenomenological level. This does not fit with what the subjects themselves report, and it does not seem at all plausible—any more than it would be plausible to hold that, as an object is moved from the periphery of the field of view to the center, the way the object looks suddenly changes at some point. The difference is one of degree. These cases, then, are not like some change-blindness scenarios in which a previously unnoticed object is suddenly noticed. There it really is as if a shape "pops out" in the phenomenology.

I might add that my proposed account of phenomenal consciousness handles phenomenological changes or differences of the sort I am getting at in the Sperling example in a straightforward and compelling way. Phenomenological detail corresponds to richness in represented features: more detail, more features represented in the content of the experience.

Block sometimes states his position in a more qualified way—and this seems to reflect best his real view of the matter, given some of his most recent comments.[7] He says that, in his view, the reason why subjects are unable to gain access to all the letters in the Sperling experiment without the tones is that "the "capacity" of phenomenology, or at least the visual phenomenal memory system, is greater than that of the working memory buffer that governs reporting."[8] The working memory system has a capacity of four items (or fewer) in humans, whereas the capacity of visual phenomenal memory "could be said to be at least 8–32 objects—at any rate for stimuli of the sort used in the Sperling and Landman experiments."[9]

I wish to emphasize again that cognitive access can be achieved via the use of the demonstrative concept *that letter*. Seeing the twelve letters, one is put in a position by one's experience to query the identity of each letter, and to so do, in each case, via a cognitive act that, in part, subsumes the relevant letter under the concept *letter*. The application of the general concept *letter* requires the use of working memory. Furthermore, it permits one to report "That is a letter."

Presumably what Block has in mind when he says that the capacity of the working memory system is four items (or fewer) under a certain restricted range of conditions is the capacity to identify (for example) letters as the specific letters they are. But now his claim about phenomenal consciousness outstripping or overflowing cognitive accessibility, while not without interest, does not have quite the bite it first appears to have. Certainly nothing that Block says here shows that there fails to be an important connection between the phenomenology of the experience one undergoes in seeing an object and the object's general cognitive accessibility.

7.5   A Further Change-Blindness Experiment

In an experiment conducted by Landman et al. (see Lamme 2003), subjects were presented with three different scenarios, as illustrated in figure 7.7. In the top scenario, cuing occurs with the presentation of the second scene; subjects are then asked whether the cued item has changed. In the middle scenario, cuing occurs with the presentation of the first scene. In the bottom scenario, cuing occurs after the disappearance of the first scene but before the presentation of the changed scene. In the middle and bottom scenarios, subjects' performance is almost 100% correct. In the top scenario, they perform poorly.

It appears, then, that cuing after the first scene but before the second scene prevents change blindness. This indicates that cuing draws the subjects' attention to one part of the entire scene, even though the scene is no longer present. Thus, when the cue occurs in the bottom scenario, there must still be a representation of the entire scene at the time of the cue. This whole scene representation has gone by the time the second scene is presented. This is why in the top scenario, unlike the other two, there is change blindness.

The conclusion Lamme draws is that the change-blindness experiments do not show that we lack visual representations of things to which we are not attending. They show, rather, that without suitable attention, some of the information in these representations does not get into working memory. Where information fails to get into working memory, it is not stored in a stable enough way for us to be able to report on what has changed after the change has taken place. According to Lamme (ibid.), the experiments do not demonstrate that we fail to *experience* many items that are not represented in working memory.

Is Lamme right? I accept that we can have visual representations of things and their features to which we are not attending. I also accept that we can experience things that are not in fact conceptually represented (in working memory or elsewhere), and that we can be conscious of things to which we are not attending. However, I want to emphasize

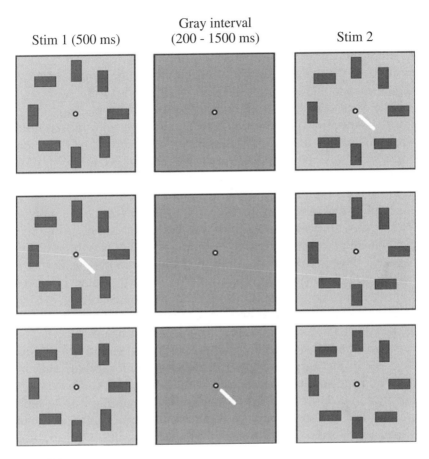

Figure 7.7
In Landman's experiment, there are three scenarios, each involving block figures and a cue. In the top scenario, the cue is presented with the final array of block figures. In the middle scenario, the cue is presented with the initial array of block figures. In the bottom scenario, cuing occurs in the period between the presentation of the two block figure arrays.

again that consciousness of a thing does not come for free as soon as there is a representation of it. For reasons already given, if the experience we are undergoing does not enable us to form a belief or make a judgment about the thing, or at least to wonder what the thing is, then we are not conscious of it.

In the change-blindness experiments, I have argued, it is sometimes the case that we are not conscious of certain things. It is sometimes as if the relevant things are not present at all. Given the direction of our attention, our experience is not sufficiently detailed with respect to the relevant regions of the field of view for it to enable us to pick out things in those regions, to discriminate them from the background. Of course, our eyes *might* have been directed just a little differently. Given the centrality of the things in the field of view, we would *then* have been able to identify them on the basis of our experience and we would not have been victims of change blindness. But the experience we would then have undergone is not the same as our actual experience. We would then have been conscious of some things of which we are not in fact conscious.

It is tempting to infer that once one's attention has been drawn to the item of which (I claim) one was not conscious in a change-blindness scenario, one must have been conscious of it originally, or at least one must have seen it. But the fact is that, with the new attentional focus and conception of the makeup of the scene, one cannot go back to how things were. One has lost one's original innocence. Recapturing it is no more possible than recovering one's youth. One is now conscious of something of which originally one was only *potentially* conscious. One now sees something that originally was only *potentially* seen.

7.6 Another Brick in the Wall

Fred Dretske (2007) takes a view of change blindness opposed to the one argued for here. He claims that in cases of change blindness we really do see the things that differ. We just don't see *that* they differ. He tries to argue for his view by reference to an interesting example involving two walls of bricks. In this section I discuss Dretske's example and his use of it.

In the example, you are asked to suppose that you are viewing the two walls, each with some bricks missing, one after the other with both eyes open from close range for several seconds each. Initially you see the wall in figure 7.8. When you look again (figure 7.9), the wall has changed. The second wall has one extra brick (called 'Sam' by Dretske). You don't see

Figure 7.8
A wall of bricks with many bricks missing.

Figure 7.9
A wall of bricks just like the one in figure 7.8 but with one extra brick.

Figure 7.10
The additional brick is a different color.

that there is any difference between the two walls. Do you see all the bricks in each wall? Do you see Sam in particular? Dretske holds that the right answer to both these questions is Yes. He argues as follows: You know how the wall would have looked if Sam had been blue (figure 7.10). You also know how the wall would have looked if Sam had been tilted (figure 7.11). You know further that the wall didn't look either of these ways. If it had, you would have noticed Sam. You would have picked out Sam immediately. Thus, you know that Sam wasn't blue or tilted. Generalizing, you know that none of the bricks were blue or tilted; and you know this on the basis of how the individual bricks look. But, according to Dretske, you are aware of an object "if your experience enables you to know things about it by the way it looks" (2007, p. 223). Thus, you were aware not only of Sam but also of every other brick in the wall. Thus, you saw Sam and every other brick in the wall.

The obvious response to this line of reasoning is to deny that you know of Sam in particular that it is neither blue nor tilted *on the basis of how it looks*. You may well know this of some bricks on the basis of how they look, but that is no reason to grant that you know this of Sam on that basis.

Dretske considers such a response but rejects it. He claims that you know of each brick in the wall that it is neither blue nor tilted. Since you

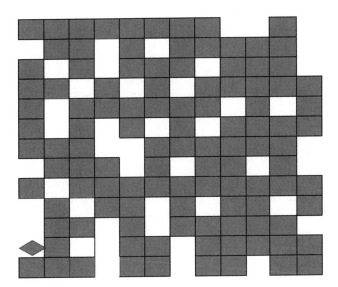

Figure 7.11
The additional brick is tilted.

know that Sam is one of the bricks, you know of Sam that it is neither blue nor tilted. He then adds:

It was, in part, the way Sam looked to you that told you that none of the bricks were blue or tilted. If some other object had occluded Sam, if, therefore, Sam did not look some way to you, you would be unable to tell whether *none* of the bricks were blue or tilted. So it is the way Sam looks that is essential for your knowing what you do about the wall. (2007, pp. 224–5)

This is not persuasive. Why should we grant that if Sam did not look any way to you then you would not have known that none of the bricks were blue or tilted? Dretske's overall reasoning seems to go as follows:

(10) You know on the basis of how the bricks look to you that none of the bricks are blue or tilted.

(11) If you know on the basis of how the bricks look to you that none of the bricks are blue or tilted then for each brick, x, you know partly on the basis of how x looks that none of the bricks are blue or titled,

Thus,

(12) For each brick, x, you know partly on the basis of how x looks to you, that none of the bricks are blue or tilted.

Given that

(13) Sam is one of the bricks,

it follows that

(14) You know partly on the basis of how Sam looks that Sam is neither blue nor tilted.

Thus,

(15) You are visually aware of Sam.

The objectionable premise in this argument is (11). You can know some fact on the basis of how certain things look to you collectively without its being true that you know that fact partly on the basis of how each individual thing in the collection looks to you.

Consider again figure 1.1. As you fixate on the central dot, you know that none of the lines on the left is blue or tilted on the basis of how the lines look, for you see the lines collectively. But you don't know the fact that none of the lines on the left are blue or tilted partly on the basis of how (for example) the fourth line away from the dot looks, for that line in particular does not look any way to you. You do not see that line (as I argued in section 1.4). This is not to say that you do not see *any* of the lines to the left of the dot individually. You do. You see, for example, the line nearest to the dot; similarly, you see the second line in. Still, it is not the case that *each* line to the left of the dot is such that you see it.[10]

Correspondingly, Dretske's opponent can insist that it is not the case that each brick is such that you see it. Given the density of the bricks, Sam could very well be like one of the lines in the middle of the grid to the left of the dot. Perhaps it will be replied that if Sam hadn't looked to you as it does then the bricks wouldn't have looked to you as they do. The way Sam looks contributes to the overall look of the wall. Thus, Sam must look some way to you; the way Sam looks enables you to know of Sam that it is neither blue nor tilted.

This is not persuasive. Consider an example from chapter 1. Suppose I weigh some marbles together on a scale. To argue that if I hadn't weighed one particular marble (in the group) I wouldn't have weighed the marbles—that my weighing this marble contributed to my weighing the marbles—and that therefore, given that I weighed the marbles, I must have weighed this marble, is to engage in unsound reasoning, at least on one plausible interpretation of the term 'weigh'. I didn't weigh this marble. I wasn't able to answer the question "How much does this marble weigh?" on the basis of what I did (which was to put the marbles together on a scale and read it). Even so, I did weigh the marbles. Thus, my weighing this marble didn't contribute to my weighing the marbles (which is not to say that the weight of each marble didn't contribute to the weight of the marbles).

Similarly, my thinking of Mark Sainsbury does not contribute to my thinking of my colleagues that they get along well together. I need not have any thought about Mark Sainsbury in thinking of my colleagues that this is the case. Here is another example. Suppose that the falling rocks dented the car roof. It need not be true that each particular rock dented the car roof. Of course, in some cases the parts do contribute to the whole in the way that Dretske supposes for Sam and the wall. If several girls are positioned in a circle, Jane's being positioned where she is contributes to the girls' being positioned in a circle (assuming that Jane is one of the girls). Similarly, if I eat Cheerios for breakfast, and this is one of the Cheerios, then my eating this Cheerio contributes to my eating the Cheerios. But Dretske needs to show that the Sam case is like the Jane case and the Cheerio case and not like the other cases above. And this he has not done.

In the passage quoted above, Dretske notes that if Sam had been occluded and thus had not looked any way, you would not have noticed Sam even if it had been blue or tilted. In that event, you would not have known of Sam that it is neither blue nor tilted on the basis of how Sam looks. But exactly what this is supposed to establish is not clear.

Dretske is certainly right that if Sam had been occluded then you would not have noticed Sam even if it had been blue or tilted. But in actual fact Sam is not occluded. Can it be true both that in actual fact Sam is not seen even though not occluded and that you know of Sam that, if it had been blue or tilted, you would have noticed it? Dretske appears to think that this is impossible. But nothing that Dretske says provides any reason to believe that this cannot be true.

Let us switch cases for a moment. Consider again the perfectly camouflaged moth on the tree trunk. I would say that it is obvious that you do not see the moth. But if the moth had been blue instead of brown, you would have seen it and noticed it even though in actual fact you cannot differentiate it from the brown background. Thus, if you are told that there is a moth on the tree trunk, you can know of the moth that if it had been blue you would have noticed it. Using this additional information, you are put in a position to form a *de re* propositional attitude with respect to the moth. The same point can be made using individual lines in the middle of the grid of lines to the left of the dot.

Likewise, on the view Dretske is opposing, you do not see Sam. Your actual experience of the second wall does not enable you directly to form any *de re* conceptual attitudes about Sam without relying on any collateral information. You are not conscious of Sam. But if Sam had been blue or tilted, it certainly would have caught your attention. Your gaze, then, would have been different, as would your experience.[11] And in these circumstances, given the different experience you would have undergone, you would have seen Sam and noticed it. Thus, given that you have been told that the two walls differ and that Sam is the difference, you know of Sam that if it had been blue or tilted then you would have noticed it.[12]

The upshot is that Dretske has not established that you know of Sam that is neither blue nor tilted on the basis of how it looks. Thus, Dretske has not established that you are conscious of Sam—that you see Sam. There is thus nothing in Dretske's example that puts pressure on the view I am proposing.

Leonardo da Vinci (1182/1880) said:

Blinding ignorance misleads us
O! wretched mortals, open your eyes.

If what I have argued is correct, then, even with eyes fully open, we may fail to see particular items in the field of view. Blinding ignorance is even more common than Leonardo thought.

8 Privileged Access, Phenomenal Character, and Externalism

As I sit here and stare at the intense blue background on the computer screen before me, I undergo a vivid color experience. In so doing, I am conscious of what it is like for me to undergo this experience. And as I reflect on my situation, it seems to me that I could not be radically wrong about the phenomenal character of my experience. Indeed, it seems to me that there is some sense in which I could not be wrong at all about that phenomenal character. Why is this? Why is it that I cannot be wrong here when surely I can be wrong about other things—for example, whether there is really a computer screen before me? After all, perhaps it just *appears* to me that there is such a screen. Perhaps I am a brain in a vat; perhaps I am having a singularly vivid dream. Why is phenomenal error impossible then?

This question is particularly pressing because of my earlier rejection of the doctrine of phenomenal concepts. The view adopted in chapter 3 seems to allow significant error with respect to the beliefs formed about phenomenal character via introspection. That view also seems to have as a consequence a form of social externalism with respect to phenomenal character; and such a position seems very implausible indeed. The purposes of this chapter are to explain why and how error is impossible with respect to phenomenal character and to show how the position I elucidate not only is fully compatible with the view adopted in chapter 3 on concepts but also does not lead to social externalism concerning phenomenal character. I also want to make some more general remarks about phenomenal character and externalism.

8.1 The Threat to Privileged Access

It is widely accepted that we have privileged access to the contents of our thoughts. On this view, we can know what we are thinking just by

introspecting without engaging in any empirical investigation of our environments. It is also widely accepted that we have privileged access to the
phenomenal character of our experiences—that is, to what it is like for
us subjectively. There is no received formulation of the *privileged access
thesis* for phenomenal character, but one common way to state the thesis
is as follows:

(PA) Necessarily, when our faculty of introspection is functioning normally, if we are in phenomenal state *S*, we can know that that we are in
S simply on the basis of introspection.

For example, necessarily, if I am feeling pain, I can know that I am feeling pain on the basis of introspection, assuming that my faculty of introspection is not impaired.

Some philosophers go further. They insist that when it comes to phenomenal character or what it is like, error is impossible. The resultant
thesis is standardly known as the *incorrigibility thesis*. Again, there is no
received formulation of the incorrigibility thesis, but the following formulation will do for present purposes:

(ICT) Necessarily, for any person *P*, and for any time *t*, if *P* believes,
on the basis of introspection, at *t* that he is in phenomenal state *S*, then
P is in *S* at *t*.[1]

One objection to (ICT) is that the phenomenal state *S* surely plays a
causal role in the formation of the phenomenal belief, at least in normal
cases, and thus must precede that belief in such cases. But according to
(ICT) the two are simultaneous. This objection can be handled by broad-
ening the time of occurrence of *S* to *t* or however long before *t* it takes *S*
to cause (in the standard way) the belief at *t* that *P* is in *S*.

A more serious objection to (ICT) is that, even with the temporal qualification, (ICT) remains an extremely strong thesis to which there are
well-known putative counter-examples. Suppose, for example, you are being tortured. A red-hot poker tip has been touched to your back nine
times. You feel excruciating pain each time. On the tenth occasion, you
see the poker as your torturer moves from in front of you to behind you,
and you expect to feel intense pain again. On this occasion, however, an
ice cube is pressed against your back. For a moment you believe that you
are feeling pain, and you cry out, but then you realize that you were
wrong. You weren't really feeling pain at all; instead you were experiencing a localized feeling of coldness.

Advocates of (ICT) typically respond to counter-examples of this sort
as follows: Even though an error is made in applying the given concept

(in this case, the concept *pain*), there is no error with respect to the phenomenal character of the state itself.[2] Error arises in *classifying* that phenomenal character (for example, as pain). The suggestion, then, is that 'pain' does not name a purely phenomenal state—that is, a state whose essence is a specific phenomenal 'feel'. For purely phenomenal states, classificatory error is impossible.

But why should classificatory error be impossible at a purely phenomenal level? The usual view is that phenomenal states are conceptualized via introspection using phenomenal concepts; and at least on some of the earlier accounts of phenomenal concepts, error is impossible. To appreciate this, consider the mental-sample view. On that view, the phenomenal concept *painfulness* refers to the phenomenal property tokened in an associated mental sample.[3] In the case that one is applying the concept to one's current state via introspection, the phenomenal concept *painfulness* refers to the phenomenal property tokened in one's introspected state (or so it is usually held). Error thus is impossible. A condition of applying the concept introspectively is that one's state token the phenomenal property to which the concept applies.

In chapter 3 I argued against the phenomenal-concepts view. I maintained that there are no phenomenal concepts, conceived of as special concepts, the possession of which requires that one have undergone the relevant experiences. The view for which I argued was that the concepts that enable us to form a conception via introspection of what it is like to experience pain, to see red, to feel a tickle, and so on are no different from nearly all other concepts. They are deferential concepts, the application of which can be corrected by others. If this view is correct, neither (PA) nor (ICT) can pass muster. Since one cannot believe that one is in phenomenal state *S* or know that one is in phenomenal state *S* without applying a concept to that state, if the concept that is applied is deferential then one is not the authority on the application of the concept any more than a layman is an authority on the application of the concept *beech* or the concept *arthritis*. One has only a partial understanding of the concept, and there is room for correction by others who know more. It appears, then, that on the view I am proposing both privileged access and incorrigibility must go. This will seem to many an unfortunate result. I shall return to it in the next section and then again in section 8.4.

8.2 A Burgean Thought Experiment

In chapter 3, following Burge, I noted that color concepts can be over-extended or under-extended. For example, someone might think that a certain shade of color on the border between orange and red was still clearly red. Such a person would likely accept correction from others who confidently agree about the right way to classify the shade. In this way, I noted, color concepts are deferential. This point extends to the phenomenal character of the experience of red. That is a general character common to all and only token experiences of red. Anyone who is willing to accept correction as to whether a certain shade should really be counted as a shade of red should be willing to accept correction as to whether a certain token experience he or she is undergoing should properly be counted as having the phenomenal character of experiences of red, assuming that she takes herself to be a normal perceiver in normal viewing conditions. In section 3.6 I gave reasons for accepting this view. I shall not repeat those reasons here. The point I wish to emphasize is that if it is possible to over-extend or under-extend the concept *red*, as one applies it perceptually, then it must also be possible to over- or under-extend the general concept one applies via introspection of the phenomenal character of the experience of red.

Suppose that the relevant concept is expressible in English in the expression "what it is like to experience red." Suppose also that I am participating in a psychological experiment in which I am shown various color patches and I am asked to report on both the color of the patch and the subjective character of my current color experience. I am shown a patch on the border between orange and red. I say, solely on the basis of my experience, "That patch is red." I am asked to say what my color experience is like. I add "This is what it is like to experience red." The color expert corrects me about the color of the patch, and I accept his correction. In these circumstances, I acknowledge that my color belief was false or at least neither true nor false. So acknowledging, on pain of incoherence, I must also acknowledge that my report of my subjective state was also false or neither true not false, and likewise for the belief I expressed in that report. Thus, privileged access goes out the window, as does incorrigibility (as I noted in the preceding section), or so it seems.

Now suppose, counterfactually, that I am a member of a linguistic community as much like the actual linguistic community to which I belong as is possible consistent with the following change: In the counterfactual community, the word 'red' has a slightly wider extension. In this community, it is correct to call patches with the color of the actual patch I am viewing 'red'. Under the counterfactual scenario, I am a microphysical duplicate of my actual self, and again I issue the reports "That patch is red" and "This is what it is like to experience red" under the same conditions.

In this situation, my belief about the color of the patch is true, as is my belief about the phenomenal character of my state. So microphysical duplicates can differ with respect to their phenomenal color beliefs (the beliefs they form using general concepts, applied on the basis of introspection, to their phenomenal states). In the actual scenario, what I believe about my experience is not true. In the counterfactual scenario, what I believe is true. Thus, what I believe in each of the two situations is different from what I believe in the other. It follows that phenomenal color beliefs "ain't in the head." But the only difference between the actual situation and the counterfactual one is how certain color words are used. Burgean social externalism[4] thus seems to hold not only for beliefs that exercise such concepts as *arthritis* and *beech* but also even for introspectively applied general concepts for phenomenal character (hereafter *PC concepts*). Or more cautiously: Anyone who is moved to adopt social externalism by the original Burge thought experiment for the concept *arthritis*[5] should be moved to hold a similar view for PC concepts.

8.3   Social Externalism for Phenomenal Character?

The question I now want to address is whether social externalism follows from my views on PC concepts for phenomenal character itself. This would be a very worrisome result. Indeed, if it did follow, it seems to me that we would have a *reductio ad absurdum* of the position I am defending.

Let us call the phenomenal character common to (or had by) all and only experiences of the color called 'red' in the counterfactual scenario the *thred* phenomenal character, and let us call the phenomenal character common to (or had by) all and only experiences of red the *red* phenomenal character. These phenomenal characters are different. The thred phenomenal character is definitely the phenomenal character of experiences of color on the border of red and orange; the red phenomenal character is not. Thus, by Leibniz' Law, these characters are not identical. Necessarily, every experience that has the red phenomenal character has the thred phenomenal character, but it is not necessarily true that every experience that thred phenomenal character has the red one.[6]

Here is a comparison: Red is not the same color as scarlet. Still, necessarily every scarlet object is red even though it is not necessarily true that every red object is scarlet.

Now let us see whether social externalism follows for phenomenal character. In the actual scenario, my phenomenal belief is not true. My experience does not definitely have the red phenomenal character, but it does have the thred phenomenal character (see above). In the counterfactual scenario, my phenomenal belief is true and my experience has the thred phenomenal character, but it does not definitely have the red phenomenal character, since the patch I am viewing has a color on the border of red and orange. Thus, social externalism for phenomenal character does *not* follow. Merely changing the meanings of color words does not suffice to generate a change in the color experience's phenomenal character.

Here is another example: Consider the experience of pain, and imagine certain other experiences on the border between the experience of pain and the experience of pressure, as in chapter 3. A person feeling such an experience might well classify it as painful. The concept being applied is one that enables the person to form a conception of what it is like for her. Still, in a typical case, she will accept correction from an expert who says that the experience is really a borderline case of pain and pressure.

Imagine now a counterfactual situation in which it is correct to call such experiences 'painful'. In this situation, the person's report "I am having a painful experience" is true as is the belief she is expressing in that report. But what she believes in the counterfactual scenario when she says "I am having a painful experience" cannot be what she believes in the actual scenario, for in the actual scenario what she believes is not true. Thus, the actual and counterfactual beliefs are different.

Let us call any experience that phenomenologically falls within the pain-or-pressure-bordering-on-pain range a *thainful* experience. In the counterfactual scenario, I am undergoing an experience that is thainful but not definitely painful. In the actual scenario, I am undergoing an experience that is not definitely painful. But it is thainful, since its phenomenal character falls within the broader thainful range. Thus, we do not have a case of microphysical duplicates who differ with respect to the phenomenal character of their internal states. The case is, rather, one of microphysical duplicates who differ in their beliefs.

8.4   A Closer Look at Privileged Access and Incorrigibility

One reaction to what I have said so far is that when it comes to phenomenal character, the subject is the ultimate authority. We can go wrong about whether something is gold or arthritis, and we are perfectly willing to accept corrections from experts or others who confidently agree on such matters, but we may reasonably reject their corrections insofar as they pertain to the phenomenal character of our experiences. If the position I am advancing requires a rejection of privileged access, so much the worse for that position.

I am happy to grant that there is something right in this reply. When I introspect an experience, I do know the phenomenal character of my experience—and I know this whatever anyone else may say. However, to the extent that the knowledge I have is factual, there will be cases in which I am prepared to be corrected by others. That is what I have argued above. I have not claimed that we could not have general concepts for phenomenal character whose application conditions are determined by my non-deferential dispositions. My claim is, rather, that this is not how the general concepts we apply to our experiences via introspection typically work. These concepts are just like other concepts. There is nothing special about them. Ordinary people possess such concepts even though they have only a partial understanding of them. And even people who have not undergone the relevant experiences can possess the concepts. Thus, error is possible in the application of such concepts. Even so, it seems to me that we do have a kind of privileged access to the phenomenal character of our experiences. Indeed, it seems to me that there is a kind of incorrigibility. It is just that the appropriate kinds of privileged access and incorrigibility are not well captured in the theses (PA) and (ICT). Those theses are false. This needs some explanation. Let me begin with the case of color.

Consider again the intense blue color of the computer monitor screen at which I am staring. It seems to me that it is conceivable that the color of which I am conscious in undergoing my present experience is not the color blue. Conceivably I am misclassifying the color. Conceivably I am wrong in believing that *that* color is the color blue. But this, of course, is a failure to know with certainty a particular truth. It is not a failure to know a thing. And in failing to know with certainty the relevant truth, I do not fail to be conscious of the color I am experiencing. Thus, I do not thereby fail to know the entity I know. I still know it simply by being directly conscious of it. I know it by acquaintance.

My knowledge of color, then, is immune from error in that there is no truth which I can doubt or fail to know such that in doubting or failing to know that truth I fail to know the color. Simply by being directly conscious of the color I know it. I may perhaps doubt that I know it; I may not know that I know it, but know it I do simply by being directly acquainted with it. As I noted in chapter 5, this was essentially Russell's view.

Consider now my *experience* of blue as I view the computer screen. I am conscious of the phenomenal character of my color experience, of what it is like for me color-wise. Is it possible that there is error with respect to the phenomenal character of my current experience? Well, yes. A certain sort of classificatory error seems possible. I may be wrong in classifying myself as having a phenomenally 'blue' experience. Conceivably the color I am experiencing is teal and I am wrong in taking it to be blue. Conceivably my classificatory mechanisms have been tinkered with by a deceitful demon intent on confusing me. Still, this is error with respect to a truth or factual error. And knowledge of phenomenal character, I urged in chapter 5, is not factual knowledge. It does not involve *de dicto* awareness.

As I view the monitor screen, I am experiencing a certain color and I know that color just by being aware of it. I am also aware of the phenomenal character of my experience by being aware of the color. I cannot conceive of the color experience's phenomenal character coming apart from the experienced color. It is a conceptual truth that if the color I am experiencing changes, the color experience's phenomenal character changes too. The explanation I offered for this in chapter 5 was that the phenomenal character of my experience just is the color my experience represents.

Thus, by knowing the color, I know the color experience's phenomenal character. And just as there is no truth which I can doubt or fail to know such that in doubting or failing to know that truth I fail to know the color, so there is no corresponding truth[7] such that in doubting or failing to know that truth I fail to know the phenomenal character of my color experience. My knowledge of the color is, in the sense just offered, immune from error; and my knowledge of my color experience's phenomenal character is immune from error in a corresponding sense too. I know that character by acquaintance.

Thus, (PA) and (ICT) are false. They are open to counter-examples. But the reason they are false is that they are stated in such a way that they involve factual knowledge and *de dicto* belief. Where deferential concepts are concerned, the ordinary users of the concepts are not the final authority. They do not have privileged access. They can be corrected by others. Error is possible.

Suppose, however, that (PA) and (ICT) are strongly restricted so that the relevant factual knowledge is demonstrative. Then the earlier criticisms no longer apply.[8] In the case of (PA), the restricted version goes as follows:

(PAdem) Necessarily, when our faculty of introspection is functioning normally, if we are in phenomenal state *S*, we can know that we are in a state having or involving *this*, where the concept *this* refers to the phenomenal character of *S*, simply on the basis of introspection.[9]

Since we have thing knowledge of the phenomenal character of S, we are put in a position to demonstrate it—to think of it as *this*—by our thing knowledge. Furthermore, our thing knowledge is provided by acquaintance with the phenomenal character of S. We have such acquaintance via our undergoing an experience that represents the quality that is the phenomenal character of S. Thus, using our faculty of introspection, we can know the truth that we are in a state involving the demonstrated property.

Corresponding to (ICT) is the following restricted demonstrative thesis:

(ICTdem) Necessarily, for any person P, and for any time t, if P believes, on the basis of introspection, at t that she is in a state with this phenomenal character, where the concept *this* P exercises in her belief refers to the phenomenal character of which P is conscious at t, then P's belief is true.

8.5   How Do I Know That I Am Not a Zombie?

I argued in chapter 3 that the general concepts I have that enable me to form a conception of the phenomenal character of my experiences do not require that I actually have any experiences at all. These concepts are ones that a zombie in our linguistic community could possess. Thus, when I feel pain, and I believe that I do, my zombie replica believes that he feels pain too. It is just that his belief, unlike mine, is false. There is, then, nothing in the general concepts I possess that rules out the possibility that I am a zombie.

However, I know that I am not a zombie. How do I know this? Fred Dretske raises this question and finds himself unable to come up with a satisfactory answer. Drestke supposes that to uncover a satisfactory answer we must find some item of which we are aware that tells us that we are aware. He comments:

What makes us so different from zombies are not the things (objects, facts, properties) we are aware of but our awareness of them, but this, our awareness of things, is not something we are, at least not in perceptual experience, aware of. So if you are, as you surely are, aware that you are not a zombie—aware, that is, that you are aware of things—what is it you are aware of that tells you this? (2003, p. 2)

It is tempting to reply that introspection tells us that we are aware of things. However, according to Drestke, what we are aware of when we introspect is not our awareness of things in the case of perceptual experience, but simply the qualities and things represented by our experience. In the case of thought, what we are aware of via introspection is the content of the thought and not the fact that we are thinking the thought.

Dretske's last claim here is very contentious. After all, it certainly seems to us that we form beliefs to the effect that we are thinking so-and-so on the basis of introspection. This being so, why not suppose that we also form beliefs that we are experiencing so-and-so on the basis of introspection?[10] Dretske claims that this is a mistake. In his view, the job of introspection is only to tell us what we are aware of and what we are thinking, not that we are aware or that we are thinking. In this respect, Dretske claims, introspection is like perception. If I perceive an orange, for example, my perceptual faculty informs me of the presence of an orange before me. That is its job. It does not tell me that I am perceiving an orange.

At the level of the things of which we are aware, then, there is no difference between a zombie and me. Thus, there is nothing of which I am aware that tells me that I am not a zombie. So how do I know that I am not?

To see that Dretske has not succeeded in raising a new and distinctively different epistemological problem here, consider the question "How do I know that there is an external world?" In this case, are there any items of which I am aware that tell me that there is an external world? Suppose it is replied that there are. At the present moment, for example, I am aware of an orange. On the assumption that the orange of which I am aware is a real, mind-independent orange and not merely a hallucinated one, the orange of which I am aware tells me that there is an external world.

One who gives this reply can say that likewise, on the assumption that the orange is genuinely *experienced* by me and not merely related to me in such a way that I mistakenly take the relationship to be one of experience, it follows that I have experiences and thus that I am not a zombie. The orange "tells" me that I have experiences just as much it "tells" me that there is an external world.

Suppose, however, it is agreed that in the perceptual case this is wrongheaded: there is no item of which I am aware that tells me that there is an external world. Then again, why not agree that there is no item of which I am aware that tells me that I am aware in the introspective case? So far as I can see, there is nothing *special* about the epistemological problem Dretske is raising. Whatever we say to the Cartesian skeptic about the external world we also can say to the zombie skeptic.

One strategy for replying to the Cartesian skeptic is to appeal to a type of warrant that, in Crispin Wright's words, "we do not have to do any specific evidential work to earn" (2004). Wright calls this sort of warrant *entitlement*. Obviously the project of developing a full account of our epistemic entitlements is a large one, but my point for present purposes is simply that there is no obvious reason why this strategy for responding to the Cartesian skeptic cannot be used to handle the zombie skeptic too.

A closely related strategy for dealing with the Cartesian skeptic is to adopt the epistemological stance of the dogmatist (Pryor 2000). According to the dogmatist, given the absence of a good reason to disbelieve the ordinary view of ourselves as living in a material world, the character of which is made manifest to us by our sense organs, we are warranted in believing that such is our situation. Again, there is no obvious reason why this strategy could not be employed with respect to the question of how I know that I am not a zombie. In the absence of a good reason to disbelieve the ordinary view that each of us is conscious of things in the environment and (in some cases) our own bodies, we are warranted in believing that view.

I am not suggesting here that there is not much more to say on the general topic of skepticism, nor am I strongly endorsing the approaches just mentioned. My point is only that *prima facie* the zombie scenario raises no special epistemological trouble.[11]

8.6 Phenomenal Externalism

Phenomenal externalism is the doctrine that it is metaphysically possible for intrinsic duplicates to differ with respect to the phenomenal character of their internal states. Given physicalism, this reduces to the doctrine that it is metaphysically possible for microphysical duplicates to differ phenomenally. In chapter 5, I opted for the radical view that the phenomenal character of an experience consists in the cluster of properties represented by the experience. This view generates a version of phenomenal externalism, if the representation of properties by experiences is itself wide or externalist. Until very recently, orthodoxy in the philosophy of mind has favored phenomenal internalism. The received view has been that phenomenal externalism is obviously false.

It does seem clear that *social* externalism for phenomenal character is a very implausible doctrine. But, in my view, there is nothing immediately implausible about phenomenal externalism when it is freed from any social ties. Some philosophers have supposed that such a doctrine cannot get off the ground, since it conflicts with privileged access. However, privileged access of the sort expressed in (PA) does not exist, and there is no obvious conflict between externalism and privileged access of the sort that is grounded in knowledge by acquaintance of phenomenal character, as expressed in (PAdem). Such knowledge is derived from acquaintance, and *prima facie* there is no more difficulty in supposing that microphysically identical creatures might be acquainted with different qualities than there is in supposing that such creatures might see different particulars. Acquaintance with a quality Q involves standing in a certain psychological relation to Q. The externalist claims that the relevant relation brings in external, environmental conditions just as seeing does.

What other reasons are there for rejecting phenomenal externalism?

The first reason that might be offered is that the immediate causes of phenomenal states are neural states. There is a direct causal dependence between the phenomenal and the neural. So, of course, if you fix what goes on in the brain, you fix what goes on at the level of phenomenology. To this I reply that causal dependence does not establish metaphysical dependence. If it did, externalism about belief contents would be refuted by the same reasoning. And nobody believes that.

A second reason is that empirical work on color vision traces the phenomenology of color experiences to opponent processing channels in the brain. Differences in color experience phenomenology are explained by reference to different activation levels in these neuronal channels (Pautz 2006). So, again if you fix the brain events, you fix the phenomenal character, or at least the phenomenal character of color experience.

My reply is that explanatory dependence does not establish metaphysical dependence. Consider the hypothesis that the fire started *because* of the short circuit. Suppose that this hypothesis is true. The fact that an identical short circuit in a different setting did not start a fire is no objection to the proposed hypothesis, for explanation is relative to a background context. The short circuit explains why there was a fire, but the short circuit alone does not metaphysically necessitate a fire. Other factors extrinsic to the short circuit are relevant. Analogously, the phenomenal externalist claims that for a state to have the phenomenal character it does, the relevant necessitating factors include matters outside the brain.[12]

A third reason is provided by the observation that I might conceivably be a brain in a vat, wired to a computer that is supplying me with inputs. This being so, how things are outside the brain does not really matter to phenomenology. If the brain states are the same, the phenomenology must be the same, whatever the external causes (Horgan and Tiensen 2002).

In response, the externalist can grant that it is both conceptually and metaphysically possible that human brains in vats have experiences. The externalist can also grant that I might now be a brain in a vat. Consistent with this, the externalist can insist that not all possible microphysical duplicates share phenomenally identical experiences, for some of these metaphysically possible duplicates differ with respect to their environmental setting or evolutionary history and some have no evolutionary history at all (in the case of accidental replicas). To assume that such possible external differences make no phenomenal difference is simply to assume the truth of phenomenal internalism.

Consider the following scenario: On the planet Xenon, there are massive trees. These trees produce many very large, hanging pods every 4 years. The pods grow gradually and depend for their development on the copious rainfall that is found on Xenon. When the contents of the pods are ready for harvesting, their shells begin to crack open. This process is hastened by the many electrical storms that occur. Lightning often strikes the trees, and the electricity is conducted throughout the tree limbs and into the bodies of the pods, thereby causing them to split apart once they have grown to a certain size.

The contents of the pods are eaten by the people who live on Xenon (Xenonites, as I shall call them). These people are very different from us. Their physiology is not brain-and-spine-based, as ours is. Instead, their minds function hydraulically. Tiny pieces of an organic metal, combined with a liquid that looks like water but is really something chemically very different, flow along the flexible tubes that constitute their internal anatomy. Sometimes, the Xenonites are so anxious to eat the pods' contents that they go out during the storms and devour them straight from the trees as the pods split open.

The pods themselves are each large enough to contain a human brain, and remarkably their contents, just before harvesting, are chemically very like human brains in which there is no activity. Even more remarkably, one particular pod (call it 'XP1'), during an electrical storm that infuses it with electricity for 15 minutes, is actually a microphysical *duplicate* of an active brain—one belonging to a human being who for the same period of time on Earth initially is having sex and then (after 8 minutes) smoking a cigarette and drinking green chartreuse.

I take it to be obvious that the pods' contents are not themselves genuine brains. On rare occasion, they may briefly be microphysically identical to live human brains, as with XP1 for 15 minutes, but brains they are not. In making this assertion I am not supposing that there cannot be brains without bodies. Clearly there can be brains in vats or brains removed from bodies that are subsequently destroyed. However, in these cases, it is at least true that the brains were *designed* to control the bodies of the creatures to which they belong or did belong, even if those creatures no longer exist or have had their usual bodies taken from them. Nor do I wish to deny that swamp brains are possible; intuitively, a molecule-by-molecule duplicate of my brain that is functioning *as* a brain inside a body is a brain even if it was accidentally created by a chemical reaction that took place in a swamp.

What I am denying is that something becomes a brain *simply* by replicating a brain microphysically. We don't suppose that something becomes a key just by replicating a key microphysically. Think, for example, of a plastic card that happens to replicate a card key but is actually designed for use as a credit card for photocopying articles at a library. Nor do we suppose that something becomes a tiger just by being a microphysical duplicate of a tiger. If the thing has the wrong evolutionary history, it isn't a tiger no matter how closely it resembles one. A voltmeter, as all will agree, doesn't become a speedometer unless it is designed (or at least used) to measure speed. An intrinsically identical voltmeter used to measure volume may be a fuel gauge instead. Similarly, a microphysical duplicate of my little finger that is actually a toe on a three-headed Martian is not also a finger. The same points apply *mutatis mutandis* to microphysical duplicates of human brains.

XP1, then, is not a brain. It was not designed by nature to function as a brain, nor has it become a brain by taking on the appropriate control role with respect to a body. Does XP1, for the period of time during the storm in which it is microphysically identical to a particular human brain, undergo experiences phenomenally identical to experiences of the relevant human on Earth? Indeed, does XP1 undergo *any* experiences? It seems to me that the *intuitive* answer to both of these questions is No. There is something it is *like* for the human being during the specified 15 minutes. She experiences a variety of pleasurable tactile, visual, gustatory, and olfactory sensations. But intuitively, I would say, there is *nothing* it is like for XP1.[13]

The Xenon example provides us with a possible case in which a standardly embodied creature with a brain and a microphysical duplicate of that brain differ phenomenally (or so it seems to me intuitively).

It does not yet involve total microphysical duplicates. However, there is a simple extension of the thought experiment that does: Let the subject on Earth be someone whose body has been destroyed and whose brain has been envatted and subsequently is supplied by inputs from a super-computer, so that XP1 is now a microphysical duplicate of a person who is systematically hallucinating the act of sexual intercourse followed by smoking a cigarette and drinking green chartreuse. Now, in my view, there is complete microphysical duplication and phenomenal difference.

Not everyone will agree with my assessment, of course. Some will, no doubt, dig in their heels and insist that XP1 is a brain and that it does have phenomenally identical experiences for the 15-minute period, however strange that initially seems. For present purposes, this does not matter. My main point is that in some cases we are all happy to grant that microphysical duplicates of normal human brains undergo experiences (as with the brain-in-a-vat scenario), but in other cases, *at a minimum*, it is far from clear-cut (as with the above scenario). Appealing to the brain-in-a-vat scenario, then, fails to provide strong evidence against phenomenal externalism.

A fourth reason for being an internalist is that the phenomenal character of an experience is an intrinsic property of the experience. So, of course, intrinsic duplicates must be alike phenomenally.

Too fast, I respond. How should we understand 'intrinsic' here? 'Intrinsic' sometimes means *essential*. Consider the token visual experience I am undergoing now, as I view the page before me. This very experience could not have had a different phenomenal character. If I had been having a visual experience with a different phenomenal character, then it would not have been *this* very experience. If the phenomenal character of my experience is essential to it, then its phenomenal character is intrinsic to it in the above sense. If this is how we understand what it is for a property to be intrinsic, then the argument of the phenomenal internalist is straightforwardly invalid.

If this is not obvious, consider the property of being caused by a mosquito. This, let us grant, is an intrinsic property in the above sense of a mosquito bite. Patently it does not follow from this that individuals who are intrinsic duplicates must be alike with respect to whether they have skin punctures that have been caused by a mosquito.

There is another sense of 'intrinsic', however, that contrasts with extrinsic, and it is on the question whether the phenomenal character of an experience is an intrinsic property in this sense that the phenomenal internalist and the phenomenal externalist disagree.

The recent literature on the metaphysics of intrinsic properties shows that it is not easy to say in full detail just what an intrinsic property is in the second sense.[14] For our purposes, however, the following remarks will suffice:

[An intrinsic property is] a property a thing has (or lacks) regardless of what is going on outside of itself. (Yablo 1990, p. 479)

The intrinsic properties of something depend only on that thing; whereas the extrinsic properties may depend, wholly or partly, on something else. (Lewis 1983, p. 197)

If some thing has an intrinsic property, then so does any perfect duplicate of that thing; whereas duplicates situated in different surroundings will differ in their extrinsic properties. (Lewis 1983, p. 197)

Thus, being a sister is extrinsic, as is being 3 feet from a table. In contrast, having mass is intrinsic, as is being round (unless the shape of a thing can be made to vary with the curvature of the space in which it is located).

Given the above understanding of an intrinsic property, once again it does not follow simply from the assumption that the phenomenal character of an experience is one of its intrinsic properties that individuals who are intrinsic duplicates cannot differ phenomenally. To see this, consider the state of shaking hands with a stranger. Touching something else is an intrinsic property of this state, but *individuals* who are intrinsic duplicates could still be such that one is shaking hands with a stranger (and thus is touching something else) and the other is not.

Furthermore, and more importantly, why should we now accept the assumption? One reply is that the truth of the assumption is revealed by introspection. But this is not so. In my view, and for reasons that by now should be fully clear, introspection does not reveal the phenomenal character of an experience either to be an intrinsic property of the experience or to be an extrinsic property of it. Indeed, introspection does not reveal phenomenal character to be a property of experience at all. The phenomenal character of my current experience, for example, is something I confront in undergoing the experience. It is a property (or better, a cluster of properties) represented by the experience.

None of the reasons discussed above for being a phenomenal internalist puts any real pressure on phenomenal externalism. In my view, phenomenal externalism is a plausible and appealing position that goes naturally with the thesis that phenomenal character is itself out there in the world.

If microphysical duplicates can have different histories, different beliefs, and different desires, and if they can see and touch different objects, why not also hold that (in some possible cases) they can be acquainted with different phenomenal characters? If meanings ain't in the head, then why insist that qualia are in there?[15] For the thoroughly modern materialist, the thesis of phenomenal internalism, like the doctrine of phenomenal concepts, should be "committed to the flames."[16] Only then will all vestiges of Cartesianism be eliminated from the materialist worldview.

Notes

Chapter 1

1. There is an ongoing debate about whether propositional-attitude states have their own proprietary phenomenal character. In some cases, it seems obvious that they do not. Patently there is nothing it is like to believe that two plus two equals four. After all, that is a belief we have when we are fast asleep. Sometimes, of course, beliefs manifest themselves in conscious thought. So manifested, is there anything it is like to have a belief? Is there an experience of consciously thinking that two plus two equals four? Most philosophers are willing to concede that *associated* with conscious thoughts are quasi-linguistic images or auditory experiences of words being spoken, where these states do have phenomenal character. But some insist that there is a further phenomenology over and above the imagistic and sensory phenomenology that may accompany conscious thoughts. This additional phenomenology is proprietary to the thoughts themselves. I fall into the deflationary camp. My reasons are given in Tye 1996 and 2003a. For the opposing view, see Horgan and Tiensen 2002; Strawson 1995; Pitt 2004.

2. For the opposing view on absent qualia, see Shoemaker 1980. Also see Tye 2006a. I should add that my 2006 view rests on an acceptance of phenomenal concepts and thus is at odds with my present position.

3. For a defense of the perceptual model for understanding higher-order consciousness, see Armstrong 1968; see also Lycan 1996. For a defense of the higher-order thought theory, see Rosenthal 1986 and forthcoming.

4. "Consciousness," Locke famously remarked, "is the perception of what passes in a Man's own mind." (*Essay Concerning Human Understanding*, book II, chapter 1, section 19)

5. The doctrine of transparency dates back to a comment made by G. E. Moore in his 1922 about the diaphonousness of consciousness. Moore held that if, for example, we try to focus our attention on the sensation of blue, our attention slips right through the sensation to the color blue. For more on transparency, see chapter 5 of the present volume.

6. This oversimplifies their view a little, but for present purposes the oversimplification doesn't matter.

7. For example, it might be held that I could undergo a color experience *e* such that, in undergoing *e*, it appears to me that surface *s* has this shade, where this shade is the determinate color of which I am directly aware at the time.

8. In this case, the color of which one is directly aware is un-instantiated (locally). Some philosophers take this to be problematic; but it is part and parcel of naïve commonsense. If one hallucinates a pink elephant, one encounters pinkness in one's experience. Pink is present to one's consciousness. On the basis of such an encounter with pinkness, one can know what it is like to experience pink. Further veridical experience is not needed.

9. For example, I can experience a finger moving now. This experience isn't just a succession of different experiences of the finger in different positions. At any given moment, it is an experience of the *movement* of the finger. That cannot occur unless there is an experienced present relative to which movement is itself experienced. Just how long the specious present is in objective time is a matter of some dispute. There is evidence that it lasts at least 30 milliseconds. See Tye 2003a, p. 87.

10. An argument of this sort is given in Dretske 2004. See also Dretske 2007.

11. For causal analyses of seeing, see Grice 1961; Dretske 1969; Tye 1982.

12. For more on the nature of perceptual content, see chapter 4.

13. I do not mean to suggest that the datum is sacrosanct. See my comments in the next two paragraphs in the text on ordinary beliefs and seeing.

14. For an appeal to differentiation, see Dretske 1969. See also Siegel 2006.

15. If indeed there is such a thing as the collection of pencils. For relevant comments on plurals, see section 1.4 below.

16. It is surprising how close to the center of the field of view the pencils need to be moved in order for the color of each pencil to become manifest. See O'Regan 2001/2002.

17. Nor, as I said in note 8 above, need the color of which I am conscious be instantiated. In cases of visual hallucination (and illusion), subjects are conscious of colors.

18. The claim that seeing an object is in certain respects like drawing a picture should not be taken to assume that intrinsic qualities of the mental picture are accessible to introspection in the way that intrinsic features of the blobs of paint on a canvas picture are accessible to perceptual awareness. Indeed, I reject this assumption.

19. I return to the issue of seeing and attention in chapter 7.

20. See Marr 1982.

21. As the time period between the presentation of the disk and the ring is increased, the ring loses its role as a mask. There is then sufficient time for information transfer and attention, and consciousness of the disk is restored. For a general discussion of time and the content of experience, see Tye 2003a.

22. For more on unilateral visual neglect, see Farah 1991.

23. In some cases, these subjects can attend to objects that are moved from outside the neglected field to inside it, provided that they focus on the objects as they are so moved.

24. People with blindsight have large blind areas or scotoma in their visual fields, due to brain damage in the post-geniculate region (typically the occipital cortex), and yet, under certain circumstances, they can issue accurate statements with respect to the contents of those areas. See Weiskrantz 1986. For example, in forced choice tests, blindsight subjects can make accurate guesses with respect to such things as presence, position, orientation, and movement of visual stimuli. They can also guess correctly as to whether an X is present or an O. Some blindsight patients can even issue accurate guesses with respect to colors in the blind field.

25. I am not claiming, of course, that one and the same experience cannot change its phenomenal character through time. Think, for example, of the auditory experience of a kettle whistle as the water boils. One experiences a change in the noise as the steam pressure increases; but intuitively there is a single auditory experience that continues as long as the noise. Throughout this book, I write as if I accept the view that there really are token perceptual experiences, considered as discrete episodes. But at a deeper level, I am opposed to such episodes. For more on this metaphysical issue, see Tye 2003a.

Chapter 2

1. Of course this is just a picture, for if God exists then there is a nonphysical concrete being and physicalism is naturally taken to be false.

2. Not all physicalists accept that physicalism should be elucidated in this way (even in first approximation). See Melnyk 2003.

3. This has been emphasized by Terry Horgan (1993), among others.

4. Sometimes 'fact' is used as a synonym for 'state of affairs'. If 'fact' is used in this way, facts are identical just in case they contain the same worldly entities structured in the same way. On this view, the fact that Michael Tye is tall, for example, is the same as the fact that I am tall. This fact is an actual state of affairs—a state of affairs that obtains—and it contains Michael Tye and the property of being tall. There is also a fine-grained use of 'fact' under which facts are partly conceptual entities that are identical just in case the components of the relevant identical worldly states of affairs are conceived in the same way. This use of the term 'fact' often figures in statements of a priori physicalism (see below); and in the context of my discussion of a priori physicalism, I use 'fact' in the fine-grained way.

5. More on this later in the chapter.

6. See, e.g., Chalmers and Jackson 2001; Chalmers 1996.

7. Unfortunately this doesn't work. See chapter 3.

8. The claim that water is a watery stuff of our acquaintance will suffice here. Chalmers and Jackson (2001) offer a less forthright way of a priori deducing the

truth of (4) from (1) and (2). They simply assert that if physicalism is true, it must be possible for a sufficiently rational subject to deduce the truth of (4) *a priori* from the microphysical and indexical facts via a complex conditional or sequence of such conditionals that is knowable *a priori*. Their view is that, given knowledge of the microphysical and indexical facts such a subject can determine *a priori* that there is a watery stuff of our acquaintance covering most of the Earth. Knowing that, the same subject can deduce *a priori* that there is water covering most of the Earth. For more here, see chapter 3.

9. This argument is offered by Chalmers (1996).

10. There is a burgeoning literature on the Mary puzzle. It has spawned two recent collections of essays (Alter and Walter 2006; Ludlow et al. 2004), and there are many published articles devoted to Mary. For those that are online (at the time of writing there were 43), see the knowledge argument at http://consc.net/online1.html#knowledge.

11. The actual semantic properties of the sounds make no causal difference with respect to the shattering of the wine glass. The sounds do not cause the shattering in virtue of their semantic properties.

12. One complaint that is sometimes lodged against physicalism is that, insofar as it permits mental properties to be non-neurological properties that are *realized* by neurological properties, it has the consequence that mental properties lose their causal efficacy just as they do on the view that they are non-physical. This complaint can be answered so long as the physicalist can point to properties of pieces of behavior, the presence of which depends on the presence of the mental properties. If the mental properties are identified with wide functional properties, for example, the relevant behavioral properties will be wide.

13. Still, it may reasonably be questioned whether the case of Merlin and Morgana is fully coherent, since we are asked to suppose that Merlin's spell brings about its effect directly without any intervening chain of transmission. In the well-known case of the major who orders "Retreat!" and the sergeant who issues the same order, where the major's order trumps the sergeant's and thereby causes the troops to retreat, the relevant counterfactual seems to me true. This is because while the situation is such that if the major hadn't issued any order *and* the sergeant had ordered "Retreat!" the troops would still have retreated, this is not the relevant scenario. In the nearest possible world in which the major does not order "Retreat!" he issues another order (rather than no order at all) and the troops follow that order. So, if the major had not ordered "Retreat!" the troops would not have retreated; this is why, according to the counterfactual view of causation, the major's order caused the retreat of the troops. However, with appropriate modifications, the standard major-sergeant case does seem to me to create real trouble for the counterfactual analysis.

14. On Yablo's account, (C) is true so long as the closest world to the actual world in which Paul is in pain without S_1 occurring is one in which another microphysical state S_2 realizes the state of Paul's being in pain, where S_2 is a state whose tokening causally necessitates screaming.

15. Leiter and Miller (1994) raise this sort of objection for LePore and Loewer (1987).

Chapter 3

1. This is to oversimplify a little. A further assumption is that the thought ascribed is a present thought. We have privileged access to the contents of our present thoughts, not to the contents of our past ones. (See McLaughlin and Tye 1998.) Attributions of past thought contents should be treated in the same way as third-person attributions.

2. For other uses of the term 'concept,' and for a helpful discussion of nonconceptual content, see Byrne 2004.

3. This is not to say, of course, that phenomenal concepts do not refer to physical entities. The concept *this* is not a physical concept, nor is the concept *I*, but it does not follow that these concepts pick out nonphysical items.

4. The notion of an image or a quasi-image is to be understood broadly here so that it covers a phenomenal memory of pain, for example. The latter is a phenomenal state that faintly echoes real pain, a state that may elicit a mental shudder or grimace.

5. Here and throughout this chapter, I write as if I accept the dogma that phenomenal properties are intrinsic properties of images and experiences. That, of course, is not my real view. (See Tye 1995, 2000.) For present purposes, whether phenomenal qualities are qualities of experiences or qualities represented by experiences does not matter. The story I have to tell about phenomenal concepts will apply to either view with minor (and obvious) modifications.

6. More on this shortly.

7. Block seems to be aware of the difficulty here. His response is: "My tentative thought is that there is a form of 'taking' that does not amount to a further concept but is enough to explain dispositions." (2006b, p. 48, n. 31) It is hard to see what he might have in mind.

8. Appealing to attention with respect to one of the properties does not save the proposal. See p. 45.

9. Balog shows some awareness of this difficulty. See her forthcoming essay.

10. See note 7.

11. This was pointed out to me by Derek Ball.

12. In general, I prefer to say that there is just one demonstrative concept, namely the concept *this* that varies in its content from context to context; but this does not matter for present purposes.

13. Note incidentally that this account itself entails that phenomenal concepts refer directly.

14. As to what counts as a physical concept, one possible view is that such concepts are expressible in the language of microphysics, chemistry, neurophysiology

or molecular biology. Another possible account of a physical concept is that it is any concept the application of which is *a priori* deducible from the microphysical truths. These two accounts are not obviously equivalent. One might reasonably question whether the application of the concepts of neurophysiology is *a priori* deducible from the microphysical truths. For present purposes, which alternative is preferred does not matter.

15. See chapter 2.

16. The notion of a aprioricity I am operating with here is the same notion used by Chalmers and by Jackson. For example, Chalmers (1996, p. 62) says that "Water is watery stuff" is *a priori* and adds: "Such a statement will be true no matter how the actual world turns out, although it need not hold in nonfactual possible worlds."

17. For further trenchant criticisms of conceptual analysis of the sort favored by Jackson and Chalmers, see Laurence and Margolis 2003.

18. Of course, if phenomenal concepts are taken to include the purely demonstrative concept *this*, then it is natural to hold right away that at least some phenomenal concepts can be possessed without undergoing any particular experience. This is not to contest the claim that, in standard cases, one cannot *exercise* the concept *this* with respect to a given experience without undergoing the experience.

19. For arguments here and a proposal about the nature of phenomenal character, see chapter 5.

20. Derek Ball (forthcoming) emphasizes this, and here and in the last argument I am influenced by a discussion with him.

21. This is the view I took in Tye 2006a. When I wrote that essay, I still accepted the phenomenal-concept strategy and the argument in it—that absent qualia are conceptually impossible—presupposes the viability of that strategy.

22. Could Mary acquire the concept 'R' expresses without having interacted with someone who introduces her to the term 'R'? Maybe not. But this is of no consequence. Could you acquire the concept that 'Tully' expresses if you had never been introduced to the term 'Tully'?

23. These points hold even on the view—which I reject—that there is no one phenomenal character common to all and only experiences of red. Let 'R' stand for the phenomenal character of *my* experiences of red. Mary in her room, by interacting with me, can acquire the concept I express by 'R'. She does not need to experience R in order to acquire the concept. She can think thoughts that exercise my concept and she can disagree with me.

24. This suggestion was made by Chalmers in a presentation, as yet unpublished, titled "From the Aufbau to the Canberra Plan."

25. I take it that full understanding does not require complete knowledge. If it did, even today's experts would not count as having full understanding of the terms they use. Furthermore, if complete knowledge were a requirement, then 'water' would not be Twin Earthable under conditions of full understanding. To appreciate this, consider someone located on earth who fully understands

'water'. On the current proposal, this person must grasp that water is H_2O. Her Twin Earth counterpart must likewise fully understand 'water', as it is used on Twin Earth. Thus, the latter person must grasp that twater is XYZ. But now these two individuals cannot be intrinsic duplicates, since their narrow verbal behavior will be different. For example, the former, if asked "Is water H_2O?" will say "Yes"; the latter will not. Thus, 'water' is no longer Twin Earthable.

26. There are also historical differences. I have discussed these various differences elsewhere (Tye 1995, 2000).

27. As he stares into the two tubes, Smith has two independent visual fields, each containing a red spot. But this is of no help to Smith in his putative deduction, since he cannot tell which of the two visual fields *is* his left field and which *is* his right.

28. Nor does it help to appeal to the statement "That is the region that appears to me to be on the left (right) of a red, round visual field." Since there is no integrated visual field, no part of the left field bears any visual phenomenal relations to any part of the right field. Incidentally, *T* cannot restrict itself to what is implied by *P* and only what is implied by *P*, since, given that there are facts not implied by *P*, namely indexical ones, *T* will then come out false. This problem can be handled by enlarging *T* to cover what is implied by *P* and the appropriate indexical truths (see chapter 2) and only what is implied by *P* and the appropriate indexical truths.

Chapter 4

1. Not everyone accepts this claim. A notable exception is Travis (2004).

2. Not all disjunctivists grant that in cases of illusion perceptual experiences have contents of the same sort as veridical perceptual experiences. See, e.g., Martin 2006. Obviously those disjunctivists who take this view cannot use the present consideration to motivate their view.

3. Assuming that the term 'singular content' is used in the usual way. For an opposing usage, see Sainsbury 2006.

4. This is an over-simplification. For example, Martin sometimes seems to hold that there is no distinctive mental event or state common to these various disjoint situations. But Martin also says that "the disjunctive view itself should be viewed as strictly neutral between views which assume that experience is a common element and those that deny it" (1997, p. 86). In the present volume, I assume that disjunctivism is a definite metaphysical thesis. For more on varieties of disjunctivism, see Byrne and Logue 2008.

5. McGinn also says in an earlier passage that we cannot deduce the identity of the object of an experience from knowledge of its content (1982, p. 38). McGinn's thought here may be that we can know the content of an experience via introspection without thereby knowing which object, if any, is present. However, this claim is open to dispute. If experiences have multiple contents (see section 4.4 below), it is not at all obvious that we can know each content via introspection. Further,

even if experiences have only a single content, it could be held that what we can know via introspection is not the content but the phenomenal character.

6. Given the thesis of strong intentionalism together with the further claim that each perceptual experience has only a single representational content, the negative thesis that McGinn advocates in the quoted passage follows. But why make these assumptions? McGinn does not say.

7. The case that follows is similar to one Grice discusses in his 1961 essay.

8. John Searle makes a proposal along these lines in his 1983 book. In Searle's formulation, the content of my experience is that *there is a yellow cube (ahead) and the fact that there is such a cube is causing this experience*. This obviously will not do as it stands. Without some restrictions on the causal connection, it is easy to construct more complex mirror-case counter-examples.

9. I am indebted to Mark Sainsbury here.

10. The problems do not end here. Veridical hallucinations cannot be handled on the causal version of the Existential Thesis. See note 18 below and the surrounding discussion in the text.

11. Of course, 'content' is a term of art, and there is no one correct way to use it. As I use the term, the content of a thought is what is thought. It is expressed in the 'that' clause and it is either true or false (or neither true nor false, on three-valued views).

12. Another possible view is that the thought is neither true nor false, since there is no object the thought is about either to have or to lack the attributed property. One difficulty for this view is that *prima facie* it requires us to give up the claim that the thought that this is a china frog is true if and only of this is a china frog in the second case.

13. Among the philosophers who emphasize the singularity or particularity of visual experience are Bach (1997), Soteriou (2000), and Sainsbury (2006).

14. The seen object need not always be a common or garden manifest object such as a tomato.

15. This is not quite true. There are cases of *de re* hallucination, as, for example, when I dream with respect to my mother that she is being strangled by a snake. Here there is a particular—my mother—and so obviously the content of my visual experience (assuming it is agreed that dreams involve visual experiences) cannot be gappy. Such an experience is singular though the object involved is not seen. For present taxonomical purposes, I am ignoring cases of this sort, but obviously they present no special difficulty for the Singular (When Filled) Thesis.

16. I do not meant to suggest here that the Russellian view is plausible for the singular or gappy contents of thoughts. As I noted in chapter 3, thought contents individuate in a fine-grained way and this is not captured on the Russellian view. My claim is that, within the framework of the Singular (When Filled) Thesis, the content schemas for *experience* are naturally taken to fit the model of Russellian singular propositions with slots in them that can be filled by objects.

17. Curiously, this is standardly denied by disjunctivists. See, e.g., Martin 2004. For trenchant criticisms of Martin's disjunctivism, see Hawthorne and Kovakovich 2006.

18. Nor can the causal version of the Existential Thesis discussed in section 4.1. According to that thesis, there can be no such thing as a veridical hallucination, since when an hallucination is present, there is no object of the relevant sort in the scene before the subject's causing his or her experience. Thus, every hallucination must be counted as falsidical. This obviously will not do.

19. Sainsbury (2006, p. 254) offers an example of this sort.

20. I return to this issue later in the chapter.

21. For further discussion leading to the same conclusion, see Schroeder and Caplan 2007.

22. One might try to handle this objection by saying that an object, o, looks F so long as o causes an experience that represents that there is something F in place p, where p is the place o occupies. But this replaces a purely singular object-based content with another partly singular place-based one. It is hard to see how this is supposed to be an improvement on the pure singular proposal. Furthermore, patently the proposed condition is not necessary, since o could look F and occupy a different location. To respond that the relevant location should be specified descriptively in the content as the place o occupies evidently does not help. The object o is now back in the content again.

23. Are there *any* visual experiences that do not have an *SWF* content? Here is one possible case. Suppose that I am surrounded by a white mist. It is not implausible to hold that my experience in this instance has an existential content on the grounds that there is no seen object. Another view is that there is a seen object, namely the portion of the mist in my field of view, and the content is of the *SWF* sort. What about the contents of experiences in the other sensory modalities? Again, I am inclined to favor the Singular (When Filled) Thesis. In the case of auditory experience, for example, the relevant particular (if there is one) is a particular sound. Things are heard by hearing the sounds they emit and sounds are particulars. Similarly, in the case of olfactory experience, the particular are smells. We smell things by smelling the odors they produce and odors are particulars. Odors begin and end. They have spatio-temporal locations, even if these locations are not at all precise.

24. This is as far as my agreement with the "real" disjunctivists goes.

25. I do not deny, of course, that the content involved in veridically experiencing a red object and the content involved in hallucinating a red object have something important in common.

Chapter 5

1. Use of 'revelation' in this context seems to be attributable to Mark Johnston (1992).

2. This claim needs one minor qualification. See later in section 5.1.

3. This too needs a minor qualification. See section 5.1 below.

4. Patently, fearing x is not the same as standing in the relation of fearing to some proposition or other about x. For example, I can fear that my dog Quigley has been bitten by a snake without fearing Quigley.

5. This oversimplifies minimally. For one qualification ignored here, see section 5.1 below.

6. For example, it seems to me plausible to suppose that I can believe of the next person who comes to the door of my house that he or she will be over 20 years of age. But I am not now acquainted with that person (in my sense of 'acquaintance'), and I may never be.

7. Encountering (or having encountered) a thing in experience is a necessary condition for acquaintance with the thing, on my view. Acquaintance with a past thing can be sustained by phenomenal memory. I make no attempt here to state conditions that are jointly necessary and sufficient for acquaintance (though earlier I stated a sufficient condition in the perceptual case). Indeed, I doubt that necessary and sufficient conditions *can* easily be stated. This should come as no surprise, given the failures of attempts to state necessary and sufficient conditions for terms of interest to philosophers elsewhere.

8. Relatedly, why couldn't such a fine-grained content be the content of some thought? Peacocke is one philosopher who adopts the fine-grained nonconceptualist view of experience. See his 2001 paper. Peacocke argues that there are differences in the phenomenology of experiences of squares and diamonds that can only be handled properly on the fine-grained proposal. For a critical discussion of Peacocke's argument here, see Tye 2006e.

9. I say "one view" here because there seem to be two different views on offer in *Mind and World*, the second of which will occupy us shortly.

10. In *Philosophy and Phenomenological Research* (1998).

11. See Hurvich 1981; Halsey and Chapanis 1951. Also see Raffman 1995.

12. Another objection is that there cannot be recognition for a first-time experience of a property, but that experience still has a specific representational content: the world still appears a certain way to the subject of the experience (Peacocke 2001).

13. For more on this, see McLaughlin and Tye 1998.

14. One nonconceptualist, Chris Peacocke, does not notice this problem. As a result, he comments: "Since these unsupplemented perceptual-demonstratives exist, and can pick out fine-grained properties, the anticonceptualist should not try to rest his case on fineness of grain." (1998, p. 610) This concession seems to me much too hasty.

15. On this picture, visual experiences do not themselves serve as reasons for beliefs. They justify or warrant beliefs but their contents do not stand to the contents of the beliefs they justify as do premises to conclusions in sound (or strong) arguments. On my usage, states of seeing-as and seeing-that do not count as visual experiences. They are, rather, hybrid states involving visual experiences plus appropriate conceptual attitudes.

16. For variants of this problem, see Clark 2000 and Byrne's entry "Inverted Qualia" in the online Stanford Encyclopedia of Philosophy (http://plato.stanford .edu/).

17. For more on this, and for a detailed presentation of a version of the adverbial theory that tries to handle the above difficulties, see Tye 1984.

18. Actually, it is a mistake to suppose that the soap and the lemon are not intrinsically the same. They are in that they have the same color and the same three-dimensional shape.

19. For an elucidation of Kaplanian character, see chapter 4.

20. For more on this, see section 5.5.

21. For a closely related alternative view, see Dretske 1995.

22. As I noted in chapter 1, the father of transparency is G. E. Moore (1922). For recent defenses of transparency, see Dretske 1995; Tye 2000, 2003a. See also Harman 1990.

23. See Dretske 1995.

24. Exactly what that role is I shall not try to spell out, but on my view (bearing in mind my remarks on Quigley in section 5.1) we can at least offer this condition: The state, in virtue of nonconceptually representing the entities it does, should enable its subject, with respect to each of those entities, at a minimum to bring the entity under a demonstrative concept and to form some attitude (wondering, judging, believing, etc.) involving the concept. The conceptual response should further be directly based on the nonconceptual content. The condition just stated is not intended to have the status of an *a priori* necessary truth. In my view, not even the claim that every experience is representational is *a priori*. The overall view I take of phenomenal character is best taken as a hypothesis justifiable in terms of its simplicity and explanatory power. For further relevant remarks about the distinctive role that experiences play, see Tye 1995, 2000. See also my replies to critics in the online symposium at http://uniroma3.it/progetti/kant/field/tyesymp .htm.

25. For a discussion of pain, see Tye 2006b. For criticisms, see Aydede 2006; Block 2006a; Maund 2006; Noordhof 2006. See also my reply to these criticisms in Tye 2006c.

26. The phenomenal many-property problem poses no threat to this view. The property complex represented by the experience of a red square has something in common with the property complex represented by the experience of a red, round thing, namely the property of being red. The property complex represented by the experience of a red square and a green triangle is different from the property complex represented by the experience of a green square and a red triangle. For example, the former complex includes the property of being a red thing to the left of a green thing (if the red thing is represented by the experience as being to the left of the green thing) whereas the latter does not.

27. See Tye 2000, Tye 2006d, and Bradley and Tye 2001.

28. I take this up in chapter 8.

Chapter 6

1. Mary's situation is fantastic, of course, but it is not *that* far removed from real world situations. Knut Nordby, a well-known Scandinavian color scientist, is an achromatope—that is, he sees the world in black and white.

2. E.g., M. Nida-Rumelin, "Qualia: The knowledge argument," in *Stanford Encyclopedia of Philosophy* (http://plato.stanford.edu).

3. I return to this topic later in section 6.1. For other relevant discussions, see Bengson and Moffett 2007; Braun 2006; Noe 2005.

4. For further discussion of the ability hypothesis that draws on recent work on the nature of knowing how, see Cath forthcoming.

5. See, e.g., Block 2006b; Chalmers 2005; Loar 1990/1997; Papineau 2002. This was also the view I took in Tye 1995, 2000, and 2003b.

6. For versions of the demonstrative reply to Mary, see Horgan 1984; Perry 2001.

7. This suggestion was put to me by David Chalmers in his commentary at a symposium on phenomenal concepts at the 2008 meeting of the American Philosophical Association's Pacific Division.

8. The view that knowing what it is like to experience red is a species of fact knowledge is espoused in Lycan 1996.

9. I take it that it can be true of Jane that she knows that this is way to ride a bicycle even at times at which she is not herself referring to the relevant way via a demonstrative. See my discussion of demonstrative knowledge in the present section.

10. Of course, Jane might be prevented from manifesting this disposition. She might be tied up and imprisoned, for example. Or she might have broken her legs in an accident, in which case she could still know how to ride a bike even though she was no longer able to do so.

11. Brogaard (forthcoming) has a different, though related, partly *de re* proposal: Mary knows, for some *e*, that *e* is what it is like to experience red. *Prima facie*, this proposal is too weak. It has the consequence that Mary can know what it is like to experience red in her room.

12. This terminology is from Alex Byrne. The case is essentially the same as that of Marianna (Nida-Rumelin 1996).

13. I owe this objection to Alex Byrne.

14. This is pressed by Chalmers (2005).

15. Zombie Mary is supplied with information about color vision by her computers and books just as Mary is. She is thus linked up with the outside world in just the same way as Mary.

16. I became aware of Conee's view after writing much of this section. His essay was brought to my attention by Tomas Bogardus. Strangely, Conee himself nowhere mentions Russell's views on knowledge by acquaintance.

17. For another version of the view that Mary lacks knowledge by acquaintance while in her black and white room, see Bigelow and Pargetter 1990. However,

their position is markedly different from either mine or Conee's. The key claim they make is that when she leaves the room, all that Mary acquires is a new *way* of knowing the things she already knows in the room, a way of knowing that involves a new mode of acquaintance with those things. This, they say, enables her to entertain a wide range of new thoughts. My claim is that (in one sense of 'know') Mary, in her room, does *not* know certain things. She knows facts about those things.

18. Here I am in agreement with Block and Stalnaker (1999).

19. For more on this, see chapter 5.

20. This simplifies slightly Chalmers's argument in his 2002 article. The further qualifications Chalmers introduces do not affect the evaluation that follows.

21. Chalmers has no objection to allowing that negative statements are positively conceivable. Indeed, his zombie argument assumes that the claim expressed by "It is not the case that someone is conscious" is so conceivable.

22. (43) is true, given the modal logic S5.

23. Chalmers has yet another version of the conceivability argument in his forthcoming that appeals to ideal primary negative conceivability. Chalmers's alternative version of the argument is susceptible to criticisms of the same sort as those adduced against the argument that appeals to ideal primary positive conceivability.

Chapter 7

1. See chapter 1.

2. On the implicit effects of the objects to which the subjects are blind, see Henderson 1997; Hayhoe et al. 1998, Fernandez-Duque and Thornton 2000; Williams and Simons 2000; Hollingsworth 2001. For a critique of some of these claims, see Mitroff et al. 2002. For more evidence on behalf of implicit visual representations of things to which subjects are blind, see Lamme 2003.

3. One obvious case where this occurs is that of ambiguous pictures. Viewing the picture and seeing the depicted item or items one way, we experience various shapes not experienced seeing the depicted item or items the other way. Think, for example, of the well-known martini glass/two faces picture. Seen as a picture of a martini glass, one experiences a bowl shape, a stem shape and a base shape. These shapes are not experienced when we see the picture as of two faces turned toward one another. For more on this, see Tye 1995.

4. The relevant focusing need not enable us to identify the thing. For example, we can attend to a thing we see through thick distorting glass. Nor by focusing here do I have in mind voluntary concentration on the thing. Subjects can see a photograph that is briefly and unexpectedly flashed across an entire screen, and they can extract the gist of the photograph even if the presentation time is as short as 30 milliseconds. This is too short a period of time for them to be able to focus mentally on the photograph in a concentrated, selective way. Still, before the unexpected presentation of the photograph the subjects are already focusing on the

screen, and their attention is reinforced by the flashing. Attention can also be paid to more than one object at a single time. Studies have shown that attention can be used to track four or five randomly moving objects simultaneously. Finally, where a demonstrative is applied to a particular object (even if only in the context of the question "What is that?"), we must focus on that object and thus attend to it.

5. Color-Changing Card Trick, at www.quirkology.com.

6. In fairness, I should add that Block seems prepared to concede this. See p. 173 below. See also Block's (2007b) reply to me. The unrestricted, general claim I take up is certainly worth discussing, however, and it is suggested by some of Block's remarks.

7. See Block 2007a,b.

8. Working memory is a global workspace. Representations in that workspace are in contact with, for example, the belief system and the reporting system, and those systems can make use of the working memory representations, but not all such representations need actually be so used. It is standardly supposed that within working memory, there is a visuo-spatial workpad. It need not be supposed that all representations in working memory are conceptual.

9. I discuss Landman's experiment in section 7.5.

10. I am not denying that you know of the fourth line away from the dot, for example, that it is neither blue nor tilted. You know this on the basis of *how the lines collectively look*; for on the basis of how the lines look you know that none of the lines are blue or tilted. Thus, given that the fourth line in is one of the lines, you know that it is neither blue nor tilted.

11. This point has come up on several occasions. See, e.g., section 1.5.

12. It is crucial to your knowledge here that you possess the additional information (that the two walls differ and that Sam is the difference). Solely on the basis of your experience, without reasoning via the additional information, you are not in a position to know of Sam that it is neither blue nor tilted.

Chapter 8

1. For a similar formulation, see Jackson 1973.

2. See, e.g., Jackson 1973.

3. See chapter 3.

4. See Burge 1979.

5. As presented in Burge 1979.

6. There is a usage of 'phenomenal character' under which no experience token can have multiple phenomenal characters. On this usage, the phenomenal character of a given token experience *e* is a conjunctive property the conjuncts of which are different aspects of what it is like overall to undergo *e*. My usage of 'phenomenal character' in the text here counts aspects of what it is like overall to undergo an experience as phenomenal characters of that experience; so, an experience may

be counted as having more than one phenomenal character. Nothing of substance hinges on which usage is adopted.

7. That is, no truth which I can doubt or fail to know.

8. Here and in the statement of (ICTdem) below, I ignore the temporal objection (section 8.1). That objection still applies, but it is easily handled.

9. I use the term 'involving' in this statement of (PAdem) since the phenomenal character of S, on my view, is not a property that S possesses. Rather, it is a property we (as subjects of S) confront in undergoing S—a property that is integral to S's identity as the phenomenal state it is. In one weak sense, the phenomenal character of S is something S has, but it is not a property belonging to S.

10. This is certainly my own view.

11. Here is a quick and dirty argument that can be brought to bear on Dretske's worry, albeit not one that will appeal to dualists: Physicalism is true. If physicalism is true, then zombies are metaphysically impossible. Thus, I am not a zombie. Since my belief that physicalism is true is itself true and I have substantial evidence for the truth of physicalism, I know that the first premise is true. So, given the second premise, which seems incontestable, I know that the conclusion of the argument is true.

12. For more on explanation and metaphysical necessitation, see Byrne and Tye 2006.

13. For more on XP1, see Tye forthcoming.

14. For a summary of this literature, see Brian Weatherstone's entry "Intrinsic versus extrinsic properties" in the online Stanford Encyclopedia of Philosophy.

15. Here I use 'qualia' as a synonym for 'phenomenal properties'.

16. This was Hume's (1748) advice with respect to any volume that contains neither "abstract reasoning concerning quantity or number" nor "experimental reasoning concerning matter of fact and existence."

References

Alter, T., and Walter, S., eds. 2006. *Phenomenal Concepts and Phenomenal Knowledge: New Essays on Consciousness and Physicalism*. Oxford University Press.

Armstrong, D. 1968. *A Materialist Theory of Mind*. Routledge and Kegan Paul.

Austin, J. L. 1962. *Sense and Sensibilia*. Clarendon.

Aydede, M. 2006. "The main difficulty with pain." In *Pain: New Essays on Its Nature and the Methodology of Its Study*, ed. M. Aydede. MIT Press.

Ayer, A. J. 1940. *The Foundations of Empirical Knowledge*. Macmillan.

Bach, K. 1997. "Searle against the world." Unpublished.

Balog, K. 1999. "Conceivability, possibility, and the mind-body problem." *Philosophical Review* 108: 497–528.

Balog, K. Forthcoming. "Phenomenal concepts." In *The Oxford Handbook of Philosophy of Mind*, ed. B. McLaughlin and A. Beckermann. Oxford University Press.

Bengson, J., and Moffett, M. 2007. "Know-how and concept possession." *Philosophical Studies* 136: 31–57.

Blackmore, S. 2003. "The grand illusion: Why consciousness is not what it seems." *Edinburgh Science Festival* 2003.

Block, N. 1980. "Are absent qualia impossible?" *Philosophical Review* 89: 257–274.

Block, N. 1990. "Inverted Earth." *Philosophical Perspectives* 4: 52–79.

Block, N. 1997. "On a confusion about a function of consciousness." In *The Nature of Consciousness*, ed. N. Block et al. MIT Press.

Block, N. 2001. "How not to find the neural correlate of consciousness." In *The Foundations of Cognitive Science*, ed. J. Branquinho. Oxford University Press.

Block, N. 2002. "Some concepts of consciousness." In *Philosophy of Mind: Classical and Contemporary Readings*, ed. D. Chalmers. Oxford University Press.

Block, N. 2006a. "Bodily sensations as an obstacle for representationism." In *Pain: New Essays on Its Nature and the Methodology of Its Study*, ed. M. Aydede. MIT Press.

Block, N. 2006b. "Max Black's objection to mind-body identity." In *Oxford Studies in Metaphysics*, volume 2, ed. D. Zimmerman. Oxford University Press.

Block, N. 2007a. "Consciousness, accessibility and the mesh between psychology and neuroscience." *Behavioral and Brain Sciences* 30: 481–499.

Block, N. 2007b. "Overflow, access, and attention." *Behavioral and Brain Sciences* 30: 530–548.

Block, N., and Stalnaker, S. 1999. "Conceptual analysis, dualism, and the explanatory gap." *Philosophical Review* 108: 1–46.

Braddon-Mitchell, D., and Jackson, F. 1996. *Philosophy of Mind and Cognition: An Introduction*. Blackwell.

Bradley, P., and Tye, M. 2001. "Of colors, kestrels, caterpillars, and leaves." *Journal of Philosophy* 98: 469–487.

Braun, D. 2006. "Now you know who Hong Oak Yun is." *Philosophical Issues* 16: 24–42.

Brogaard, B. Forthcoming. "What Mary did yesterday: Reflections on knowledge-how." *Philosophy and Phenomenological Research*.

Burge, T. 1977. "Belief *de re*." *Journal of Philosophy* 74: 338–362.

Burge, T. 1979. "Individualism and the mental." *Midwest Studies in Philosophy* 4: 73–121.

Burge, T. 2003. *Reflections and Replies: Essays on the Philosophy of Tyler Burge*, ed. M. Hahn and B. Ramberg. MIT Press.

Byrne, A. 2001. "Intentionalism defended." *Philosophical Review* 110: 49–90.

Byrne, A. 2004. "Perception and conceptual content." In *Contemporary Debates in Philosophy*, ed. E. Sosa and M. Steup. Blackwell.

Byrne, A., and Logue, H. 2008. "Either/or: Disjunctivism for dummies." In *Perception, Action, Knowledge*, ed. A. Haddock and F. Macpherson. Oxford University Press.

Byrne, A., and Tye, M. 2006. "Qualia ain't in the head." *Noûs* 40, no. 2: 241–255.

Cath, Y. Forthcoming. "The ability hypothesis and the new knowledge-how." *Noûs*.

Cavanagh, P., He, S., and Intriligator, J. 1999. "Attentional resolution: The grain and resolution of visual awareness." In *Neuronal Basis and Psychological Aspects of Consciousness*, ed. C. Taddei-Ferretti and C. Musio. World Scientific.

Chalmers, D. 1995. "Facing up to the hard problem of consciousness." *Journal of Consciousness Studies* 2.

Chalmers, D. 1996. *The Conscious Mind*. Oxford University Press.

Chalmers, D. 2002. "Does conceivability entail possibility?" In *Conceivability and Possibility*, ed. T. Gendler and J. Hawthorne. Oxford University Press.

Chalmers, D. 2003. "The content and epistemology of phenomenal belief." In *Consciousness—New Philosophical Perspectives*, ed. A. Jokic and Q. Smith. Oxford University Press.

Chalmers, D. 2004. "Phenomenal Concepts and the Knowledge Argument." In *There's Something About Mary: Essays on Phenomenal Consciousness and Frank Jackson's Knowledge Argument*, ed. P. Ludlow et al. MIT Press.

Chalmers, D. 2005. "Phenomenal concepts and the explanatory gap." In *Phenomenal Concepts and Phenomenal Knowledge: New Essays on Consciousness and Physicalism*, ed. T. Alter and S. Walter. Oxford University Press.

Chalmers, D. Forthcoming. "The two-dimensional argument against materialism." In *Oxford Handbook of the Philosophy of Mind*, ed. B. McLaughlin. Oxford University Press.

Chalmers, D., and Jackson, F. 2001. "Conceptual analysis and reductive explanation." *Philosophical Review* 110: 315–361.

Chisholm, R. 1957. *Perceiving*. Cornell University Press.

Clark, A. 2000. *A Theory of Sentience*. Oxford University Press.

Conee, E. 1994. "Phenomenal knowledge." *Australasian Journal of Philosophy* 72: 136–150.

Davies, M. 1992. "Perceptual content and local supervenience." *Proceedings of the Aristotelian Society* 92: 21–45.

Da Vinci, L. 1182/1970. "On foolishness and ignorance." In *The Notebooks of Leonardo da Vinci*, ed. J. P. Richter. Courier Dover.

Dennett, D. 1991. *Consciousness Explained*. Little, Brown.

Dennett, D. 1992. "Filling in versus finding out." In *Cognition: Conceptual and Methodological Issues*, ed. H. Pick Jr. et al. American Psychological Association.

Donnellan, K. 1966. "Reference and definite descriptions." *Philosophical Review* 75: 281–304.

Drestke, F. 1969. *Seeing and Knowing*. University of Chicago Press

Dretske, F. 1995. *Naturalizing the Mind*. MIT Press.

Dretske, F. 2003. "How do you know that you are not a zombie?" In *Privileged Access: Philosophical Accounts of Self-Knowledge*, ed. B. Gertler. Ashgate.

Dretske, F. 2004. "Change blindness." *Philosophical Studies* 120: 1–18.

Dretske, F. 2007. "What change blindness teaches about consciousness." *Philosophical Perspectives* 21: 216–230.

DuBois-Reymond, E. 1885–1887. *Reden*. Leipzig.

Evans, G. 1982. *The Varieties of Reference*. Oxford University Press.

Farah, M. 1991. *Visual Agnosia*. MIT Press.

Fernandez-Duque, D., and Thornton, I. 2000. "Change detection without awareness: Do explicit reports underestimate the representation of change in the visual system?" *Visual Cognition* 7: 324–344.

Grice, H. 1989/1961. "The causal theory of perception." In *Studies in the Ways of Words*. Harvard University Press.

Grimes, J. 1996. "On the failure to detect changes in scenes across saccades." In *Perception*, ed. K. Akins. Oxford University Press.

Hahn, M., and Ramberg, B. 2003. *Reflections and Replies: Essays on the Philosophy of Tyler Burge*. MIT Press.

Halsey, R., and Chapanis, A. 1951. "Number of absolutely identifiable hues." *Journal of the Optical Society of America* 41: 1057–1058.

Harman, G. 1998. "The intrinsic qualities of experience." In *The Nature of Consciousness*, ed. N. Block et al. MIT Press.

Hawthorne, J., and Kovakovich, K. 2006. "Disjunctivism." *Proceedings of the Aristotelian Society*, Supplementary Volume 80: 145–183.

Hayhoe, M., Bensinger, D., and Ballard, D. 1998. "Task constraints in visual working memory." *Vision Research* 38: 125–137.

Heck, R. 2000. "Nonconceptual content and the 'space of reasons.'" *Philosophical Review* 109: 483–523.

Henderson, J. 1997. "Transsaccadic memory and integration during real-world object perception." *Psychological Science* 8: 51–55.

Hinton, J. 1973. *Experiences*. Clarendon.

Hollingworth, A., Williams, C., and Henderson, J. 2001. "To see and remember: Visually specific information is retained in memory from previously attended scenes." *Psychonomic Bulletin and Review* 8: 761–768.

Horgan, T. 1984. "Jackson on physical information and qualia." *Philosophical Quarterly* 34: 147–183.

Horgan, T. 1993. "From supervenience to superdupervenience: Meeting the demands of a material world." *Mind* 102: 555–586.

Horgan, T., and Kriegel, U. 2007. "Phenomenal epistemology: What is consciousness that we may know it so well?" *Philosophical Issues* 17: 123–144.

Horgan, T., and Tienson, J. 2002. "The intentionality of phenomenology and the phenomenology of intentionality." In *Philosophy of Mind: Classical and Contemporary Readings*, ed. D. Chalmers. Oxford University Press.

Hume, D. 1748/1993. *An Enquiry Concerning Human Understanding*. Hackett.

Hurvich, L. 1981. *Color Vision*. Sinauer.

Jackson, F. 1973. "Is there a good argument against the incorrigibility thesis?" *Australasian Journal of Philosophy* 51: 51–62.

Jackson, F. 1975. "On the adverbial analysis of visual experience." *Metaphilosophy* 6: 127–135.

Jackson, F. 1977. *Perception*. Cambridge University Press.

Jackson, F. 1982. "Epiphenomenal qualia." *Philosophical Quarterly* 32: 127–136.

Jackson, F. 1998. *From Ethics to Metaphysics*. Oxford University Press.

Jackson, F. 2004. "What Mary didn't know." In *There's Something About Mary: Essays on Phenomenal Consciousness and Frank Jackson's Knowledge Argument*, ed. P. Ludlow et al. MIT Press.

Jeshion, R. 2002. "Acquaintanceless *de re* belief." In *Meaning and Truth: Investigations in Philosophical Semantics*, ed. J. Campbell et al. Seven Bridges.

Johnston, M. 1992. "How to speak of the colors." *Philosophical Studies* 68: 221–263.

Kaplan, D. 1989. "'Demonstratives' and 'afterthoughts.'" In *Themes from Kaplan*, ed. J. Almog et al. Oxford University Press.

Kosslyn, S. 1980. *Image and Mind*. Harvard University Press.

Kosslyn, S. 1994. *Image and Brain*. MIT Press.

Kriegel, U., and Williford, K., eds. 2006. *Self-Representational Approaches to Consciousness*. MIT Press.

Kripke, S. 1980/1972. *Naming and Necessity*. Harvard University Press.

Kripke, S. 1982. *Wittgenstein on Rules and Private Language*. Blackwell.

Lamme, V. 2003. "Why visual attention and awareness are different." *Trends in Cognitive Sciences* 7: 12–18.

Laurence, S., and Margolis, E. 2003. "Concepts and conceptual analysis." *Philosophy and Phenomenological Research* 67: 253–282.

Leiter, B., and Miller, A. 1994. "Mind doesn't matter yet." *Australasian Journal of Philosophy* 72: 220–228.

LePore, E., and Loewer, B. 1987. "Mind matters." *Journal of Philosophy* 93: 630–642.

Levine, J. 1983. "Materialism and qualia: The explanatory gap." *Pacific Philosophical Quarterly* 64: 354–361.

Levine J. 2001. *Purple Haze: The Puzzle of Consciousness*. Oxford University Press.

Levine, J. Forthcoming. "Conscious awareness and (self-) representation." In *Consciousness and Self-Reference*, ed. U. Kriegel. MIT Press.

Lewis, D. 1973. "Causation." *Journal of Philosophy* 70: 556–567.

Lewis, D. 1980. "Veridical hallucination and prosthetic vision." *Australasian Journal of Philosophy* 58: 239–249.

Lewis, D. 1983. "Extrinsic Properties." *Philosophical Studies* 44: 197–200.

Lewis, D. 1990. "What experience teaches." In *Mind and Cognition*, ed. W. Lycan. Blackwell.

Loar, B. 1997. "Phenomenal states." In *The Nature of Consciousness*, ed. N. Block et al. MIT Press.

Locke, J. 1690/1975. *An Essay Concerning Human Understanding*. Oxford University Press.

Ludlow, P., Nagasawa, Y., and Stoljar, D., eds. 2004. *There's Something About Mary: Essays on Phenomenal Consciousness and Frank Jackson's Knowledge Argument*. MIT Press.

Lycan, W. 1996. *Consciousness and Experience*. MIT Press.

Lycan, W. 1997. "Consciousness as internal monitoring." In *The Nature of Consciousness*, ed. N. Block et al. MIT Press.

Marr, D. 1982. *Vision*. Freeman.

Martin, C. 1994. "Dispositions and conditionals." *Philosophical Quarterly* 44: 1–8.

Martin, M. 1997. "The reality of appearances." In *Thought and Ontology*, ed. M. Sainsbury. Franco/Angeli.

Martin, M. 2002. "The transparency of experience." *Mind & Language* 17: 376–425.

Martin, M. 2004. "The limits of self-awareness." *Philosophical Studies* 120: 37–89.

Martin, M. 2006. "On being alienated." In *Perceptual Experience*, ed. T. Gendler and J. Hawthorne. Oxford University Press.

Maund, B. 2006. "Michael Tye on pain and representational content." In *Phenomenal Concepts and Phenomenal Knowledge: New Essays on Consciousness and Physicalism*, ed. T. Alter and S. Walter. Oxford University Press.

McDowell, J. 1994. *Mind and World*. Harvard University Press.

McDowell, J. 1998. "Reply to commentators." *Philosophy and Phenomenological Research* 58: 403–431.

McGinn, C. 1982. *The Character of Mind*. Oxford University Press.

McGinn, C. 1991. *The Problem of Consciousness*. Oxford University Press.

McGinn, C. 2004. "What constitutes the mind-body problem." In *Consciousness and Its Objects*. Oxford University Press.

McLaughlin, B., and Tye, M. 1998. "Externalism, Twin Earth, and self-knowledge." In *Knowing Our Own Minds: Essays on Self-Knowledge*, ed. C. Macdonald et al. Oxford University Press.

Mellor, H. 1992. "Nothing like experience." *Proceedings of the Aristotelian Society* 93: 1–16.

Melnyk, A. 2003. *A Physicalist Manifesto: Thoroughly Modern Materialism*. Cambridge University Press.

Millar, A. 1991. *Reasons and Experiences*. Clarendon.

Mitroff, S., Simons, D., and Franconeri, S. 2002. "The siren song of implicit change detection." *Journal of Experimental Psychology: Human Perception and Performance* 28: 798–815.

Moore, G. 1922. "The refutation of idealism." In Moore, *Philosophical Studies*. Routledge and Kegan Paul.

Nagel, T. 1974. "What is it like to be a bat?" *Philosophical Review* 83: 435–450.

Nida-Rumelin, M. 1996. "What Mary couldn't know." In *Conscious Experience*, ed. T. Metzinger. Imprint Academic.

Nida-Rumelin, M. 2002. "Qualia: the Knowledge Argument." In *Stanford Encyclopedia of Philosophy*, ed. E. Zalta. http://plato.stanford.edu.

Nemirow, L. 1990. "Physicalism and the cognitive role of acquaintance." In *Mind and Cognition*, ed. W. Lycan. Blackwell.

Noe, A. 2005. "Against intellectualism." *Analysis* 65: 278–290.

Noordhof, P. 2006. "In a state of pain." In *Phenomenal Concepts and Phenomenal Knowledge: New Essays on Consciousness and Physicalism*, ed. T. Alter and S. Walter. Oxford University Press.

O'Regan, K. J. 2000/2001. "Experience is not something we feel but something we do." Manuscript.

O'Regan, J., and Noe, A. 2001. "A sensorimotor approach to vision and visual consciousness." *Behavioral and Brain Sciences* 24: 883–975.

Papineau, D. 1993. *Philosophical Naturalism*. Blackwell.

Papineau, D. 2000. *Introducing Consciousness*. Icon Books.

Papineau, D. 2002. *Thinking about Consciousness*. Oxford University Press.

Pautz, A. 2006. "Sensory awareness is not a wide physical relation." *Noûs* 40: 205–240.

Peacocke, C. 1983. *Sense and Content*. Oxford University Press.

Peacocke, C. 1992. "Scenarios, concepts, and perception." In *The Contents of Experience: Essays on Perception*, ed. T. Crane. Cambridge University Press.

Peacocke, C. 1998. "Review: Nonconceptual content defended." *Philosophy and Phenomenological Research* 58: 381–388.

Peacocke, C. 2001. "Does perception have a nonconceptual content?" *Journal of Philosophy* 98: 239–264.

Perry, J. 2001. *Possibility, Consciousness and Conceivability*. MIT Press.

Pitcher, G. 1971. *A Theory of Perception*. Oxford University Press.

Pitt, D. 2004. "The phenomenology of cognition or, what is it like to think that P?" *Philosophy and Phenomenological Research* 69: 1–36.

Price, H. 1932. *Perception*. Methuen.

Putnam, H. 1970. "Is semantics possible?" In *Languages, Belief and Metaphysics*, ed. H. Keifer and M. Munitz. State University of New York Press.

Pryor, J. 2000. "The skeptic and the dogmatist." *Noûs* 34: 517–549.

Pryor, J. Forthcoming. "An epistemic theory of acquaintance."

Raffmann, D. 1996. "On the persistence of phenomenology." In *Conscious Experience*, ed. T. Metzinger. Schoning-Verlag.

Rensink, R., O'Regan, J., and Clark, J. 1997. "To see or not to see: The need for attention to perceive changes in scenes." *Psychological Science* 8: 368–373.

Rosenthal, D. 1986. "Two concepts of consciousness." *Philosophical Studies* 49: 329–359.

Rosenthal, D. Forthcoming. "Higher-order theories of consciousness." In *Oxford Handbook in the Philosophy of Mind*, ed. B. McLaughlin and A. Beckermann. Clarendon.

Russell, B. 1912. *The Problems of Philosophy*.

Sainsbury, M. 2006. *Reference without Referents*. Oxford University Press.

Schaffer, J. 2000. "Trumping preemption." *Journal of Philosophy* 9: 165–181.

Searle, J. 1983. *Intentionality*. Oxford University Press.

Searle, J. 1992. *The Rediscovery of Mind*. MIT Press.

Schroeder, T., and Caplan, B. 2007. "On the content of experience." *Philosophy and Phenomenological Research* 75: 590–611.

Shoemaker, S. 1975. "Functionalism and qualia." *Philosophical Studies* 27: 291–315.

Shoemaker, S. 1981. "Absent qualia are impossible—A reply to Block." *Philosophical Review* 90: 581–599.

Siegel, S. 2006. "How does visual phenomenology constrain object seeing?" *Australasian Journal of Philosophy* 84: 429–441.

Simons, D. J. 1997. "Change blindness." *Trends in Cognitive Sciences* 1: 261–267.

Simons, D., and Ambinder, M. 2005. "Change blindness: Theory and consequences." *Current Directions in Psychological Science* 14: 44–48.

Simons, D., and Rensink, R. 2005 "Change blindness, representations and consciousness: Reply to Noe." *Trends in Cognitive Sciences* 9: 219.

Snowdon, P. 1990. "The objects of direct experience." *Proceedings of the Aristotelian Society*, supplementary volume 64: 121–150.

Soteriou, M. 2000. "The particularity of visual perception." *European Journal of Philosophy* 8: 173–189.

Sperling, George. 1960. "The information available in brief visual presentations." *Psychological Monographs* 74, no. 11: 1–29.

Stanley, J., and Williamson, T. 2001. "Knowing how." *Journal of Philosophy* 98: 1–40.

Strawson, G. 1995. *Mental Reality*. MIT Press.

Sturgeon, S. 1994. "The epistemic view of subjectivity." *Journal of Philosophy* 91: 221–235.

Travis, C. 2004. "The silence of the senses." *Mind* 113: 57–94.

Tye, M. 1982. "A causal analysis of seeing." *Philosophy and Phenomenological Research* 42: 311–325.

Tye, M. 1984. "The adverbial approach to visual experience." *The Philosophical Review* 93: 195–225.

Tye, M. 1995. *Ten Problems of Consciousness*. MIT Press.

Tye, M. 1996. Review of Galen Strawson, *Mental Reality*. *Journal of Philosophy* 93: 421–424.

Tye, M. 1999. "Phenomenal consciousness: The explanatory gap as a cognitive illusion." *Mind* 108: 705–725.

Tye, M. 2000. *Consciousness, Color, and Content*. MIT Press.

Tye, M. 2003a. *Consciousness and Persons: Unity and Identity*. MIT Press.

Tye, M. 2003b. "A theory of phenomenal concepts." *Philosophy*.

Tye, M. 2006a. "Absent qualia and the mind-body problem." *Philosophical Review* 115: 139–168.

Tye, M. 2006b. "Another look at representationalism about pain." In *Pain: New Essays on Its Nature and the Methodology of Its Study*, ed. M. Aydede. MIT Press.

Tye, M. 2006c. "In defense of representationalism: Reply to commentaries." In *Pain: New Essays on Its Nature and the Methodology of Its Study*, ed. M. Aydede. MIT Press.

Tye, M. 2006d. "The puzzle of true blue." *Analysis* 66.

Tye, M. 2006e. "Nonconceptual content, richness and fineness of grain." In *Perceptual Experience*, ed. J. Hawthorne and T. Gendler. Oxford University Press.

Tye, M. Forthcoming. "Phenomenal externalism, Lolita, and the planet Xenon." In a volume of essays in honor of Jaegwon Kim. MIT Press.

Weiskrantz, L. 1986. *Blindsight: A Case Study and Its Implications*. Oxford University Press.

Williams, P., and Simons, D. 2000. "Detecting changes in novel, complex three-dimensional objects." *Visual Cognition* 7: 297–322.

Wittgenstein, L. 1953. *Philosophical Investigations*. Blackwell.

Wright, C. 2004. "Warrant for nothing (and foundations for free)?" *Proceedings of the Aristotelian Society*, supplementary volume 78: 167–212.

Yablo, S. 1990. "Intrinsicness." *Philosophical Topics* 26: 479–505.

Yablo, S. 1992. "Mental causation." *Philosophical Review* 101: 245–280.

Yablo, S. 1999. "Concepts and consciousness: Comments on Chalmers, *The Conscious Mind*." *Philosophy and Phenomenological Research* 59: 455–464.

Index

Representation and Mind
Hilary Putnam and Ned Block, editors

Hilary Putnam, *Representation and Reality*

Fred Dretske, *Explaining Behavior: Reasons in a World of Causes*

Jerrold J. Katz, *The Metaphysics of Meaning*

Jerry A. Fodor, *A Theory of Content and Other Essays*

Cora Diamond, *The Realistic Spirit: Wittgenstein, Philosophy, and the Mind*

Stephen L. White, *The Unity of the Self*

Michael Tye, *The Imagery Debate*

Christopher Peacocke, *A Study of Concepts*

John R. Searle, *The Rediscovery of the Mind*

John Campbell, *Past, Space, and Self*

Galen Strawson, *Mental Reality*

Michael Tye, *Ten Problems of Consciousness: A Representational Theory of the Phenomenal Mind*

Robert Cummins, *Representations, Targets, and Attitudes*

Peter J. McCormick, *Starmaking: Realism, Anti-Realism, and Irrealism*

Hao Wang, *A Logical Journey: From Gödel to Philosophy*

Daniel C. Dennett, *Brainchildren: Essays on Designing Minds*

Jerrold J. Katz, *Realistic Rationalism*

Jose Luis Bermudez, *The Paradox of Self-Consciousness*

Jerry Fodor, *In Critical Condition: Polemical Essays on Cognitive Science and the Philosophy of Mind*

Jaegwon Kim, *Mind in a Physical World: An Essay on the Mind-Body Problem and Mental Causation*

Jerry Fodor, *The Mind Doesn't Work That Way*

Susana Nuccetelli, *New Essays on Semantic Externalism and Self-Knowledge*

Michael Tye, *Consciousness and Persons: Unity and Identity*